# The Germans

# The Germans

By Erich Kahler

Edited by Robert and Rita Kimber

Princeton University Press

Princeton, New Jersey

LCC: 73-21751
ISBN: 0-691-05222-0

Library of Congress Cataloging in Publication data will
be found on the last printed page of this book

Publication of this book has been aided by
a grant from the Whitney Darrow Publication
Reserve Fund of Princeton University Press

This book has been composed in Linotype Caledonia


Printed in the United States of America
by Princeton University Press,
Princeton, New Jersey

# Contents

## Contents

# Editors' Foreword

ERICH KAHLER originally wrote *The Germans* as a series of lectures on German cultural history. He delivered these lectures while teaching at Cornell University in 1951-1952, and in 1955-1956 he again presented the material under the auspices of the Lord Simon Lectureship at the University of Manchester. In June 1969, he began preparing the manuscript for publication. At the time of his death a year later, he had revised the first eighteen lectures; these are chapters one through fourteen of the present book.

*The Germans* draws on materials and develops certain themes that appeared in Kahler's earlier work, *Der deutsche Charakter in der Geschichte Europas* (Zürich: Europa Verlag, 1937); but the second book is not merely a translation of the first. *Der deutsche Charakter in der Geschichte Europas* is an attempt to define the "German character" as manifested in European history. Kahler's approach in this study is not chronological but topical: how, he asks, does the "German character" express itself in German intellectual life, in the growth of the German cities, in the German economy. These concerns are reiterated in *The Germans*. This work, too, is a characterological study that offers highly personal interpretations. Kahler's basic assumption is that a nation, just like an individual, is possessed of a distinct "character" and that it, too, proceeds in its growth from childhood to maturity. He argues that what makes Germany unique among the major European nations is that she did not experience normal growth and never achieved anything like maturity. She never, he asserts, progressed beyond a "protracted puberty," an "endless becoming" (*Der deutsche Charakter*, p. 41), and achieved national coherence only in the intellectual realm but never in the political one.

The reader who knows *Der deutsche Charakter* will find himself on familiar ground in the present book. Not only are the central themes identical, but many passages from the earlier study, often abbreviated and reworked, have been incorporated into the later one: the outline of Prussian history, the account of the Germanic tribes and of their encounter with Roman civilization, the long section on the growth of the German cities. The thesis of the Luther section in *The Germans* also goes back to the earlier book, but there Kahler does not present such a detailed account of the Reformation or of Luther's career.

Sharing themes and a certain amount of material, the two books cannot help sharing in the element of polemic. Kahler wrote *Der deutsche Charakter* during the last years of the Weimar Republic, and the distress he felt over political developments in Germany is clearly evident in that volume, so evident that when he submitted the manuscript to a Munich publisher, an editor sympathetic to the Nazi cause denounced Kahler to the party. Shortly after the elections of 1933, the police searched Kahler's home for the manuscript but failed to find it. Kahler was in Austria at the time and never returned to Germany. The manuscript was later smuggled to him in Zürich, where he lived until he emigrated to the United States in 1938. In view of these circumstances, it is not surprising that the polemical tone became even sharper when Kahler wrote of the German character again in 1951-1952.

But despite the similarities that exist between these two studies, there is also one crucial difference. *Der deutsche Charakter* investigates the phenomenon of the "German character" from a number of perspectives. The book is a reflective, philosophical one that walks around its subject and focuses on it ever more sharply from all the vantage points Kahler's broad learning let him assume. *The Germans*, on the other hand, was conceived as a series of lectures for undergraduate students. While Kahler wanted to illuminate the same problems he had dealt with in *Der deutsche Charakter*, he also wanted to narrate the history of the German people. He therefore organized the second book chronologically rather than topically, presenting a cultural history of the Germans from the Great Migrations up to World War II and including in it much basic information that had no place in the earlier study.

In editing the manuscript, we were able to shorten it considerably by omitting the recapitulation at the beginning of each lecture and by eliminating other repetitions that were doubtless useful in the context of a lecture series but that are unnecessary in print. Since it was impossible to locate all the sources quoted throughout the book, we decided to dispense with documentation altogether. The brief bibliography contains titles Erich Kahler himself provided as well as a number of more recent studies of general interest. Unless otherwise noted, the translations of quoted texts are Erich Kahler's.

We are grateful to Alice Kahler for providing us with the information on the publishing history of *Der deutsche Charakter* and on the history of the manuscript for *The Germans*.

ROBERT KIMBER
RITA KIMBER

*Deutschland? aber wo liegt es? Ich weiss das Land nicht zu finden.*
*Wo das gelehrte beginnt, hört das politische auf.*

*Germany? But where is it? I cannot find such a country.*
*Where erudition begins, politics comes to an end.*

    FRIEDRICH V. SCHILLER — "Das Deutsche Reich," *Xenien*

# The Germans

# Introduction

THIS STUDY is a somewhat heretical undertaking since it does not fit into any of the commonly accepted scholarly categories. It is intended as a characterological history of the Germans, German history viewed as the formation of the German character. Conversely, the character of the German people emerges as a creation of German history. The general assumption is that the history of a people is that people's character—their characteristic being—as revealed in time.

This book is not meant to be a history of Germany in the usual sense, political or otherwise. Such presentations describe a sequence of events and conditions in a given geographic and linguistic area. If any specifically German features are stressed at all, they are seen merely as incidental results of circumstances, not as the consistent expression of a people's way of reacting to the world and of creating their world. The emphasis is on what happened and why it happened, not on how it happened. Historical terms and concepts are often used abstractly, as if "kingdom," "state," or "city" had the same meaning for different peoples and periods and therefore required no definition. But it is precisely the peculiar form and significance an institution has taken on in the course of a people's history that reveals the special quality of that people.

A characterological perspective is particularly relevant for German history. In contrast to French, English, or Spanish history, the record of what happened in Germany cannot be unequivocally called German history. It is neither a plainly *German* history, nor is it German *history*. It is not exactly *German* because it lacks a consistent substratum. It comprises manifold histories: the history of the Germanic tribes; the history of the Holy Roman Empire; the histories of Austria, Prussia, Bavaria, and many other regional territories and dynasties; the history of a forty-year German *Kaiserreich* and of an ill-starred, ill-famed Third Reich; as well as the histories of various estates, classes, and movements.

3

*Introduction*

It is not *German* history but a segment of world history. Nor is it German *history*, for it does not represent the evolution of a clearly defined historical entity. During a long succession of intricate, diversely centered processes, common characteristics and concepts have developed. They can be seen as the unintegrated elements of a still unfinished nationality toward which Germany, particularly its intellectual elite, has been striving for so long. A truly homogeneous German nation has not been achieved to this very day. What is generally understood as "German history" is not the history of an established *being* that has grown to maturity and completeness. It relates the perpetual *becoming* of an entity whose very being consists of becoming and whose identity is in constant question.

It is hardly possible to understand Nazi Germany, for example, without considering the characterological and psychological implications of earlier German history. Conversely, an attempt to describe the character of a people without looking into its historical origins is bound to remain erratic, resting as it does on casual observations of isolated phenomena. An account of the characterological features of a people can attain a fair degree of accuracy only if it is based on a study of that people's entire history. The disposition of the German people can be traced back to the historical constellation at the time of the Great Migrations. It is there that the character and destiny of the German people originated: in the encounter of barbarian Germanic tribes with the highest civilization of the epoch, the Roman Empire. Everything that has happened in Germany since can be viewed as a consequence of this fateful encounter.

The statement just made touches on a fundamental problem of special relevance to the understanding of history. My assertion that a primal situation gave rise to all further developments in Germany seems to imply the strictest determinism. It raises the question of whether there is such a thing as freedom of will, freedom of choice, freedom to shape one's destiny. Before I enter into the substantiation of my thesis, I would like to make a few preliminary remarks on this problem.

As in the life of an individual, there are two main determinants in the life of an ethnic group: heredity and environment. Heredity represents what is transmitted from within and from the past by generation and through previous generations. Environment in-

4

cludes all influences from without, the circumstances into which any organism is born and the changing conditions that accompany its development. The life of a people, like that of a person, proceeds in the constant interaction of inner and outer determinants. A certain disposition, produced by ancestry and tradition, meets environmental actuality; and a mutual transformation, an intercreation, takes place.

Psychoanalysis has shown that the most important age in the life of a human being is his childhood, the earliest, formative age, in which he is most flexible and receptive. At this age, the main processes of life occur in the unconscious. Freud's view that the experiences of earliest childhood determine the course of a person's entire life strikes me as too extreme. I am inclined to believe that quite a bit may be changed by later events and that the process of intercreation between disposition and environment goes on as long as life lasts. But a direction is certainly set at the beginning, and with advancing age the adaptability of the human being decreases. Less and less can be changed in later periods.

If the life of a person or the career of a people is shaped by the interplay of two powerful forces, what function can be left to human volition and conscious effort in this closely knit web of objective determinants? Human will and conscious striving obviously exist and make themselves felt in the course of history. We often find personal decisions, personal initiative, personal achievements exerting a decisive influence on the turn of events. This problem is of particular importance in the development of Germany because, as we shall see later, the whole career of the German people suffers from a lack of balance between volition and determination.

The answer to our problem seems to lie in the fact that the capacity for reflection, for making a choice, for deliberate willing and acting, is part of human nature and one of its determinants. A particular shape of mind, including vitality and will, may in itself be regarded as a product of hereditary and traditional forces; and whether an individual carries out an action successfully or not depends on the relationship between his vitality and sensibility and the magnitude of the task presented by circumstances; in other words, it depends on a person's or a people's capacity to meet the challenge of the environment.

An individual making full use of all his faculties acts with a

5

sense of complete freedom. Freedom is experienced in thought, choice, and decision; and it seems boundless because the vital resources of a human being are indeed without limits. Yet when we view decisions in retrospect, when we delve deeply enough into the motives of an act or into modes of thinking, we are sure to find that they were determined by transpersonal factors.

The same is true in the history of a people. There is an age-old dispute between the "materialistic" and the "idealistic" schools of historical thought. One holds, with Marx, that historical events are determined by social and economic conditions. The other, represented by the German historian Leopold von Ranke, maintains that the course of history is affected by the will of men, by human ideas, and by the initiative of great personalities. In the life of ethnic groups, free will is embodied in outstanding personalities. "Great men" articulate a state of consciousness which remains unexpressed in the confused drives and longings of their people. They define and enact the unformulated resolves of the masses. They may be at odds with the attitudes of their people, as the wisest men usually are; but to the extent that they express the unconscious inclinations and decide the destinies of their people, they will come to be regarded as historical personalities.

Just as an individual's consciousness, reason, and free will are influenced by heredity and environment, so, in the history of a people, the thoughts and actions of leading men are influenced by the traditions of their people and the climate of their epoch. Their ways of thinking, their explorations and innovations, are determined by developments far beyond their individual range. Yet these explorations and innovations are no less their own achievements.

The special relevance of this problem for Germany becomes evident when we consider the role of Martin Luther in the evolution of the German people. His powerful personality represents a great divide in this evolution. No other European nation has been affected to such a degree by the character and acts of one single man. Luther created a common German language. This was the initial step toward German unification and remained its only lasting foundation. Luther approached this task in a deliberate, scholarly manner, fully conscious of its historical importance. Indeed, he boasted of this language as his own creation, unlike Dante, who reverently elevated the traditional Tuscan vernacular to a common Italian language. Luther's religious reform disrupted Christianity throughout Europe; but in Germany, it created a more lasting division than in any other country. Religious reformers before him had established only insignificant sects or national churches. Also, by transferring the supreme authority of the church to secular rulers, Luther instituted the peculiar authoritarianism of German governments and the peculiar submissiveness of the German middle class, the mentality of *Obrigkeit* and *Untertan.* In fact, there is hardly any aspect of the character and history of modern Germany, including National Socialism, which cannot be traced back to Luther.

Nowhere in Europe can we find a single personality whose impact on a nation's history is comparable to Luther's. But if we look closer, we shall see that this man, who was so influential in German history, was himself subject to emotional and intellectual forces that have their origin in the social and cultural configurations of medieval Germany. His anxieties, his inner insecurity, and his insatiable yearning for support and approval reflect the conflicts of Germanic man caught between a dying paganism and an unattainable Christianity. In Luther's vacillation between boundless devotion and unbridled revolt, we recognize the ambivalent attitude toward Rome which pervades all of medieval Germany. Conditions in the anarchical Germany of the time contributed greatly to the success of the Reformation. It was the diffusion of power in the empire and the emperor's lack of control that account for the spread of Luther's ideas and for his very survival. This key figure in German history seems much less the master of his own mind and conduct, seems much more controlled by external events and his own reactions to them, than do comparable figures in the Latin countries who had far less influence on national destiny.

In order to understand Luther and the impact he had on modern Germany, we have to go back to the Middle Ages, back to the encounter of the Germanic tribes with the Roman and Christian world.

# Part One

---

## MEDIEVAL GERMANY

# 1.

---

## THE UNIQUENESS OF GERMANY

THE HISTORICAL COMPLEX called Germany presents a unique case both in European history and in world history.

Germany's history is unique, first of all, because her population never achieved national homogeneity. In certain parts of the country—in Frisia, Lower Saxony, Schleswig-Holstein, Franconia, the Alemannic regions, and Upper Bavaria—some strong ethnic connections with Germanic origins have persisted. In other parts—in Saxony and Prussia—the amalgamation of stocks is complete; and if any ethnic traits prevail, they are Slavic rather than Germanic. Also, in the course of German history, the center of cultural and political life shifted constantly from region to region and from dynasty to dynasty.

The second unique feature is a geographical one. All other major European nations developed within well-defined geographical limits. Their natural boundaries seem to have predestined them to form historical units and to expand and integrate their national dominions up to these natural limits. France, Italy, Spain, England, the Scandinavian countries, and Russia were all physically defined by coastlines, mountain ranges, great rivers, bordering wastelands, or, as in the case of Russia, by a great protective remoteness from the scene of complex historical processes. Bohemia, Hungary, and old Serbia are well situated in mountain and river confines where their tribal founders settled in the early Middle Ages. Even Scotland is naturally separated from England by the Cheviot Hills and the Tweed. The southern and western nations were preformed as administrative units of the Roman Empire long before their emergence as independent nations. Belgium and the Netherlands are nearly identical with the Roman provinces of Belgica and Germania inferior.

11

The situation in Germany is characteristically different. The North Sea, the Rhine, and the Alps constitute natural boundaries to the north, west, and south; but the expansion and intermingling of the Germanic tribes prevented these natural borders from evolving into political ones. Eastern Germany was open to the repeated onslaughts of various tribal masses—Huns, Slavs, Arabs, Magyars, Turks—and it came to be a buffer zone in constant turmoil. Roman conquest stopped in the middle of the country along the Rhine and the Danube; this dividing line, the Limes, created a first, basic rift between the southern and the northern parts of Germany. The Limes would later mark the division between the Protestant North and the Catholic South.

Lacking ethnic homogeneity and the organizing influence of Roman administration, Germany began as a vast, shapeless area populated by half-nomadic tribes under constant pressure from eastern invaders. Even later, centuries after an East Frankish kingdom had come to be identified with the Holy Roman Empire, Germany still lacked definition as a geographical concept and remained an indeterminate region with fluid, contested boundaries. It seemed predestined to become the center of European crosscurrents, the perpetual battlefield of Western conflicts.

This condition is reflected in the multiplicity of names for both country and people. The names of all other European nations have their origins in distinct tribal or local entities. Germany and the Germans, however, are named differently in different languages; and the basic designations, *Germania* and *deutsch*, did not even arise indigenously, but were introduced from without.

*Germania* is a Latin word, probably of Celtic origin. It appears first in Hellenistic and Roman sources, and was used by the Gallic Celts and by Roman writers to designate the population or the dwelling places of the various barbarian tribes beyond the Rhine and the Alps. These tribes had no distinct feeling of ethnic community and called themselves by their tribal names. The Germans later claimed that *Germania* derives from the Germanic *Ger-mannen*, spear-men, but this etymology has proved to be pure fantasy.

*Deutsch* goes back to the old German word *diutisc* (from *theoda*, folk); but originally it referred only to the language. It too makes its appearance in Latin and occurs for the first time around A.D. 800 in documents of the Frankish church. It designates the vernacular of the tribes beyond the Rhine, and is an ecclesiastical, not a popular term. Otfried, who uses *theodisce* when writing Latin, speaks of his language as *thiu frenkiska zunga* (the Frankish tongue) in a vernacular text of A.D. 860. Only in the twelfth century does the meaning of the word *theodiscus* expand to include the people. But by then the word had been largely confused with and replaced by the term *Teutonicus*, which derives from the Teutons, a tribe that clashed with the Romans in the second century B.C. and was of Celtic rather than of Germanic origin. Later, it was again the sense of a shared language that led to the revival of the term *deutsch* (*teutsch*) as a designation for both country and people.

This long uncertainty about a common name accounts for the variety of names foreign languages have for Germany and the Germans. In Italian the country is called *Germania*, the people *Tedeschi*; the French names, *Allemagne* and *Allemands*, derive from the Alemanni; the Slavic designations are *Germanija* for the country, *Niemzij*, *Němci*, *Nijemec* for the people.* The Swedish *Tyskland* and *Tysk*, as well as the Dutch *Duitsland* and *Duitsers*, are derived from *deutsch*. The Finnish and Estonian *Saksalaiset* goes back to the name of a Germanic tribe, the Saxons.

But the most important German anomaly is the unique character of Germany's evolution. We may distinguish four main types of national evolution. They are: 1) the centrifugal type, the expansion of a nation from a nucleus. Italy developed from Rome, Spain from Castile, France from the Île de France, England from its south, Switzerland from three original cantons, the United States from the thirteen original states. 2) the transformative type, the conversion of primitive, "underdeveloped" ethnic groups, already established as nations, into modern nations by the revolutionizing effects of intellectual, social, and technological trends of the nineteenth and twentieth centuries. Such was the genesis of the smaller Slavic nations and of Hungary. We are seeing a similar transformation today among the liberated colonial, or semi-colonial, peoples in Asia and Africa. It could even be said that Russia became a modern nation through the revolutionizing

---

* These Slavic terms mean "mutes, stutterers," i.e., foreigners. Similarly, in Greek, the onomatopoeic word *barbaros*, barbarian, means "stutterer," a man who speaks an unintelligible language.

influence of western European thought. 3) the divisional type, the separation of a regional group from a larger unit, as in the case of the Netherlands and of Portugal. 4) the centripetal type, development from the periphery toward the center. This is in fact no "type" at all; it is the unique history of Germany.

To understand Germany's development, it is helpful to contrast it with the evolution of the Romanic nations. Rome was their prototype. Comparable to the natural growth of all living creatures, its development followed the pattern of organic consecution, proceeding by expansion from a nuclear cell. Initially a small, rudimentarily urban center, Rome extended its territorial and cultural sway by responding to the outside world in a succession of conflicts with neighboring peoples; and these defensive actions turned into aggressive conquests. By absorbing and integrating more and more territory, Rome gradually became extensive enough to create a civilization of its own. The Italian city-republics of the Renaissance, evolving from Roman emporia or trade centers, were direct offsprings of Rome. Like France and Britain, which were former Roman provinces, they followed the Roman pattern. All of them grew around capital and residential cities. This metropolitan origin (*metropolis* means "mother city") determined their national history socially, culturally, and intellectually. In these countries, the nobility established city life, "urbanity," and "civilization" as the norm. In Rome, the nobility originated in the city and grew with it. In the Italian cities, noblemen mingled with the burghers. In France and Britain, the rulers compelled their refractory feudal grandees to live in the residential city and participate in the life of the court. This urban life softened the manners of the nobles and developed in them a taste for the arts and for the uses of the intellect. Court society set the tone for the country and created a unifying national tradition.

The development of Germany is the exact reverse. Vaguely defined borders and the inheritance of the Roman Empire determined Germany's early history, and throughout almost two millennia, her repeated efforts to establish a national center failed. Superficial national unification was finally achieved in 1871, only to be abolished again in 1945. No leading residential city, no national court, no national tradition, no national civilization could develop. As a consequence, Germany never achieved

14

that concentration of power which enabled other western nations to exert political and cultural hegemony over Europe.

There is one final and crucial anomaly I would like to mention before we begin our detailed study of the German past, an anomaly that has deeply affected the psyche and character of the German people. All European nations, those of the east as well as those of the west, evolved from their own territorial base, however small. Their evolution was determined by their own immediate interests. Only after they had achieved their identity did their cultural development attain European and universal significance. This could happen only because these countries had assumed their national character naturally in the pre-conscious period of their history. Germany, on the other hand, started from a base not entirely her own; she started from the broad foundations of a universal "Roman" Empire; and, as I said before, a unified, truly *German* Germany was never achieved, although it remained the ultimate goal of long intellectual striving.

The intellectual effort to realize this goal developed rather late; and, being intellectual, it was carried on in the full light of consciousness, a consciousness that was not a reflection of the physical chaos of the country but a reaction to it, an attempt to counteract despair over that chaos by seeking models in envied foreign cultures. Philosophers and poets, applying lofty, universal principles and disregarding the actual state of affairs, worked out political and cultural prototypes for a national style of life; but the final result was the narrowly materialistic, Machiavellian German nationalism of the nineteenth and twentieth centuries with its contempt for the humanistic mentality of the Classic and Romantic periods and for the intellect in general. This divergence of material and intellectual interests added another rift to the many inner conflicts of the German people.

For centuries, Germans have been aware of their country's unusual situation among more fortunate European nations, and a sorrowful intelligentsia has bewailed this situation time and again. After the defeat of 1918, which put an end to the triumphant progress of the Second Reich, the Germans tried to overcome this age-old inferiority complex and to compensate for repeated national failure by fabricating a new interpretation of their past. This interpretation drew on old popular legends, on Richard Wagner's revival of Germanic mythology, and on

Gobineau's race theory. Wagner's *Bayreuther Blätter* had propagated Gobineau's theory in Germany, and this theory was further elaborated by a whole school of German archeologists and anthropologists. The new interpretation tried to convert the German national deficiency into a Nordic racial superiority, indeed, to explain this deficiency away by placing the blame for it on other nations.

In this view, Germany's peculiar situation is due to the predominantly Nordic character of the German people and to the qualities inherent in this character. Nordic man is pictured as a born fighter who loves to live dangerously. He challenges all the fiendish powers he encounters on his way—dragons, death, and the devil. He is a conqueror by nature and by vocation and, therefore, a non-conformist who cannot adapt himself to the humdrum ways of modern middle-class civilization.

Several motifs come together in this interpretation. There are Wagner's figures from pagan times: Siegfried, Parsifal, Tristan; there is the medieval knight, fighting dragons, going on crusades, and seeking adventures, as in Dürer's engraving *Ritter, Tod, und Teufel*; and there is a reminiscence of Nietzsche's superman and "blond beast."

This image of the Nordic hero absorbed two other traditional figures: *der deutsche Michel* and *Doctor Faustus*. Both reflect the German situation. Siegfried was killed by a stab in the back, and Parsifal was seen as *der reine Tor*, the naive dupe who is not aware of the insidious ways of the wicked world. This innocence is personified in the *deutsche Michel*, the good, honest, trustful simpleton wearing a nightcap that symbolizes his drowsiness and sluggishness. It is he who is constantly cheated and made a fool of. The Germans often see themselves in this role. Every misfortune is attributed to the deceit of others: the crafty Jews, the perfidious British (*das perfide Albion*), the treacherous Italians, and so forth. The defeat in the First World War was blamed on a diabolic *Dolchstoss*, a stab in the back. The efforts of the German army had supposedly been undermined by Jewish or enemy elements.

*Der deutsche Michel* represents the lower aspect of the Nordic hero. *Doctor Faustus* represents a higher form. He is the intellectual adventurer who wants to conquer the forces of the universe, fathom the secrets of nature, unlock the past and the future, and so transcend all human limits. He is the Nordic version of Prometheus stealing the fire from the gods. His lust for spiritual power even leads him to make a pact with the devil. Goethe transformed this figure of the black magician into a symbol of modern man, and Spengler identified it with the Nordic type. For Spengler, Nordic man and Faustian man were one.

This self-image of the Germans is not wholly unfounded. The Germans are an important people in human history, a people without whose contributions the development of Western man is inconceivable; and their contributions are a direct result of their tendency to overstep human limitations. Lacking the sense of a human community with established bounds and traditions, the Germans also lack the common sense that such a community imparts to its members. They are given to extremes of both good and evil. They are capable of reckless self-sacrifice for causes or objects, because they have no mainstay in the self; it is the outer goal—ideal or material—that sustains them and gives them security. In their disregard for reality, they are cheated time and again, not by men but by circumstances.

That is the element of truth in the German self-image, distorted as that image may be by resentment and self-aggrandizement. What is demonstrably untrue in it is its racial factor: the "Nordic" quality of the Germans. The Germans are as much a blend of different ethnic groups as any other European people. They have absorbed Celtic, Slavic, Magyar, Mediterranean, and so-called Alpine elements. What there is of a Nordic, i.e., Germanic, strain in the Germans is shared with all European nations and even with the Berber tribes of North Africa. This Nordic strain is physically more conspicuous in the peaceful, temperate Scandinavians. These descendants of the Vikings have succeeded in forming distinct nations and, having attained their national identity, have never dreamed of creating a Nordic world empire. Gobineau, the forerunner of German race theory, extolled what he believed to be the descendants of the Germanic conquerors in the French nobility; but he by no means regarded the German people as paragons of racial excellence; he considered them mongrels in which Germanic traits no longer dominated. Nor did Richard Wagner pretend that the Germans as he knew them were basically Germanic. What he and his Nazi followers wanted to accomplish was *Aufnordung*, nordification, a revival of Nordic qualities. The com-

17

plex mixture of ethnic groups in Germany clearly made this impossible.

Thus, despite certain residual Germanic characteristics in the German people, the racial explanation of Germany's unique and anomalous situation is not tenable. What happened to Germany and in Germany can only be understood if we trace her history step by step from its very beginnings, for the entire course of that history seems determined in large measure by the constellation under which the Germanic tribes first emerged from primeval dusk into the light of history.

# 2.♦

## THE CONFRONTATION

### The Roman Empire

ROME's confrontation with the Germanic tribes was the initial phase of German history proper, and to understand the significance of that encounter for Germany's development, we must take into account the vast cultural gap that existed between Rome and the Germanic tribes that conquered her.

The city of Rome, which was to become the nucleus of the Roman Empire, was an essentially urban community, even in its earliest, most primitive stages. At first it was a kingdom, then, from about 500 B.C. on, a republic. In defending herself against rival Italic peoples, she gradually conquered them and extended her sway over the entire Italian peninsula. Interfering in the affairs of Sicily brought the Romans into conflict with Carthage, a Phoenician city in North Africa, which at that time was the undisputed master of the Mediterranean and its trade routes. After a long and arduous struggle, Rome finally defeated Carthage and destroyed her. In the course of these wars in the period between 264 and about 133 B.C., Rome extended her rule far beyond Italy. She won control over Sicily and the Mediterranean islands in the south, Spain and the coast of North Africa in the west, and Macedonia in the east.

The first transalpine intruders in Italy were the Celts, who came from the east and swept over Europe ahead of the Germanic tribes. The bulk of the Celtic population finally settled in France and on the British Isles. After 500 B.C., the Celtic Gauls, who inhabited what is now France, began to push down across the Alps. In 390 B.C., they penetrated as far as Rome itself, but were eventually driven back. This period from about 500 to 133

B.C., ending with the conclusion of the Carthaginian Wars, was the first stage of Roman history, the first round of expansion and consolidation beyond the Italian mainland.

Even this first colonial expansion was accompanied by the development of an elaborate system of administration, by vastly increased trade, and by the accumulation of wealth among leading families. The source of this wealth was not trade alone but, more important still, the exploitation of high offices, particularly the governorships of provinces. This led in turn to an opulent style of life in the capital and, consequently, to sharp divisions in the society: divisions between the metropolitan, genuinely Roman elements of the population and those of provincial extraction; divisions between the upper classes with full, unrestricted citizenship and the lower classes who were either restricted in their civil rights or excluded from citizenship altogether. Domestic disorder could not but result from such division in a growing population. The masses struggled to gain their political rights, and rivalries developed among political leaders who resorted to demagogy and exploited the aspirations of the masses in their efforts to win control of the state.

Ambitious men could rise to power through two principal offices: "tribune of the people," the traditional protector and attorney of the plebeians, and "imperator," the commander in chief of the army. Frequently, the imperatorship was the first step on the way to a powerful consulate or even to the dictatorship. A clear distinction has to be made between the offices of imperator and dictator. In the republican period, an imperator was primarily a military officer. He had unlimited power, but only over the armies under his command and over the provinces in which they were fighting. The dictator held a civilian office. He was to be appointed only in times of emergency and for a strictly limited period, but he was given unlimited control over the entire state.

The second period of Roman history, from 133 to 31 B.C., was that of the civil wars. This was a time of crisis for the republic, characterized by increasing transgressions of traditional law, savage upheavals, and massacres. It started with the popular reforms of the Gracchi, two brothers who were tribunes of the people and who enforced much-needed legal innovations by illegal and ultimately violent means. The period was also marked by internal strife between Marius and Sulla, Caesar and Pompey,

Octavian—Caesar's grand-nephew and adopted son—and Mark Antony, all of them imperators and consuls, some of them dictators and tribunes of the people.

One might think that this period of continuous unrest and temporary anarchy would mean the end of Rome. It did spell the doom of the republic, but it also saw the expansion of Roman rule to the borders of the known world—to Egypt and Mesopotamia, to central Europe, and to the British Isles. The foundation of the Roman Empire had been laid. The civil wars also increased the power of the city. They spurred the ambitions of competing leaders who outdid each other in saving the state from foreign assaults and in conquering new provinces.

The Roman Empire was the first and last world empire, the first and last one that could truly be called universal. It was not just an agglomeration of territories but an organized whole with an imposing civilization and an unequalled system of administration. The roads, the aqueducts, the baths, the theaters, the majestic buildings, all the technical innovations and comforts of urban life that spread wherever Rome governed—all this was implied in the Roman name and gave it its incomparable prestige. To be a Roman citizen was to hold a title of honor unmatched by any other in the world. The splendor of the name outlived the empire itself; it persisted long after the complex structure of Rome had collapsed and left her an easy prey to invading hordes.

What seems most significant historically in the rise of Rome is the impact of a few individual actions that transformed Rome and created concepts, offices, and titles that have become central to the vocabulary of government. The first was Caesar's famous decision to cross the Rubicon, the border of the province legally under his imperatorial command. He thus defied the Senate, which, swayed by Pompey, ordered him to lay down his command and release his army. Caesar's act was clearly a revolutionary one, lacking even that semblance of formal authorization which previous leaders had always sought. Caesar went on to defeat Pompey and his associates in Italy both in the east and in the west. He then returned to Rome, celebrated his four triumphs, and assumed control of the state. He had himself elected consul for ten years and dictator and *praefectus morum* (supervisor of morals) for life. He also assumed tribunicial powers, including *sacrosanctitas*, and the title imperator as a personal surname. By accumulating all these offices and titles, he established a totally new kind of monarchy. Its precursory form, the Greek *tyrannos*, achieved only transitory and purely personal significance. But the Caesarian regime, founded on a huge, elaborately organized dominion, gradually perpetuated and legitimized itself, finally becoming a European institution.

Caesar established this monarchy *de facto*, not *de jure*. He left the republican constitution intact; he merely took over its offices as special, well-deserved privileges. His private family name, Caesar, Greek *Kaisar*, and his title, imperator, thus became the common designations for the new type of monarch. Kaiser and tsar derive from the personal name Caesar, emperor from imperator. *Imperium*, which originally designated a temporary function and area of command, developed into the concept of a large, multifarious, yet politically unified domain, the empire. The use of imperial titles by monarchs like the Napoleons, who came to power by their own efforts, evokes the revolutionary origin of the *Imperium Romanum*. The rise of Napoleon Bonaparte is particularly reminiscent of Caesar's, and his rule was equally "imperialistic." Imperial titles, harking back to the universality of the Roman Empire, seemed to carry more prestige than royal ones.

Like Caesar, Octavian exploited civil strife to gain power. Under Octavian the transformation from the Republic of Rome to the Roman Empire was completed. After defeating his rival Mark Antony, Octavian began to consolidate the monarchy by limiting but not fundamentally changing the republican constitution. He insured that his stepson and adopted son, Tiberius, would succeed to power by bestowing an extensive secondary *Imperium* and the tribunicial power upon him. Tiberius, a successful commander, continued the established but now hypocritical practice of submitting his imperial election to a senate which was no longer strong enough to refuse approval of it. Thus, a perpetual *Imperium* gradually became established, and the transformation of state and society was well underway.

The use of personal names to designate offices reflects the role a few individuals played in the creation of the monarchy. Just as Caesar became a title, the epithet Augustus, first bestowed on a triumphant Octavian by the people, then solemnly conferred on him by the senate, became the regular attribute of succeeding emperors, Roman and medieval. The customary designation for an eminent senator, *princeps senatus* (first among the senators), was accorded Octavian as a personal tribute. In the forms *principatus* and *principium*, it became another title of the imperial ruler and a designation of his office. The title was later restricted to heirs to the throne or "princes."

The third period of Roman history extends from about 31 B.C. to A.D. 323, the year of Emperor Constantine's conversion to Christianity. This period marks the end of Rome's expansion but also the beginning of her decline.

In A.D. 212, the emperor Caracalla extended Roman citizenship to all free people living within the bounds of the empire. Thus, people who had been connected with Rome only indirectly through their provincial governments, their proconsuls, and their procurators now had a direct relationship to the great city. They enjoyed all the privileges of citizenship, including access to the highest ranks and offices, even that of emperor. This gradually changed the structure of the city and the empire. The old city-state with its sacred offices and authorities, its nucleus of Roman nobility surrounded by populations at various stages of development, became a leveled, centralized bureaucratic state in which new imperial offices and functions displaced the old ones. But these changes did not affect the basic principle on which the Roman Empire was built: the preeminence of the city of Rome over the provinces.

These changes had a democratizing influence at first. Stoicism, with its ideal of human equality and tolerance, gained ascendancy in Rome when Marcus Aurelius (A.D. 161-180) came to the imperial throne. As a ruler, he was guided by "the concept of a state," as he put it, "with one law for all, and founded on freedom of speech, a government that sets the freedom of those governed before all else." The old senatorial nobility was displaced by an aristocracy based on wealth. By way of positions in the imperial administration, these "equestrians" from provincial families attained to the highest offices in Rome. Similarly, under the pressure of more frequent foreign assaults, the Roman legions and the Praetorian Guards, which had formerly consisted of citizens of the capital only, were opened to rural provincials. Even barbarians served in Augustus' "auxiliary" units. This trend culminated in the accession of Septimius Severus (193-211) to the imperial throne. He came from a Romanized African family and rose to the emperorship through a bloody struggle among military commanders. His sweeping reforms inaugurated an era of military rulership. The role the barbarized Praetorian Guards played in the selection of emperors constituted a social revolution. It expressed not only the overweening self-assertion of the armies that protected the state from ever increasing foreign attacks and domestic revolts, but also the antagonism toward the rich and cultured Roman citizenry felt by the country people who now formed the bulk of the armies.

Thus, initial democratization ultimately had just the opposite effect. It led to a thorough bureaucratization of the state and so to a form of totalitarianism. All Rome's equal citizens were subject to equal harassment by the centralized government of an absolute monarchy. Diocletian (284-305), an Illyrian said to have been an enfranchised slave, surrounded himself with a large, ostentatious retinue and introduced an elaborate court ceremonial, the famous "Byzantine" ceremonial, prototype of later Western court rituals. Although he himself had come to power through the army, he put an end to military usurpation by separating the civil administration from the military command and by reinstating succession by heredity and adoption. He had to reorganize an economic system disrupted by inflation. A huge increase in taxes was necessary to maintain large mercenary armies and the court. There were, in fact, two courts, since the defense of such an extensive empire required its division into western and eastern realms with coequal emperors. The government had to resort to forced levies in kind and to compulsory state service from which only the specially privileged were exempt. These measures gradually exhausted the resources of the population.

The Roman Empire originated in a city-state, and it never abandoned this original concept. Its base was the city, not the country. It converted its peoples to an urban life and civilization; they became accustomed to thinking and acting in urban terms. The ruling city gave the state identity. The surrounding country was only an adjunct; it had no life and meaning of its own and existed solely to feed and support the city. The Roman government regarded the provinces merely as territories to be exploited through the cities. But consistent adherence to a principle often tends to be self-defeating. In the case of Rome, extreme urbanization resulted in the disruption of city life and so led to the development of feudalism.

In the fourth and final period of Roman evolution, the empire merged with the Christian religion. The lofty, spiritual concept of Christianity penetrated the structure of the empire and contributed as much to its luster as it did to its political decline. The administrative system of the Church, formed by analogy with the empire, absorbed what was left of the gradually failing Roman authority and replaced it when the Western Empire collapsed in the fifth century. Canon law continued the tradition of Roman law. The spiritual empire of the Church extended to all the Roman provinces, reaching north to Britain, Gaul, and the Danube; and it endured even when these provinces were lost to the barbarian tribes. Materially powerless though it was, the Church incorporated into its own spiritual authority the prestige of the Roman civilization it had inherited.

If we contemplate the entire course of Roman history, what astonishes us most about it is not merely the logical consistency of its development but the emergence of this consistency from a continuing interaction of chaos and order. Anarchical passions and fierce rivalries, acting as agents of change, were always counterbalanced by a prudence that restored order to a threatened society and, at the same time, laid the foundations of order for societies to come.

This was the impalpable but ineluctable force the Germanic tribes encountered when, with naive and savage impetuosity, they conquered the crumbling Roman Empire.

## The Germanic Tribes

The first known site of the Germanic tribes was Scandinavia, where they can be traced back to the second millennium B.C. Around 1000 B.C., they started to push south, probably because of overpopulation in their homeland. A western branch moved up the Elbe and the Rhine, reaching the river Main around 200 B.C. and southern Germany around 100 B.C. These tribes made their first appearance within the Roman orbit when they clashed with Roman armies in Styria, Carinthia, and the Rhone valley. This western, Teutonic branch of the Germanic tribes settled in what is now Germany, and even today we distinguish the regional and linguistic sections of Germany by the names of these Teutonic

25

groups: Alemanni ("all men") and Suevi (Swabians) on the upper Rhine; Franks ("free men") on the lower and middle Rhine; Saxons ("swordsmen") between the Weser and the Elbe and in the Harz mountains; and Thuringians south of the Saxons. (The territory once occupied by the Saxon tribe is nearly identical with what is now called Old Saxony or Lower Saxony. Upper Saxony became the site of mixed Germanic and Slavonic settlements and was later divided into various principalities, including the eastern territory of the Kingdom of Saxony.)

An eastern branch of the Germanic tribes crossed the Baltic Sea between 600 and 300 B.C., pushed up the Vistula to the Carpathian mountains, and moved down toward the Black Sea, where they arrived in the second century A.D. The Vandals settled in Silesia, the Markomanni in Bohemia. The Goths, after reaching the Black Sea, divided into Visigoths and Ostrogoths (West and East Goths), mingled with the native population, and established vast kingdoms in southern Russia. The Ostrogothic kingdom at the peak of its power in the middle of the fourth century A.D. stretched from the Black Sea to the Baltic.

Some of the Germanic tribes stayed in their native Scandinavia; they have remained the purest bred of what may be called the Germanic peoples. They later sent out a second wave of migration. Bands of Norsemen, the "Waräger" or confederates, crossed the Baltic Sea after A.D. 800 and subjected the Slavic and Finnish populations. The conquered peoples called these invaders "Rûs" (Russians). Advancing along the Dnieper in 864, the Rûs settled in Kiev, which became the center of their political power and the nucleus of what would later be Russia. In the west, the Scandinavians invaded England in the eighth century and established a stronghold on the west coast of France (Normandy) in the ninth century. From Normandy, they penetrated into southern Italy and Sicily where they founded a powerful kingdom in the eleventh century.

The gradual expansion of the Germanic tribes was a kind of chain reaction. Their basic social form was the clan. Clans grew to tribes from which new clans branched off, migrating, campaigning, and seeking new homes. These clans formed new tribes in turn, either alone or by merging with others. In this way tribes and tribal names appeared for a time and disappeared again to

26

be replaced by others. Some of these ephemeral kingdoms left their mark on history, but only a very few, like the Franks, the Saxons, the Burgundians, and the Langobards ("long-beards"), had a lasting influence on it.

These Germanic migrations constituted an increasing threat to Rome. Warding off the advancing tribes had become a considerable task for the Romans in the period from 71 B.C., when the Swabian chieftain Ariovistus first crossed the Rhine, to A.D. 260, when the Alemanni broke through the Limes. But the main thrust that started the upheaval known as the Great Migrations originated in northern China, far away from the scene where it was to have its most important effects. After their defeat by the emperors of the later Han dynasty, the western branch of the Hiung Nu, or Huns, set out westward around A.D. 300. They overran the peoples of the Sarmatian steppes, north of the Caucasus, and defeated the eastern Germanic tribes of the Goths, the Gepids, and the Scyrri, pursuing them into Roman territories. The stream of Germanic peoples from the north—Burgundians, Vandals, and Langobards—met the westward sweep from the Black Sea. The result was that gigantic whirlpool of mingling populations in which the Roman Empire succumbed.

One aspect of this process is of great importance for the later development of German-Roman relations. I have already mentioned the magic power of the Roman name and the pride people of diverse extraction felt in belonging to this venerable community. As Joseph Vogt has noted in his book on Constantine the Great, it would have been easy for some non-Italic commanders and rulers to sever their homelands from the empire in the frequent periods of anarchy and to form independent dominions of their own. But having become Romans, they remained more passionately loyal to the universal and eternal city than their native Roman predecessors. In the face of mounting Oriental influence, the Illyrian emperors from Decius to Diocletian were ardent champions not only of imperial unity but also of the Latin tradition. Later, when the empire disintegrated, this same reverence for the Roman name accounted for the ambivalence the Germanic conquerors felt toward everything Roman and Christian. This ambivalence determined the nature of Germanic involvement with the Roman Empire. It manifested itself most clearly in the

27

conflicting positions of the medieval emperors who were torn in their loyalty to their Germanic origins and to the Roman dignity they had assumed.

This ambivalence did not have purely emotional origins; it also arose from the peculiar political and military relations established between Rome and the Germanic tribes. Even under the Roman Republic, conquered populations were admitted into the Roman dominion as allied peoples or *foederati*. Caesar employed Germanic detachments as *auxilia* fighting side by side with the Roman armies; and, beginning with the reign of Severus, these *auxilia* were rewarded with land in their own provinces as payment for their military service. The auxiliaries gradually became the mainstay of the Roman army. Germanic tribes often fought with the Romans against their kinsmen, and occasionally they shifted sides. Their situation was ambiguous and confusing. They were both tribesmen and Roman soldiers. They were only superficially Romanized and Christianized. They were aware of the incomprehensible but majestic rule of the Roman and Christian civilization, but they were unable to overcome their barbarian nature.

In the conquering Germanic chieftains, this ambivalent situation was reflected in a deeply ambivalent state of mind. Confronted with the intangible power and prestige of Rome, they vacillated between physical force and respectful humility. Victorious Germanic chieftains who took possession of Roman territories were suddenly paralyzed by some mysterious fear or shame or repentance. They felt the need to submit to what they had subjugated.

According to the report of the contemporary theologian and historian Orosius, the Visigoth Ataulf, who joined his brother-in-law Alaric in the sacking of Rome, confessed that "he first had the ardent desire to wipe out the name of Rome and to make all of Rome into a Gothic empire. Ataulf wanted to become what Caesar Augustus had been. But long experience had taught him that the Goths, because of their unrestrainable barbarism, could not be forced to obey laws, and that to abolish laws would mean that the state ceased to be a state. Therefore, he, Ataulf, finally decided to seek fame in reinstating and enhancing the power of the Roman name through Gothic might and to go down in posterity as the restorer of the Rome he was unable to replace. This is why he desisted from war; this is why he strove for peace."

This was also the policy of the Ostrogothic king Theodoric the Great. After wresting Italy and Sicily from the Scyrian Odoacar, he decided to abandon his successful military campaign and devote himself to preserving and reviving the traditional Roman institutions whose administration he left in native hands. The famous *Edictum Theodorici*, a codification of his decrees, was largely a confirmation and reinterpretation of Roman legislation. He even undertook restoration of buildings in the Roman Forum. His intention was to rule jointly with the eastern emperor, to whom he wrote: *Regnum nostrum imitatio vestri*—Our rule shall be an imitation of yours.

This ambivalent attitude of the Germanic chieftains has no precedent or parallel in history; no other conquerors have ever felt a similar awe before their victims. Only in this instance was a lofty, universal, yet dying empire conquered by a primitive people who, by contact with this empire, had come to recognize its greatness. Even the most ruthless of the Germanic tribes, the Vandals, felt respect for Roman greatness. Under their leader Geiseric, they plundered Rome but did not destroy it. Attila the Hun, whose contact with the empire was quite brief, was totally devoid of this respect.

At the time of the Germanic migrations and for a long time thereafter, the landscape of central Europe was bleak and inhospitable. Vast primeval forests were interspersed with steppes, moors, and swamps. "Who," Tacitus asks, "would be tempted to leave Asia, Africa, or Italy for Germany, a geographically uninviting country with inclement weather and poor soil, a sad place to contemplate for anyone not native to it." This region lacked all the amenities that the southern coastal areas offered their populations. It is no accident that Western civilization started in the amphitheater of the Mediterranean. This sunny and protected sea favored communication among diverse peoples. Trade and cultural exchange flourished. Roman colonization first brought the skills and knowledge of Mediterranean civilizations to the less advanced peoples of northern and central Europe. In the gentle Mediterranean climate, where the struggle for existence was not as harsh as in the north, technical and cultural advances

29

served to enhance the quality of life. But in northern Europe, the new skills were more than amenities. They became powerful tools in the battle for survival, and it was the need for such tools, combined with the ingrained habits of struggle against the environment, that eventually prompted the northern peoples to outstrip their teachers.

It seems futile to speculate why the Germanic tribes migrated south toward the Mediterranean and the Black Sea instead of developing their own lands or spreading into the vast, sparsely populated areas of the east. The prospect of booty, the lust for adventure, and the pressure of the Huns all may have been contributing factors, but the appeal of a warmer climate and the attractions of a more advanced civilization were probably the main motivations.

Due to a lack of concrete evidence, there has been much debate about the cultural level of the Germanic tribes, and recent attempts to present their barbarism as a peculiar Germanic civilization have added to the confusion. Not only Roman and Christian writers but Germanic sources as well attest to the primitive social and economic conditions of the Germanic tribes. Fierceness in battle was the highest virtue among the tribes. Peaceful occupations were looked down upon and held unworthy of a man. The whole early record of the tribes is one of perpetual feuds, plunder, raids, and massacres; and the custom of human sacrifice is confirmed up to the seventh and eighth centuries A.D. by Roman, Greek, and Christian sources. To call this state civilization is to deprive the word of its meaning. Emphasis on the heroic in the early history of the tribes should be neither decried nor glorified. It belongs to the past of all civilizations.

Neither wholly nomadic nor wholly sedentary, the tribes were always ready to settle but equally ready to move. They developed no residential centers, no sanctuaries or temples. Their only structures even vaguely resembling towns were walled encampments (*Fluchtburgen*) of which traces have been found. These were primitive fortifications made of clay and situated on hills or in remote places in the forest. The concept of a city was so foreign to the Germanic peoples that when they saw the magnificent buildings, temples, baths, and arenas of the Roman cities, they did not think of using them or imitating them. As the Roman historian Ammianus Marcellinus noted, the Germanic tribes con-

30

sidered cities "tombs surrounded by labyrinths." They either avoided them or leveled them whenever they could. Even later, after the Frankish kings had adopted Roman customs and become Roman emperors, they still refused to reside in cities. They wandered about from one estate to another, living off each one in turn. This hatred of cities is a Germanic characteristic that persisted in the German feudal nobility and had an unfortunate influence on the social and intellectual development of Germany.

The Germanic tribes lived by a combination of hunting, stock farming, and such planting as their perpetual warring and traveling allowed. Tillage was left largely to women, children, and old people—to all those unable to bear arms. The land was owned by the clan or tribe, and every year both tillage and harvest were divided among the families or clans. The rotation of agricultural work among members of the tribe or clan insured that no one would settle into it and so become sedentary or unfit for military action. This appears to have been the rule, but customs varied among different tribes and at different times. In some Germanic tribes individual property and cultivation did develop; in others, both common and individual tillage existed side by side. But even where individual cultivation occurred, some land was still reserved for common use, particularly as pasture land. This institution survives to this day in the English "common" and in the German *Allmende*.

Equality and communality were the rule among tribal members, but the belief in the magic power, the "mana," of certain individuals offset this principle of equality. Victorious warriors were rewarded with preferred positions and with large grants of land. Then, because of the belief in the magic of their blood, their families and descendants were elevated above ordinary freemen (*Gemeinfreie*) to a rank of nobility. In some tribes, especially in those that established domains of at least transient significance, the supreme commander, the *Herzog* (*herizogo*, i.e., the leader of the troops), or the *Fürst* (*furisto*, the "first") was elected from these noble families; and the families of these leaders were, so to speak, elected with them. These "first" men of their tribes were given the title *rex* by the Romans, although this term does not really correspond to the German titles.* Tacitus was aware of this

---

* The appropriate Roman terms would have been *praetor* (*prae-itor*, the marcher in front) or *princeps* (the first among equals).

31

incongruity, and at a point where he uses the word *reges* in connection with Germanic tribes he adds: "as far as the idea of *regnare*, ruling, can be said to apply to Germanic chieftains." The German word *König*, used as an equivalent for the Latin *rex*, stems from the Germanic *kunis*, which means simply "descendant from a noble family" or "representative of the family (*chunni*)."

Thus, Germanic leadership was partly electoral, partly hereditary; the people chose their leader, but they chose him as a representative of a special family believed to be endowed with supranatural gifts. This peculiarly Germanic combination established a pattern that persisted throughout the German Middle Ages and contributed to the incapacity of the German kings and emperors to establish lasting dynasties. It also gave rise to still another paradox in the German character: a powerful drive for independence combined with an equally strong need for submission to a sanctified authority. German history is characterized by the interaction of these two motivations; and we shall see later how extreme self-assertion eventually led to self-repression through collective discipline.

The Germanic tribes show definite characteristics of peoples at a primitive, pre-individualistic stage: the custom of communal property; the equality of tribal members; the belief in the magical gifts of shared "blood" in selected families; and the uncodified, half-totemistic state of their mythology and religion. But for a people at this cultural level, their tribal bonds appear exceptionally weak. The Germanic people entered history in innumerable but related groups. Clans and tribes formed and vanished, divided and united; but they never developed a coherence that brought them all together, nor did single tribes develop enough stability to survive as independent cultural entities. The enduring kingdoms of the Franks, Anglo-Saxons, and Normans were formed on the pattern of Roman and Christian institutions.

A precocious individualism is reflected in the unbridled independence of some tribesmen. But even more striking evidence of the weakness of tribal bonds is the Germanic institution of *Gefolgschaft*. This principle of absolute loyalty to an individual leader was a crucial element in the rise of medieval feudalism. We find it mentioned in the accounts of Caesar and Tacitus, and it occupies a central position in eighth- and ninth-century epics like *Beowulf* and the *Heliand*. The latter, written by a Christian cleric, makes the story of Jesus Christ understandable to Germanic minds by telling it in terms of a warring chieftain and his following or *Gefolgschaft*.

Tribal leaders were elected by all the free men of the tribe, but it was also customary for a single warrior to summon personal followers for a campaign he wanted to start on his own initiative. This arrangement was purely private. It guaranteed the leader the unswerving loyalty of his followers, loyalty to the death if need be, in exchange for protection, subsistence, instruction in arms, and a share of any booty taken. *Gefolgschaft* was based solely on personal fidelity and trust between the leader and the follower. A breach of faith on either side annulled the bond. The very lack of legal definition gave this personal relationship its moral force and sanctified its bonds. Personal loyalty (*Treue*) was the supreme Germanic virtue, not only in the tribal period but throughout the Middle Ages. It held the feudal system together, taking precedence over tribal bonds and ties of kinship.

In the process of occupying conquered territories, the Germanic tribesmen became increasingly concerned with cultivating the lands their leaders had given them, and hierarchical differences developed which foreshadowed the feudal system to come. Converging forces created this system. Paramount among them was the fusion of the Germanic custom of the *Gefolgschaft* with similar forms of personal dependency that had developed in the declining Roman Empire. The medieval feudal empire originated in mutual obligations between individuals, and it remained based on them throughout its history. It was not a genuine state but a complex system of mutual bonds, an immense, intricate hierarchy of vassals and feudal lords. Each lord was the vassal of a higher lord in turn. The hierarchy ended with the emperor who was subject only to God. Whatever transformations and elaborations the institution of the *Gefolgschaft* may have undergone, it still remained the basic force behind the organization of the feudal empire.

When the Germanic tribes conquered Rome, they assumed control of an empire that was not just Roman but Christian as well. The gap between Christianity and Germanic religion was as great as the gap between Roman civilization and tribal society; and the ambivalence that characterized the tribes' attitude toward Rome also characterized their attitude toward Christianity. The

33

need for submission and independence would make itself felt throughout the history of German religious life, too.

In terms of the evolution of religion, the mentality of the Germanic tribes was still at the earliest, most primitive stage. Lucien Lévy-Bruhl has called this the stage of participation. In this stage, man personifies natural forces, endowing them with a will and emotions like his own. The entire universe is animate; the visible and the invisible, the inner and outer life, dream, hallucination, and reality are all of the same order. All forces are in close communication and are capable of passing into one another. Man can become an animal, plant, or mineral; and these in turn can assume human attributes.

Because there is no fundamental distinction between the animate and inanimate, there is also no fundamental distinction between the living and the dead. Death is simply a removal to some distant region; it does not mean total or final absence. The dead return in the newborn or as ghosts, souls released from their former bodies and ready to inhabit new ones. From the ancestral dead a personified spirit of the species takes shape, a First Ancestor or legendary Elder Brother who represents both the origin and the substance of the species. He lives in a remote place and can be perceived only in dreams or visions that medicine men, shamans, or priests communicate to the people.

The transformation of participation into religion involves an objectification of the ancestral spirit and an awareness of the distinction between time and eternity. At this state of religious evolution, man confronts the question not only of his own origin but of the origin of all things. Here, the deity ceases to be a blood relative and becomes the universal creator.

The final evolutionary step from religion to world religion could only be accomplished at a stage of intellectual maturity and in a social situation that favored the realization of a deep human affinity between people of diverse extraction. World religion, as it developed out of the Jewish experience and as we find it in the teachings of the prophets and of early Christianity, is the free belief in a universal God as creator, lord, and redeemer. The emphasis gradually shifts from the creator to the ruler and savior. The physical bond between man and deity disappears. Man's allegiance to God is established by a covenant and based solely on faith and confidence. It is therefore not religion in its original sense; it is a creed, a purely spiritual confession of faith in a supreme being who is in no way related to any particular people and does not appeal to a tribe or nation but speaks directly to each human being.

Original Christianity severed the pagans from their tribal roots, leaving them with a universal spiritual God as their only inner support. But this concept of divinity was so foreign to them that a savior in human form was needed to make Christianity meaningful to the pagan world. Christianity had to be transformed into Christology before it could become a world religion. Paul was able to accomplish this transformation because the message of Jesus' divinity and death on the Cross had already been anticipated in Hellenistic cults enacting sacrificial death and resurrection. The ancient Mediterranean peoples were prepared for the Pauline message. They had already known highly developed religions incorporating pantheons, rituals, sanctuaries, and priesthoods. The mingling of cults and ideas in Hellenistic civilization and the influence of the Stoa and of proselytizing Judaism had made the peoples of the Near East susceptible to the Christian message. Indeed, the first Christian communities formed among pagan worshippers of the Jewish god.

The transition to world religion was a long and difficult process even for the religiously advanced peoples of the Mediterranean. But for the Germanic peoples, who were at an earlier stage of religious evolution, this transition was more difficult still; and the persistence of Germanic religious elements into modern times would seem to indicate that it was never fully accomplished. Seen in terms of religious evolution, the figures of Germanic mythology are the products of a stage between participatory cult and actual religion. Like the social forms of the Germanic tribes, they lack clear definition. A single natural power, capable of assuming many shapes, permeates the Germanic world. The principal god, Wuotan (Norse "Odin"), is a sorcerer or shaman with varied magical gifts. He lacks the omnipresence of a universal god, but he is felt to be ubiquitous because he can suddenly appear anywhere, literally transported by ecstasy, trance, or fury.*
His perpetual disguise is his very identity.

Because nature itself forms the substratum of Germanic my-

* His name is based on Old High German *wuot*, rage, madness. Wuotan means "the bearer and creator of rage."

35

thology, there are no sharp distinctions between demons, gods, or heroes; and we do not find highly individualized figures like those of classical antiquity. Pan, for example, the Arcadian god of woods and pastures and the patron of the idyllic natural life, has no parallel in Germanic mythology. The fact that Germanic figures represent natural forces lends them their fairy-tale quality and also explains why they could survive intact into the modern period. A late and allegorical form of myth, the fairy tale evolved at a point in history when nature was no longer considered divine but when natural phenomena still remained incomprehensible and were therefore personified and demonized. The dragons, giants, and dwarfs; the witches, elves, and imps of the Germanic world stayed alive in northern fairy tales precisely because they lacked the clear outlines of the Greek nymphs and satyrs and thus could assume changing roles, eventually appearing as devils in a Christian context.

The predominance of natural forces in Norse mythology also prevents the evolution of a fixed cosmic order. In Greek mythology, the ascendancy of the Olympians was established early when the gods defeated the Titans. Northern myths show no such clear-cut superiority of the divine over the natural. On the contrary, the battle between gods and natural forces is a long struggle that ends in the defeat of the gods. War, nature, and destiny come to be identical; both gods and humans are subject to destiny, to warring nature, which destroys in order to create anew. In Germanic mythology, war is the order of nature and the basic element of life. The cosmic struggle begins between two clans of deities. One clan consists of the Vans, fertility spirits reflecting the milder, more settled tribal life in the Scandinavian homelands and on the northern shores. The Vans are defeated by the Ases, mythical figures originating among the migrating central European tribes. The climactic event of Germanic mythology is Ragna- rök. In this gigantic Armageddon, the Ases themselves succumb to giants and dragons gone berserk, and the whole world is destroyed. The Fenriswolf swallows Odin and the sun; the Midgard- snake, slain by Thor, kills him with its poisonous breath. The sky collapses, and its debris crushes the earth. This preordained orgy of destruction must occur so that the gods may die a heroic death and a new world may arise.

Although the gods appear as the friends and prototypes of

Germanic man, their battle with the monsters, unlike the Persian contest between Ahuramazda and Ahuramanu, is not a battle between Darkness and Light, Good and Evil. Even the most tenuous moral presuppositions would have required the defeat of the monsters. "Behind this myth," Hans Naumann states, "lies the experience that nothing lasts on earth, that birth itself is a death sentence. . . . No one is punished because everyone is slain." No sacred morality, no divine law could evolve from this glorification of heroism. Other mythologies include figures or concepts in which law and destiny are united: the Indian Dharma, the Greek Themis, the Roman Fas and Fatum. There are no equivalents in Germanic mythology. Germanic destiny is simply the process of nature, devoid of any values; and in this view, it is unclear whether death means defeat or self-realization.

It is obvious enough how far removed from Christianity this Germanic religion was. The absence of a just god, the lack of a divine law, and the meaninglessness of history all stand in direct contrast to the underlying tenets of Christianity. The Germanic peoples did, of course, eventually succeed in bridging this gulf, too; but elements of this early, primitive religion remained alive and continued to exert an influence on German history well into our own times. Richard Wagner and the Nazis after him were able to draw on Germanic mythology and turn it to their own purposes because it spoke of a heroic age that the German people, divided and embittered, had never experienced in their history and that they were willing to recover at the cost of the Roman and Christian heritage they had never quite made their own.

# 3.

## THE EARLY FRANKISH KINGDOM

IT HAS often been argued, especially by German historians, that when the Germanic tribes assumed the inheritance of the Roman Empire, they had progressed far beyond the state that Tacitus and other Roman historiographers describe. This argument has some validity. Contact with Roman civilization had existed for six centuries, and an exchange of influence did occur during that time. But even after six centuries of increasing familiarity with Roman and Christian civilization, the Germanic people were still thorough barbarians. The Merovingians, the Frankish rulers from the fifth to the eighth century and the founders of the Germanic Roman Empire, had not had any direct contact with the center and the source of Roman civilization. Their experience had never gone beyond the Roman Celtic province of Gaul, even after they had become Christians and had ruled Gaul as Roman grandees. Contemporary sources like the *Historia Francorum* of Gregorius, bishop of Tours, give us an impression of the culture and mentality of the Frankish rulers. Gregorius was a Gallic or Gallo-Roman nobleman of great erudition and genuine devotion to the Christian faith. Despite the enmity of the Frankish rulers, he remained impartial and did not bear any grudges against the Germans. He is one of the best and most reliable authorities on the history of his epoch. We also have the reports of Venantius Fortunatus, a Roman poet who lived for a time as a highly honored guest at the courts of the Gallic grandees and rulers and eulogized them in flattering poems and letters.

These accounts show that the Merovingians were still essentially barbarian. The term Merovingian stems from their ancestor Merovig, an early Frankish leader who fought with the Romans in the

38

battle against the Huns at Châlons-sur-Marne in 451. Rising from the position of Germanic war leaders, the Merovingians displaced the Roman provincial governors of Gaul. In the battle of Soissons in A.D. 486, the Frankish leader Clovis defeated Syagrius, the last Roman governor of Gaul. Syagrius' rule had been practically autonomous because the Western Roman Empire had ceased to exist ten years earlier when the last emperor was deposed. Clovis also took possession of the large estates of the Roman fisc in Gaul. Like the other Germanic chieftains, Clovis recognized the authority of the Byzantine emperor and accepted the title of Roman Consul from him. He also became a Christian; but, being subject to western influence, he followed the Catholic or Athanasian doctrine, not the Arian one.* From his new position as the practical successor of the deposed Western Roman emperor, Clovis, and later his descendants, subjected the Frankish territories beyond the borders of Gaul. The Merovingians rewarded their personal followers with land from these newly acquired fiscal estates. Thus, Gaul and the Frankish illegitimate kingdom there became the nucleus of the medieval empire.

These Frankish "kings" were intoxicated with their new power but unprepared to handle it. They displayed the same ambivalent state of mind that was common among the German chieftains, reveling in their despotic power yet eagerly emulating Roman ways. They were, at first, quite unfamiliar with what remained of Roman administration and governed only their private estates without interfering in the affairs of the rest of the country. Gaul was in a state of utter confusion. The cities were depopulated and partly destroyed. In the country, the Roman and Romanized Gallic landowners lived on their estates as before. The Frankish rulers courted them and the influential clergy, hoping to win them over and to learn from them. Some of the Merovingian chieftains even had ambitions as poets, theologians, or legists, all to the hardly concealed amusement but trembling applause of the Gallo-Roman nobility. But these pursuits did nothing to temper the greeds and passions of the Frankish rulers.

The Merovingians were constantly feuding with their sons or

---

* The doctrine of the Alexandrian presbyter Arius, who denied the divine nature of Jesus Christ, had been adopted earlier by the eastern Germanic tribes.

brothers, snatching inheritances, pieces of land, or treasure from them, making and breaking treaties at will. In 561, Chlotar crushed a revolt of one of his sons and had this son burned alive together with his wife and children. Soon after returning to his estate at Braine he himself died in the excitement of an autumnal hunt. Hilperik, one of the three remaining sons, immediately rushed to his father's main estate, took all the treasures kept there, and distributed part of them among his father's followers, accepting their oath of fealty in return. He then went to Paris, the former capital of the Roman province, appropriated the imperial palace there, and set out to conquer as much land as possible before his brothers could interfere. They joined forces against him, however, and defeated him. The result was turmoil—a succession of treaties, breaches of treaties, and divisions by lot.

A similar case is that of Theodehilde, wife of the king Haribert. After the death of her husband, she seized the treasure of the king, and in order to keep her rank as queen, proposed marriage to her brother-in-law, the king Guntram, enticing him with the promise of treasure. Guntram accepted, but when she came to him, he took the treasure, some of which rightfully belonged to his brothers, and had her promptly escorted into a monastery in Arles, where she ended her days in powerless rage.

All the Merovingians had innumerable wives, and the jealousies and intrigues among these Merovingian women defy the imagination. They were ferociously independent, commanding their own attendants and warriors, bribing them with treasures or love, dispatching them with sword or poison whenever they wanted them out of the way. These wild Germanic women often determined their husbands' policies, urging them on into new battles and rivalries; and it was they who finally destroyed the Merovingian dynasty.

For a whole generation the political events of Gaul were dominated by a feud between two women, Brunhildis, the wife of King Sigibert, and Fredegundis, the wife of his brother, King Hilperik. Fredegundis, as beautiful as she was shrewd, had incited her husband to murder another of his wives. The victim was Brunhildis' sister, Galasvintha. Brunhildis countered by inducing her husband Sigibert to make open war upon Hilperik. Fredegundis sent some of her men to murder Sigibert, and she provided the murder weapon herself, a *scramasax* or long hunting knife which she had taken care to poison. Finally, having done away with all the sons of Hilperik's former wives, she had her son Chlotar II, who succeeded Hilperik, put Brunhildis to death.

Such was the mentality of the Merovingians. Their era was one of chaos and violence. The few noble figures of the time were Roman or Gallo-Roman landowners.

Endless feuding over inheritances caused the downfall of the Merovingians. Instead of adopting the principle of hereditary succession established by Roman law or following the old Germanic custom of popular election, they divided the rulership among their offspring as though it were personal property. This primitive conception of government is characteristic of their regime.

From the many divisions of the Frankish territory three main dominions emerged. Neustria (Neosterriki) was centered around Paris and Soissons; Austrasia (Osterriki) incorporated the area around Metz and Reims; Burgundy included its present territory as well as the Provence. Later, the center of Austrasia shifted to the east, that of Burgundy to the southeast.

A new family, the Carolingians, rose to power from the office of major-domo under the Merovingians. The *major domus*, an office originating in the administration of the big Roman senatorial estates, was the chief administrator of the royal household. In this capacity the Carolingians learned the discipline of administration. They came to understand the distinction between responsible government and the arbitrariness of the Merovingians. They acquired moderation in manners, the rudiments of political thinking, and a taste for civilization.

Step by step the Carolingian administrators gained influence over their masters and eventually took over the Frankish kingdom. They too accepted Roman titles, but unlike the Merovingians, they took Christianity seriously and became active defenders and propagators of the faith. It was they who repelled the advance of the Islamic Arabs from Spain into southern France. Indeed, the Carolingian monarchs and the Roman Church were united by a bond of mutual protection and promotion which ultimately led to the crowning of Charlemagne as the first emperor of the Holy Roman Empire.

The reasons for this alliance can readily be found in the circumstances of the Church after the collapse of the Western

Roman Empire. The bishop of Rome had no material power to protect Italy or the estates and properties of the Church. He was still formally dependent on the Byzantine emperor, who remained the nominal head of the Church. But the Byzantine emperor could not guarantee the safety of the bishop of Rome. Also, these two Christian leaders were divided over the so-called iconoclastic question. To combat the influence of the monks and decrease the wealth of the eastern monasteries, which were exempt from taxation, the Byzantine emperor prohibited the worship of images and the performing of miracles. Since the prestige and the influence of the monks depended on these practices, the emperor alienated a great part of his own clergy as well as the bishop of Rome and the Western Church. This clash resulted in a lasting enmity between the two Churches.

The bishop of Rome had to look elsewhere for aid and protection, and he turned to the Frankish monarchs, who had political reasons for wishing to strengthen this bond. The bishop asked Charles Martel, nominally the major-domo of the Merovingian household but virtually the ruler of Gaul, for assistance against the threatening Lombards (Langobards) who had established a kingdom in northern Italy. To win Charles's favor, the bishop conferred on him the titles of *subregulus* and *princeps* of the Franks. Charles Martel's son, Pepin, actually came to the bishop's aid. In return the bishop encouraged Pepin to assume the throne and anointed him in 754, formally deposing the last Merovingian. In addition, he made Pepin a *patricius Romanorum*, a title and function which could be conferred legally only by the Byzantine emperor. The title carried with it the imperial governorship of Italy and the right and duty to protect the Roman Church. With this act, the bishop of Rome took the first step toward emancipating himself from Byzantine rule. He gained much more than he had expected because Pepin, by virtue of his new office, bestowed upon him all the land he had conquered from the Lombards. By law, this land should have gone to the Byzantine emperor.

The increasing commitment of succeeding popes and Frankish rulers to this alliance culminated in an event that laid the foundations of the medieval world. Pope Leo III, threatened by a powerful opposition among his own clergy, appealed to Charles, later Charlemagne, for help. When the Frankish ruler appeared in Rome to investigate and settle these quarrels, Leo crowned him *Imperator Romanorum* at the holy mass on Christmas day in A.D. 800. Leo seemed to be implying by this act that from then on Rome was to be considered the seat of a renovated empire.

It has been said that Leo's action angered Charles. We do know, in any case, that Leo did not act with Charles's prior knowledge and that Charles would have wanted the Byzantine emperor's consent to the coronation. By this *fait accompli*, the bishop of Rome not only made Charles the supreme secular ruler in the West, but also emancipated himself from Byzantine control and became the head of Western Christendom. On the very same day that the Frankish king was made emperor, the bishop of Rome became pope. The papacy and the Holy Roman Empire, the spiritual and temporal successors to the Roman Empire, were founded simultaneously. The popes who promoted Frankish chieftains to dominant positions in the temporal world intended to keep their barbarian protectors in permanent spiritual submission and to become themselves the real rulers of a new ecclesiastical empire. Yet, in effect, they created a temporal authority that later proved to be their strongest rival.

These two great institutions—the papacy and the Holy Roman Empire—were inextricably bound to each other. They jointly rose to power and jointly fell from it. They successively aided and destroyed each other. In the great struggle for supremacy that developed between them, the popes sought to best the emperors in worldly power while the emperors hoped to usurp the spiritual authority of the popes. The result was the debasement of both Church and empire.

# ♃.

---

## CHARLEMAGNE

THE CORONATION of Charles was the culminating event in a historical process that had begun centuries before and that was destined to place the inheritance of the Roman Empire in the hands of the German people, but before we consider the implications of this event for German history, we should cast a glance at the personality and achievements of Charlemagne. He was not the flawless legendary hero that both German and French patriots have pictured him to be, but he was nevertheless a great man and a crucial figure in German and Western history. As I mentioned before, the early Carolingians were culturally and ethically more advanced than the Merovingians. Clovis was the only Merovingian of real stature, but the Carolingian line began with a whole succession of powerful and astute men. If Charles Martel and the three Pepins (Pepin of Landen, Pepin of Héristal, and Pepin the Short) had not been outstanding figures, they could not have risen to the positions they achieved; but Charlemagne surpassed them all.

Charles was born in 742. His mother seems to have been a woman of unusual strength of character who exercised a powerful and beneficial influence over her two sons. From her, Charles had his first lessons in Christian piety, and he must have had some additional schooling. We know that he could read, and it is probable that he could write. His literacy is noteworthy in a time when most rulers could not read the decrees and treaties they signed with crosses. Clerks, usually monks, were employed to read and write for them.

Charles distinguished himself from his predecessors and from all Germanic chiefs of his time in other respects as well. He was a fervent Christian who never wavered in his faith and who did his utmost to follow the dictates of his religion. He made the Christian cause his own, promoting Christianity by militant as well as peaceful means. He drove the Arabs out of Spain, and he Christianized the Germanic heathen, resorting to fire and sword where missionaries failed. His dedication to the faith, however, did not blind him to the political machinations and ambitions of the Church.

Although he was a physically powerful man, an excellent swimmer and hunter and a ruthless warrior, Charles still appreciated civilized life and had a genuine bent for education and the arts. He was the first European ruler to establish schools that were accessible to the people. There had been earlier schools at some monasteries and cathedrals. It has even been contended that Pepin the Short maintained a court school. But the main function of the monastery and cathedral schools was to train candidates for the priesthood; and later investigations have shown that Pepin did no more than keep a tutor for the royal children. The mass of the people had no access to education.

Charles established a school at court and sent his own children to it. He also ordered that the children of his courtiers attend it. It is reported that Charles occasionally went to the school himself and sat side by side with the children of the lowliest. The schools Charlemagne founded were truly public in the sense that they were open to all. The king expressly stipulated that the children of the poor should have equal rights with the children of noblemen. We have this information from the annals of an anonymous monk of St. Gall. The reliability of this source has been questioned; but Charles's democratic decree is so unusual for its time and so in keeping with what we know of his character that it should not be dismissed as a mere invention. Charles preferred plain people to his grandees and sometimes picked able men of low extraction for responsible offices. He had modest personal tastes as well, preferring simple clothing to the rich oriental silks other Frankish noblemen imported from Italy.

He planned to introduce Roman architecture into his country, and to this end, he brought home models and sketches from Italy. He incorporated these examples of Roman pillars, capitals, friezes, and facades into his palaces at Aachen, Ingelheim, and Nymwegen. He hoped to build a replica of St. Peter's basilica, and he even thought of founding a capital in the Roman style. This notion of a permanent residence and seat of government was a novel one for a Germanic chieftain. Charles's successors had no desire to act on this idea, and he never realized it himself because he was engaged in warfare for so much of his own lifetime.

Charles's architectural innovations seem all the more impressive if they are viewed in the context of his time. The basic industrial skills had been lost. Men had forgotten how to forge iron, and ancient monuments like the Roman Colosseum were torn down to obtain the iron clamps holding the stones together. The art of making glass and the even simpler one of brickmaking had disappeared. There was little glass except in the churches. The huts of the common people consisted of one room without windows, and a hole in the roof allowed the smoke to escape. Chimneys were unknown, even in the most elaborate palaces.

Music, too, was in a state of neglect. Charles took great interest in it and tried to improve the quality of choral singing in particular. He visited the churches frequently and publicly rebuked any choir he heard singing off key. The famous chorale *Veni, creator spiritus* is attributed to him.

Charles is also responsible for the preservation of innumerable literary texts, both sacred and profane. Since mechanical printing was unknown at that time, all literary reproduction was done by hand. Charles contributed a new minuscule to the art of writing, and he employed monks as copyists to duplicate the documents extant in his kingdom. If he had not collected and recorded these texts, scores of them would be lost to us. Some that he did preserve have, of course, been lost anyhow. One of these, mentioned by Charles's biographer, Eginhard, is a collection of pagan poems in which the prodigal adventures and feats of old Germanic chieftains were glorified. Jacob Grimm discovered a Frankish manuscript, however, which contains fragments from primitive versions of both the Edda and the Nibelungen sagas and which may well have come from Charlemagne's collection. Charles's interest in this area extended to language itself. He knew Latin and some Greek, and he even commissioned a Frankish grammar.

He also concerned himself with astronomy, theology, and law. He acted as a judge himself, as did all Germanic chieftains; but in this capacity, he tried to establish legal standards and put an end to arbitrary practices. In his famous *Capitularia,* circular letters sent out to bishops, counts, governors, and other persons in authority, he gave explicit instructions on the conduct of various offices. These letters served as a legal code and as a legislative and executive organ as well. They dealt with moral legislation, ecclesiastical affairs, political subjects, and the administration of law. Charles made a sincere effort to apply his religion to all aspects of his life. In this, his simplicity and naivete were great assets. He displayed none of the hypocrisy that characterizes rulers at more advanced stages of civilization.

Finally, he gathered around him a group of extraordinary men, the like of which could not be found anywhere else in Europe at that time or for centuries afterwards. They lived at his palace, pursued their studies under his protection, taught in his schools, and were his favorite company whenever he had a moment of relaxation. The most eminent among them was Alcuin, a native of Northumberland in England and one of the leaders who made the monastery at York a dynamic center of learning in a dark world. There were also two monks from Ireland, Paulus Diaconus and Theodulf. Eginhard, a young monk from Fulda, later wrote the famous biography of Charlemagne. This company, or academy, lived in a most informal way, had their meals together with the king, and afterwards read and discussed classical authors or St. Augustine. They put aside their titles and original names and called each other by familiar names: Charles was David; Alcuin, Albinus; Pepin, the king's son, was Julius; Queen Liutgarde was Ava.

The reign of Charlemagne with its unique blend of religiosity and early rationalism has often been celebrated as a period of incipient enlightenment and has even been called the Carolingian Renaissance. The term is misused, though, because there was no rebirth of culture but only a premature and short-lived flowering of it.

Given his tastes and inclinations, it is not surprising that Charles was a man of moderation and self-discipline, qualities that were practically unheard of in the Germanic world. He showed admirable restraint, for example, in dealing with his brother Carloman. The brothers hated each other heartily and early in Charles's reign, Carloman deserted him in their joint campaign against the Aquitanians. Carloman died soon after, not at Charles's hand, however, but of natural causes. His widow fled precipitously, crossing the Alps into Italy in mid-winter. She feared the avalanches less than her brother-in-law, but she had misjudged Charlemagne's nature.

Charles displayed this same magnanimity toward one defeated enemy after another. He spared Hunald, the leader of the Aquitanians; Tassilo, who headed the Bavarian uprisings; Desiderius, chief of the Lombards; and even Widukind, the Saxon chieftain who broke treaty after treaty and repeatedly led his savage tribe against Charlemagne. The only flaw in his reputation for mercy is the wholesale slaughter of 4,500 Saxon prisoners at Verden on the Aller, but here we have to remember that Charles resorted to this measure only after eighteen encounters with the ever refractory Saxons.

Charlemagne's modern biographer, C. E. Russell, aptly sums up this aspect of Charles's character: "Charles of the Franks may well be believed to have been by far the most enlightened and merciful ruler of his times. But how many removes was even Charles from the woods and the stone hatchet? Education, reflection, and his religion had chastened and mollified the spirit of the wild man, but not so that a reversion was impossible. The instinct that moved Widukind to kill priests and torture converts was still rudimentary in the king of the Franks. Under ordinary conditions it lay dormant in him; when he was disturbed by savagery he responded in kind."

But perhaps the most remarkable thing about Charles was his talent for statesmanship and administration. To build a kingdom from a number of small states was in itself no great achievement. It required an iron will, a hardened conscience, and a strong army. But to hold such a kingdom together after it had been established was a colossal task. This is exactly what Charlemagne achieved. To be sure, he was an invincible warrior. Whenever he appeared on the battlefield, the enemy was doomed. His very name instilled fear. He developed tactics of surprise that were studied by military experts up to the time of Napoleon. When we consider the scope and size of his campaigns and conquests and the extent of the empire he consolidated, we can hardly believe that a single man could accomplish so much. He put down the Aquitanian revolt and conquered the Lombards, incorporating their kingdom into the Frankish empire. He established his rule in Venetia, Istria, Dalmatia, and Corsica. He Christianized the Bavarians and the Saxons, subdued the Avars of the

Lower Danube, and pushed back the Arabs in Spain. He established marches (*Marken*) or fortified borderlands from the Atlantic to the North Sea, from the Pyrenees to the Carpathians. All these marches—from Denmark (Dane Mark) to Friuli, from Austria (Ostmark) to Barcelona—were at the same time centers of colonization, Germanization, and Christianization. Charles even contemplated reuniting the Eastern and Western Roman Empires, and he maintained special diplomatic relations with the khalif Harun al-Rashid in Baghdad. But again, the truly impressive point here is not the vast range of Charles's kingdom but the fact that he could hold it together. If we consider that hardly any of the medieval emperors after him were capable of controlling their territories, Charles's achievement seems to border on the miraculous.

## THE FEUDAL SYSTEM

In Charlemagne's empire, the Germanic and Romanic worlds became one. The most far-reaching consequence of this fusion was the rise of the feudal system. The decline of Rome had brought her closer to the level of the Germanic tribes, and long contact with the empire had made the tribes more receptive to Roman values. The preconditions for the growth of feudalism were inherent in these transformations.

Two crucial changes took place in the structure of the empire. One was the decline of city life, accompanied by a shift from a commercial to an agricultural economy. The other was the disintegration of the old impersonal hierarchy of government and the rise of a new one based on personal bonds and obligations. These two changes are closely related and should be considered together.

We have already noted how the organizing principle of Roman government ultimately led to the decline of the empire. Rome originated as a city-state, and all the resources of the empire were devoted to serving the city. Rome was administered exclusively from the city, and the city regarded the provinces as territories to be exploited for its own ends.

The provincial cities were organized along the pattern of the metropolitan city-state. They had provincial senates, consisting of rich landowners who lived in the city and who, like the Roman senators, had their estates cultivated by slaves or by free tenants. These provincial senatorial bodies were called *municipia*, municipalities (from *munia*, official duties), indicating their obligation to provide duties in kind or in money for the metropolis, the armies, and the state. Only Roman senators were exempt from all duties.

50

Under the centralized regimes of Diocletian and Constantine, modeled after the totalitarian rule of the Ptolemies in Egypt, these provincial municipalities and their officials, the *decuriones,* were held responsible for the delivery of ever increasing duties and taxes. The term *decurio,* originally a military designation for the commander of a *decuria,* a unit of ten horsemen, later became an administrative designation; and in the provinces it came to mean simply a senator of a municipality.

The taxes became so heavy that free men tried to escape all positions of responsibility. They deserted the cities, fled to the country, and, if escape upwards into the ranks of the Roman senators was impossible, they became soldiers, monks, or peasants. Rome took measures to close these routes of escape. Every trip, every sale or lease of property, every bequest was made subject to the approval of the provincial governor. Donations, however, were exempt from this control. A member of a municipality could give his estate to some powerful patron—a Roman senator, a high official, or a bishop—who was free from taxation. The donator than received his estate back in tenure. Since this agreement was private and not protected by law, it was made on the basis of confidence. No money changed hands. The receiver of the donation took possession of the property; the receiver of the tenure retained all the rights of possession, but he retained them only through the benevolence of his patron. He had no legal claim to them whatsoever. Such an agreement was called a *precarium,* because it came about by means of *preces* (requests or petitions). The English word "precarious" derives from *precarium* and reflects the uncertain nature of these agreements. They put the receiver of the tenure completely at the mercy of his benefactor.

The lower strata of the population were no better off. The craftsmen and artisans of the cities were organized in hereditary guilds that had originally been formed as cultic groups to honor the patron deities of the different crafts. (Later, the role of the patron deities in the guilds was taken over by Christian saints.) Membership in these guilds was made compulsory so that the state could control the crafts and make artisans captives of their trades.

In the rural districts, taxes were assessed according to acreage and the number of free laborers on an estate. In order to increase revenues, the government freed the slaves. They could no longer be bought and sold, and, theoretically, their condition should have been improved. But in fact they became serfs bound to the soil rather than to their masters. This system of taxation worsened the condition of the free tenants as well because it increased the power of the landlords over them. Since the landlord was obliged to deliver their taxes and had both police powers and legal jurisdiction over them, the free tenants too became tied to the soil. Their position was practically the same as that of the serfs, and these two groups began to fuse, forming one single caste. Small landowners also suffered from taxation. They had no desire to improve or extend their property because they did not want to become members of the city municipalities, a rise in rank that only meant additional tax burdens.

These conditions brought disaster to the cities. The urban centers were soon deserted and their life paralyzed. Even the senators of Rome itself preferred to spend most of their time on their estates where they lived quietly among friends and servants, undisturbed by dangerous court intrigues and political events in which they no longer took an active part. Political power resided in the courts of the emperors and in the army. Since the state's only function was to exploit the people, it gradually lost its hold over them. It could not prevent them from seeking and finding ways of life free of the burdens imposed by imperial bureaucracy and taxation. Many fled into arrangements of a purely private nature.

Besides the donation of property in exchange for tenure, another kind of private arrangement was the surrender of one's person to a patron in return for relief from administrative pressure, state service, and taxes. This agreement was similar to the one used for a donation of property. It too was based on loyalty and trust; it too was private and unacknowledged in law. The patron offered protection; the "client" offered personal attendance and services. This agreement was called *clientela*.* It had a long history in Rome, and many free individuals of all ranks and classes made use of it to escape the increasing influence of the state.

The Roman *precarium* and *clientela* bear an obvious resemblance to the Germanic *Gefolgschaft*. The Roman practices grew

* *Clientela* comes from the Latin verb *cluere*, to hear. It is interesting to note that other verbs whose basic meaning is "to hear" also include the sense of "to obey," e.g., Latin *obedire* from *ob-audire* and German *gehorchen*.

52

from different origins and served different purposes, but *precarium, clientela,* and *Gefolgschaft* are all identical in their purely personal nature. Thus, through the decline of the cities and the proliferation of personal dependencies, the gap between the social structure of Rome and that of the Germanic tribes was gradually closed.

The Celtic tribes had an institution very similar to the Germanic *Gefolgschaft,* but the Celtic relationship was not wholly private. It was incorporated into the tribal system, and the bond between follower and leader was permanent, not temporary. In Latin, the Celtic follower was called *vassus* (vassal). Because the Celts had been thoroughly Romanized by centuries of Roman rule, their custom of vassalage was the first to fuse with the Roman *clientela*; and because the medieval empire had its origins in Celtic Gaul, the Celtic word vassal became the standard term for a feudal follower.

As we have seen, the relationship between the Frankish king and the pope also evolved from a personal bond. But in this case it was never made clear who was the patron and who the follower. Since spiritual power and temporal power were completely different, no clear dominance emerged for some time. The question of supremacy, however, became the subject of constant disputes between the emperor and the pope, and each attempted to appropriate both powers for himself. But mundane affairs soon took precedence over spiritual matters; the result was the emancipation and secularization of the empire.

We can see how various currents converged in the development of the feudal system. Still another factor, stressed by the Belgian historian Henri Pirenne, is the shift from a commercial to an agricultural economy. This shift was partly due to the decline of city life and partly to the loss of the Mediterranean trade routes to the Saracens. The Mediterranean had been the dominant trade center, and its closure to the Western world from the seventh century on had a revolutionary effect on economic conditions. The loss of trade proved disastrous for city life in the West. For a time, trade ceased almost entirely. But the decline in foreign trade was not the only reason for shrinking markets. Trade became less important to medieval society as a whole as monasteries and feudal estates became more self-sufficient and as increasing numbers of people left the cities. In what local trade remained, a money economy gave way to a barter economy. All these factors contributed to the rise of the feudal system, and we can now turn to the historical development of that system.

The Merovingian chieftains took control of the Roman province of Gaul and of the estates of the Roman fisc. As Christians and landholders, they had severed their tribal bonds, but they had not become "kings" as we understand the term. Their "courts" were large country estates like those of the Gallo-Roman grandees, but unlike the grandees, the Frankish rulers led an unsettled life and kept moving from one of their estates to another. The distinction between private and public affairs does not apply in the Merovingian period. The Frankish rulers held only private property and maintained only private retinues. From these beginnings, medieval feudalism and the Holy Roman Empire evolved.

The Romans called the Merovingian chieftain king of the Franks, *rex Francorum,* and his estates were called a *regnum.* *Regnum* did not originally mean kingdom but simply "land of the king." Only gradually did this "land of the king" become an actual kingdom. The administration of the Frankish kingdom and of the later empire evolved from the private management of the king's estates, and the feudal lords evolved from his personal retinue or *clientela.*

In the course of their campaigns, the Frankish kings had adopted Roman military organization; and they rewarded their followers with lands from their own estates or from newly conquered territories. As a result, administrative offices came to be modeled after military ones, and the ranks of count and duke came to be identified with important roles in the medieval empire. The word count derives from the Latin *comes. Comes* means escort or companion and was an imperial title which, in the later empire, was attached to every kind of office including the military command of a unit approximately the size of a modern regiment.

When Frankish troops settled on conquered lands, the counts retained their positions of leadership and became the staff of the civil administration. As the "land of the king" and the number of settlers increased with each new conquest and as more warriors became farmers, the counts became extraordinarily powerful. In their capacity as mediators between the people and the king, they decided on the exemptions from military service and collected the fees paid for such exemptions. Like the old Roman *comites*

54

*civitatis* (governors of provincial districts) and the Gallo-Roman landowners, the counts also assumed legal jurisdiction over their people. In doing so, they appropriated the function of the Germanic *thinginus*, an elected judge who had also presided over the *thing* or popular assembly. This office was not abolished entirely but was absorbed into that of the Roman *centenarius*, the commander of a hundred men. These officials were the counts' delegates and bore the title of viscount, derived from *vice comes*.

The counts came to represent their people in assemblies called by the chieftains. Originally, all the warriors had attended these assemblies to express their wills and opinions. But as peasants on widely scattered farmsteads, they could no longer attend in person. Now, when rulers changed, the counts simply forced a collective oath of loyalty on their people, abrogating the old custom of personal agreement between leader and follower. Thus, as the power of the counts increased, the common people gradually lost their rights and freedoms.

In the office of duke, which was still higher than count, attributes of the Germanic tribal chieftain and of the Roman *dux* were combined. Diocletian had created the rank of *dux*, the supreme military commander of a province, when he separated civil and military administration in the provinces. (The Venetian *doge* and the fascist *duce* both stem from *dux*, which means leader.) The Frankish kings found that they had to appoint dukes to replace the chieftains of conquered Germanic tribes like the Bavarians, Saxons, Swabians, and Thuringians. The original tribal *Herzöge*, the Tassilos and Widukinds, had to be removed or they would continue to incite their people to rebellion. The appointed *Herzöge* were usually chosen from foreign tribes.

The personal retinues or *clientelae* of the Frankish leaders were largely composed of bishops and Gallo-Roman landowners. The Frankish chieftains were eager to attract these influential men, and they offered large parcels of land to them. During their quarrel over their inheritance, the Merovingian heirs disposed of large tracts of land in an effort to win powerful supporters. Now it was the large landowners who were the followers of the king, not the Frankish people, who had been reduced to the status of mere subjects.

But land was not the only reward for joining the king's clientele. When a count or duke was to be chosen, the king naturally selected one of his personal followers. In this way, the king's clients acquired high offices as well as extensive property. They used their wealth to increase their power, and they used their power to increase their wealth.

When the Carolingians assumed rule of the Franks, they had to contend with powerful lords who controlled extensive territories and large numbers of people. The Carolingians could not rely on a general levy if they needed troops. They depended on the people their lords could raise. In other words, they depended on the personal followers of their own personal followers, relying on the old Germanic tradition of the *Gefolgschaft* and combining it with the Gallic system of vassalage. Lord and vassal were bound by a solemn pledge. The vassal promised his unswerving loyalty and support to his lord, and in return the lord granted the vassal the use of certain lands. The pledge was mutually binding for life. When the king's vassals concluded similar agreements with lesser lords, the feudal system began to take shape.

Feudalism never became a legal institution. It was always based on personal agreements. Since feudal agreements were not defined and protected by law and since no higher authority existed to enforce them by law, they depended entirely on trust and loyalty. This explains the importance of fidelity as a concept in the medieval world.

Even in feudal society, the Roman administrative system remained alive for a time in such offices as duke and count. But since the holders of these offices were, as a rule, powerful feudal lords as well, the offices lost their original significance and became appurtenances of the feudal system. Eventually, they became fiefs in themselves; and, like other fiefs, their importance depended on the power of the individuals who held them. When all fiefs, landed and administrative, became hereditary, power no longer resided in individuals alone but remained permanently invested in fiefs and therefore in the families that held them.

# 6.

---

## THE GROWTH OF THE FRENCH NATION

UNDER the later Carolingians, Charlemagne's realm disintegrated. The intrinsic differences between the eastern and western parts of Charlemagne's kingdom became increasingly evident, and the same feudal institutions developed differently in the Frankish and Germanic parts of his domain.*

After Charlemagne's death the power of the Carolingians came to an end, and their decline was even more rapid than that of the Merovingians. One reason for this decline was the weakness and ineptitude of Charlemagne's successors, but there were other reasons for it as well. The customary division of an inheritance had always led to disputes, but the vast size of Charlemagne's empire and the growing power of both secular and ecclesiastical lords intensified these conflicts.

Charlemagne's son, Louis the Pious, was able to preserve the unity of his kingdom only with great difficulty. The suppression of revolts took all his energies, and his consequent neglect of foreign policy and defense hastened the breakup of the empire. Louis' inheritance was divided several times among the three sons who survived him. In the final territorial division of 843, the famous Treaty of Verdun, the division between the French and the Germans was foreshadowed. Indeed, this division had already become evident in the so-called oaths of Strasbourg. As commanders of their respective armies, the two brothers Charles the Bald and Louis the German took these oaths in 842 to confirm a treaty they had made with each other. The oaths were bilingual,

* In England and in southern Italy, feudalism developed only at the end of the eleventh century, in the eastern countries in the twelfth and thirteenth centuries, in Scandinavia in the fourteenth century.

employing the vernacular of the countries assigned to the brothers by this treaty. Charles the Bald and his people used the Romance language of the western part; Louis the German and his people, the Germanic language of the eastern part of the Frankish kingdom. The Treaty of Verdun forced a family compact upon the third brother, Lothair, and divided the administration and control of the Carolingian empire among the three brothers. Charles the Bald, as king of the West Franks, received a realm mainly Romance in speech and custom and approximating medieval France in general outline. Louis the German, as king of the East Franks, took a kingdom ethnically, geographically, and linguistically Germanic. It extended from the Rhine to the eastern frontier of the empire but did not include Frisia. The third and eldest brother, Lothair, kept the empty title of emperor and became king of an amorphous realm between the western and the eastern kingdoms. Lothair's domain extended from the Dutch and Frisian shores through Burgundy and Provence down to Italy. The northeastern part of his kingdom, called Lotharingia (Lorraine) after him, became the site of a mixed and creative culture; and the struggle between France and Germany for this territory was to go on for many centuries. The Treaty of Verdun determined the history of western and central Europe for more than a millennium. With this treaty, the Gallic and Germanic kingdoms became separate entities, not just geographically and politically but culturally as well. From this point on, the territories that became modern France and Germany would develop along completely different lines. Though nominally still part of the empire, the French kingdom assumed a separate existence for all practical purposes. Unlike Germany, France remained uninvolved in the affairs of the empire and could mature naturally, growing into one of the great political and cultural powers of history. She had already acquired the attributes of nationhood when Italy was still an agglomeration of independent cities and regions, when Britain was still a colony of French Normandy, and when Germany was not even a geographical term, much less a nation.

We would do well to clarify here exactly what we mean by a "nation," for the concept of nationhood is central to this study. All the major countries of Europe, with the exception of Germany, became nations early in the modern period. The fact that Germany did not achieve nationhood but has struggled to achieve it throughout her history is one of the main factors that constitute her uniqueness.

The term nation is often used rather carelessly. Many ancient peoples—Egyptians, Persians, Greeks, and Jews—have been called nations. This seems to me incorrect and inexact, since a nation, in my view, has a definite structure of its own, encompassing special features and premises that had not existed before the founding of the French nation. All the so-called ancient "nations" were either tribes, tribal kingdoms, or sacred city-states; consequently, their origins were religious. This is clearly evident in the tribes and is equally true of the city-states of the Greeks and the Romans. In all those cases, the beginnings of earthly community were still determined by religious bonds. Even the Catholic creed, in its early history, can be seen as an expression of hope for a universal community, a hope realized to a certain degree in the Roman Empire.

Northern Europe developed new political structures, purely secular in nature. They expressed the folk character of their peoples, taking over the function religion had had in the tribes and in ancient civilizations. The Christian world religion was not an integral part of this process. Its appeal was universal, directed at humanity in general and at the human being as such. Whenever the Church did play a role in the formation of a secular political entity, it did so in violation of its own nature.

Thus, properly speaking, a nation is a political structure that develops after the creation of a world religion. Its growth is independent of religious concerns, no matter how strong the spiritual influence of the world religion may be. Religion is no longer fundamental to the political structure. A nation is a temporal community derived from the folk character of its people and influenced by the geography of its region. Even if its ethnic make-up is varied, it evolves toward a homogeneity of life and culture. The sum of the profane customs and achievements of a national community gradually becomes a body of subconscious memories and constitutes what we call a tradition. Tradition in turn acquires an authority of its own and takes over some religious functions, becoming, as it were, a profane religion for the nation.

France is the first country to develop a homogeneous way of life, a tradition, and a true nationality; she thus provides the perfect countertype of Germany. Arising in the Île-de-France and in its main city, Paris, French nationality gradually spread through-out the territory that is the France of today. Several factors account for this process. The thorough Romanization of the country was one of them. Roman customs and institutions as well as the Roman principle of central administration were firmly entrenched. In Gaul, the urban tradition of Rome survived among the Gallo-Roman magnates and especially among the bishops, whose offices compelled them to remain in the cities. The monasteries assumed control of religious life in the rural areas. The land-owning clerics, particularly the bishops, played an important part in shaping the French kingdom and establishing the Capet dynasty.

Another crucial factor in French national development was the continuity of the Capet dynasty. For 340 years the direct succession from father to son was not interrupted. The Capet kings did not follow the Frankish-Germanic custom of splitting the inheritance among their descendants. In order to avoid the division of property, they adopted the Roman principle of primogeniture,* and the great feudal lords of the country followed their example. Another means the Capets used to insure succession was the crowning of the eldest son during his father's lifetime. The old Germanic custom of electing the king was gradually forgotten, and the dynastic principle was established as a national tradition.

But the most significant factor in the development of the French monarchy, and therefore of French national unity and homogeneity, was the strength of the French feudal system. The Roman principle of central administration had never been completely abandoned, and it had a decisive effect on French feudalism. There were practically no allodial properties left,** and as the authority of independent landholders shrank to virtually nothing, the authority of royal administrative offices continued to grow, fused, of course, with the power of the feudal lords holding these offices. As dukes and counts, the lords could utilize the still extant structure of Roman administration to consolidate their feudal

* The younger sons were granted fiefs or offices which reverted to the crown if these sons had no male heirs.

** Allodial property was a free inheritance, a property entirely one's own and not granted in exchange for vassalage. *Od* is the old Frankish word for property, *all* for "full" or "complete," hence, *allod*, "full ownership." By contrast, a *feod* is land granted by a superior for use only, not as a permanent possession. *Feod*, and hence feudalism, derives from the old Germanic *fehu*, "cattle," that is, movable property.

power and to enforce military service both among their followers and among the remaining independent landholders. This helped spread the feudal system in France, and it gave rise to the saying: *Nulle terre sans seigneur* (No land without a lord).

This concentration of extensive territories in the hands of relatively few feudal lords promoted uniform administration throughout the country. At first, this concentrated power of the lords was a threat to the king's authority, but later it proved advantageous. The kings had to deal with only a small number of lords whose power and territories they gradually came to control. The kings obtained some lands by marriage and inheritance, some by seizing forfeited fiefs. They also acquired territories by direct confiscation. If a lord was found guilty of a breach of faith toward his vassal, the king could proceed against the lord and confiscate his fief. Kings were even known to encourage complaints of this kind so that they would have a pretext to act against a powerful lord. They used similar methods in dealing with the cities. Offering special patronage and subsidies in exchange for prerogatives of government, they undermined the authority of the urban feudal lords and gradually gained control of the cities themselves.

The French kings were also the first to take scholars of Roman law into their service as private counsellors. These so-called legists were usually petty clerics or monks, but there were also burghers and even serfs among them. These legists helped effect a gradual restitution of Roman law, and they also helped establish the principle that in Gaul the authority of the French king should equal that of the Roman emperor. Eventually, the weapon of Roman law would be used to break down the feudal system and locate all power in the monarchy. From these legal advisers, a new class of nobility developed, the *noblesse de robe*. The legists were particularly devoted to the monarchs and the monarchy as such and called themselves *milites regis*, soldiers of the king. They were the predecessors of the great ministers of the later French kingdom, the Cardinals d'Amboise, Richelieu, and Mazarin.

In the course of their efforts to outmaneuver the lords and consolidate their own power, the kings also created a supreme court of appeal that began as a jurisdictional institution and developed into a political one: the parliament. Its role in the unification of the law, and so of the nation, cannot be overestimated.

But the most important Roman legacy to France was the concept of a capital city. Paris took on the authority of the Capet kings who resided there, and in turn Paris lent authority and even immortality to the monarchy. As the city endured, so too did the king. *Charles, Henri, Louis meurent, mais le roi ne meurt pas.* The authority of Paris affected all aspects of national life, social, cultural, and intellectual as well as political. From the end of the eleventh century on, the great scholars of the medieval world gathered in Paris, and it was here that all the controversial points of Scholastic philosophy were debated. At the end of the twelfth century, the Parisian "guild of masters" developed into one of the first universities of the Christian continent.

Paris also set the standards of behavior for the whole country. The language spoken on the Île de France became the foundation of modern French, and the civilizing influence of the capital extended to the feudal lords, eventually transforming them into courtiers. At first, the king summoned magnates to the *curia regis* (assembly of the king) only occasionally. But with the inclusion of the legists, the *curia regis* became a permanent governing body and gradually expanded into an elaborate royal court. When the monarchy was at its height in France, only a member of court society had social standing. Anyone who wanted to obtain a position had to attend the court. As we shall see, this presents a striking contrast to conditions in Germany where no capital existed and where it was the mark of nobility *not* to go to court but to live on one's own estate and to keep a court of one's own, no matter how miserable.

France modeled her capital city after Rome, but there is a distinct difference between Rome and Paris. Rome and her dominions were identical. City and empire were one. The republics of the Italian Renaissance were a later incarnation of the city-state. Their surrounding territories were identified with the capital cities and bore their names—Milan, Florence, Venice. But in France, Paris was the center and symbol of the country, not the country itself. The surrounding territories were not absorbed by it. They contributed to it, had a share in it, and were represented by it. Capital and country were independent but at the same time mutually dependent entities. In this seemingly contradictory but eminently viable relationship, the legacies of both feudalism and Roman administration remained alive.

# 7.

---

## IMPERIUM ET SACERDOTIUM

THE FACTORS that encouraged the growth of a unified nation in France were completely lacking in Germany. This eastern Frankish kingdom, originally part of Charlemagne's realm, was now detached from France or Francia, the country that was the home of the Franks and that still bore their name. The eastern kingdom consisted of peripheral territories populated by various Germanic tribes that had been gradually subdued and incorporated into the Frankish kingdom. Roman rule and civilization had never reached most of these territories. There were no cities and no definite frontiers. The cities that finally did develop grew from bishoprics, founded by the kings as the Christian missions advanced, and from *Pfalzen*. The word *Pfalzen* derives from the Latin *palatia*, but these "palaces" of the kings, counts, and dukes were in fact no more than crude wooden houses fortified against attack.

In geography and climate, France is a much more favored region than Germany. French soil had been under cultivation since Roman times; and, with the exception of the Norse invasions, France was relatively untroubled by foreign incursions during the Middle Ages. In contrast, Germany had not progressed very far beyond the most primitive stages of agriculture. The beginnings of steady soil cultivation under the guidance of the monasteries had been repeatedly cut off by the invasions of the Magyars, Slavs, and Danes. The Magyars were a particular scourge of the eastern kingdom. In 899 they swept through the Bavarian *Ostmark* into the Lombard plains; in 907 they defeated the Bavarians; and in 919 they harried Saxony and penetrated as far as Lorraine. Wherever the invasions occurred the effects were the same. There was a marked decline in the population and, consequently, a decline in the amount of land under cultivation.

63

Old boundaries disappeared, and the land returned to nature. The situation in these eastern regions was a permanently unsettled one in which no stable system of administration and no durable social order could take root.

Five great duchies emerged during the period of the invasions: Franconia, Saxonia, Thuringia, Swabia, and Bavaria. These duchies corresponded essentially to the territories of the Germanic tribes that had been incorporated into the Frankish kingdom generations before. Earlier historians have interpreted the rise of the duchies in the late ninth century as a rallying of the Germanic tribes around their natural leaders and as a rebirth of the old Germanic tribes. These historians claim that the tribes were unaffected by the partitioning of their territories and formed again on the basis of their individual customs and dialects, thus reasserting their true moral personalities.

This account of the rise of the German duchies does not reflect all the known facts. The German "tribes" were not homogeneous racial or territorial units any more; nor were they held together by common languages, since local dialects had developed within far narrower bounds. What customs and legal institutions existed were not of tribal origin but reflected new class and political structures. More important still, the leaders who rose to power in the German duchies at the end of the ninth century were not, as a rule, tribal representatives. They were Carolingian administrators—counts and margraves—who assumed ducal titles or were appointed to them by the kings in times of war. The roots of this ducal authority were military, not tribal. However, tribal differentiation was preserved in military organization. In the west, the Carolingians directed their summons to armed service to "all inhabitants between Seine and Loire." But in Germany, the troops were summoned tribe by tribe. In 869, for example, Louis the German divided his army into local units, sending the Saxons and Thuringians against the Slavic Sorbs, the Bavarians against Moravia, and retaining the Franks and the Swabians under his own command.

In the eastern kingdom dukes still retained the position of military leaders. As guardians of the frontiers, they were compelled by the invasions to extend their authority throughout their provinces. The authority of Charlemagne persisted long after his death, and even the later and weaker Carolingians commanded respect and had no difficulty in controlling the eastern dukes. But with the end of the Carolingian dynasty, the struggle for supremacy in the eastern kingdom began.

Here we see another striking difference between France and Germany. In France, the Capet dynasty was ready to take over. Working within clearly defined geographic limits, it created a stable administrative order that could gradually be extended. In the vast, unsettled German territories, a struggle between the various dukes and ducal families ensued, a struggle that would never be clearly resolved. Because the kings and emperors were either designated by their predecessors or elected by their peers or appointed by a combination of these methods, they always remained on the same level as the other chiefs of tribal regions. Regardless of the seemingly higher rank, they still remained chiefs among other chiefs and were never regarded as superiors. None of them, no matter how able, ever succeeded in establishing lasting and undisputed authority over the others; none of them ever succeeded in completely abolishing the election of the king by the lords, a custom held over from the popular elections in the Germanic tribes; and none of them ever succeeded in founding a lasting dynasty. Four or five direct successions within one family did occur, but this was extremely rare, and the successions were always challenged. The imperial crown passed from one family and region to another. At various times, it was Frankish, Saxon, Bavarian, and Swabian, even Swiss and Luxemburgian. It was sometimes claimed by individuals from one ducal family or another, sometimes by several contenders at once; and at one point, in the interregnum of 1256 to 1273, no one held it at all. Since most dukes were foreign usurpers or appointees, they could not even count on the support of people in their own regions, much less in others, if they became kings or emperors. They all depended on the good will of the lords, who were usually more powerful than they were themselves. This dependence on the lords—a dependence that not even the boldest and most energetic of the German emperors could overcome—was the main source of all the confusion and strife that make up the greatest part of German history.

One consequence of this situation was that every decision, appointment, or reform had to be bought from the lords with concessions, rights, land, or even money. Not only were the vast territories of the empire gradually traded away, but all the offices, prerogatives, claims, and jurisdictional rights of the crown were also given away as fiefs or in some other form. Lands, fiefs, offices, and rights were so torn asunder by changes of ownership, division through inheritance, bargaining, and usurpation that anarchy resulted.

The German rulers had to divide their energies among three main tasks: they had to ward off constant invasions, protect themselves against the lords, and maintain imperial authority against the rival claims of the popes. The French kings had only one task: the consolidation and integration of their national kingdom.

Before we examine the German variety of feudalism and the conflicts that arose from it more closely, we should understand exactly how the legacy of the Roman Empire fell to the eastern Frankish king and not to his western counterpart.

Arnulf was the last Carolingian to achieve a precarious reunion of the western and the eastern Frankish kingdoms. He temporarily pushed back the foreign invaders and had himself crowned emperor by the pope. In the period of anarchy after his death, the inner structure of the kingdoms deteriorated, and the ties between the pope and the Frankish rulers were broken. The weak Carolingians of the western kingdom lacked all power and ambition to claim the old imperial title.* When Hugh Capet rose to power, the transfer of the imperial dignity to the East Frankish rulers was an accomplished fact. The Capet kings had the good sense not to aspire to the imperial crown.

After the end of Carolingian rule, both the empire and the papacy were torn by internal strife. The Italian dominions of Charlemagne had been divided between the kings of Burgundy and Lombardy. The unity of imperial power seemed destroyed for all time. But the memory of Charlemagne's empire lived on, and some 150 years after Charlemagne's coronation, circumstances allowed the Saxon leader and Frankish king, Otto I, to win the imperial title. Building on the work of his father, Henry I, Otto was able to repel the Magyars and Slavs, subdue his rebellious peers, and unite the East Frankish kingdom. Otto took every precaution to insure the loyalty of the duchies. He appointed his

* The names of these last western Carolingians characterize their personalities. Louis IV was called Louis d'Outremer because he had to flee from his vassals. Louis V was le Fainéant, the do-nothing, the idler.

relatives as dukes, adding the tie of blood to that of vassalage; at his coronation as Frankish king in 936, the dukes expressed their submission to him by assuming the ceremonial roles of marshal, chamberlain, butler, and steward. Otto was able to retain control over the lords despite the constant recalcitrance of the Bavarian and Swabian dukes, the latter of whom was his own son, Liudolf. These two dukes threatened to conduct a foreign policy of their own and hoped to increase their power by annexing Italian territory. Otto had to become involved in the affairs of the Burgundian and Lombardic kings in Italy if he was to prevent his own rebellious dukes from gaining additional power. He dealt with this problem by pocketing both Burgundy and Lombardy and by marrying Adelaide, a Burgundian princess and heiress. About ten years later, having pacified his kingdom and become the most powerful monarch in Europe, Otto, like Charlemagne, received a call for assistance from the pope, who was under attack from Otto's vassal, the Lombardian chief Berengar. The resulting campaign ended with the crowning of the Frankish king as emperor.

Unlike Charlemagne, Otto had consciously set out to attain the imperial crown; and now the relationship between pope and emperor was made more explicit. The emperor took an oath to defend the pope, and in return the pope swore allegiance to the emperor. This mutual agreement became an integral part of a papal election. An aspirant to the papacy had to pledge his allegiance to the Frankish king before he could become pope. Once elected and confirmed, the pope then crowned the Frankish king emperor. By this Ottonian stipulation, the imperial title became a permanent attribute of the East Frankish, or German, king. From then on, no other claim to the imperial position could gain recognition; and the empire became identical with the dominions—real or imaginary—of the East Frankish or, as it was later called, Teutonic kingdom. This brought about an important change in the nature of the empire. The emperor was no longer an emperor in the Roman sense but a supreme feudal lord over a hierarchy of lords and, at the same time, a vassal of God.

Germany and the empire exerted a mutual influence on each other. The empire and even the papacy became feudalized by Frankish institutions, and the German kings became increasingly obsessed with the mission of preserving the Roman Empire. Otto

I was a sober, energetic man and certainly one of the most Germanic among the German emperors. German affairs were his main concern. Although the memory of Charlemagne was very much alive for him, he was chiefly interested in consolidating his Frankish realm and in asserting his claims to the Lotharingian kingdom, which he was able to bring back into the eastern kingdom for the next 300 years. But the designs of his dukes on northern Italy and the historical tie between Lotharingia and the imperial title drew him inevitably into his commitment to the empire. Otto had originally intended to achieve what the Capets had accomplished in France: the creation of a firmly established domestic regime. But his very desire to unify his kingdom obliged him to form an alliance with Rome, and it was this alliance that would determine Germany's destiny once and for all. Even Otto, this most Germanic of the German emperors, was forced to spend ten years in Italy, fighting Italian chiefs, deposing and appointing popes, and clashing with the Byzantine emperor over southern Italy.

From this point on, the Roman and imperial idea with all its massive tasks and burdens became an obsession of the German rulers. Otto's grandson, Otto III, son of a Byzantine princess, was so dominated by the Roman idea that he wanted to be a Roman before all. He hoped to fuse Germany and Italy, empire and papacy, into one theocratic empire similar to the ancient Roman and Byzantine empires. He aspired to be an emperor of emperors yet "the humblest servant of Christ." Otto's vision of a new, universal Roman Empire initiated the feudalization of the *Patrimonium Petri*—the administration of the papal dominion—and foreshadowed Frederick II's complete integration of the Germanic and Roman worlds.

Germany's permanent ties with imperial and ecclesiastical Rome were to have far-reaching consequences. Otto I tried to strengthen the Church materially and morally, hoping that the Church would support him in his struggles with the secular lords. His efforts failed both in Germany and in Rome. The German bishops and archbishops belonged to the same families as the secular lords and shared their political ambitions. Feudal lords and landowners themselves, they joined in the intrigues and rebellions of the secular lords. In Rome, Otto I and succeeding German emperors tried to combat the instability and corruption of the Vatican. In an attempt to purify and revitalize the papacy, Otto III encouraged and protected the reform movements of the Camaldulian and Cluniac monks. Henry III, the great Salian Frankish monarch of the eleventh century, carried on this policy and made it one of the keynotes of his reign. But the emperors soon found that they had not made strong allies of the popes but had simply helped them became dangerous rivals of the crown. In the reign of Henry IV, open conflict over the question of investiture broke out, the pope contesting the emperor's right to appoint German bishops. This led to an increasingly violent struggle between the temporal and spiritual powers. The Italian city-republics, and some foreign powers as well, were dragged into the conflict, and the emperors soon found themselves engaged on two fronts. They had to assert their authority and maintain their imperial prestige in Italy if they wanted to hold their position at home, but at the same time, they had to quell domestic revolts and establish at least a provisional order in Germany if they wanted to be free to pursue their imperial ambitions. Anarchy resulted, and no national consolidation could be initiated, much less achieved, in Germany proper. The Hohenstaufen dynasty collapsed under these pressures, and in the years of the interregnum from 1256 to 1273, the last remnants of legal order disappeared.

The German princes exploited the downfall of the Hohenstaufens to secure lasting power for themselves. Seven of the princes joined together in a college of electors to keep the electoral process in their own hands. A century later, the Luxemburg emperor, Charles IV, bargaining to perpetuate his own dynasty, sanctioned the electoral college in his Golden Bull, a statute that ceded to the electors the right to select the emperor and thus enhanced the power of the territorial states within the Reich.

## GERMAN FEUDALISM AND
## ITS DISINTEGRATION

THE GERMAN rulers' permanent involvement in the affairs of Italy and of the empire could not help affecting the internal development of Germany. First, power was never centralized in Germany, and the feudal system was never as extensive there as it was in France. Allodial properties existed among the feudal estates, and the owners of these independent properties were exceedingly proud of the fact that they were nobody's vassals. Even the most insignificant of these landowners considered themselves equals of the emperor, and they felt superior to the feudal peers who held their fiefs from the emperor and conceded him some temporary prerogatives as supreme feudal lord. These free landowners owed allegiance to no one; they did not even rise to salute the emperor if he happened to pass by. This strain of fierce individualism in medieval Germans forms a striking contrast with the cringing submissiveness of modern Germans. We shall see later how this extreme individualism evolved into extreme conformity.

The existence of independent landowners prevented the growth of a universal feudal hierarchy extending in an unbroken chain from the king down to the lowliest vassal. It created instead a number of minor hierarchies, because independent landowners granted fiefs themselves and, within the limits of their own properties, behaved like major feudal lords. Also, as mentioned in the previous chapter, further division of power took place because the dependence of the emperor on his lords forced him to grant not only lands but crown offices, privileges, and jurisdictional rights as fiefs. In the course of time, these fiefs changed hands and gradually lost any connections they had once had with spe-

70

cific places or people. This meant that power was separated from its human sources and became an object that could be bought and sold.

We can see what the concrete results of this process were if we compare a map of Germany at the time of the Saxon emperors with one from the Hohenstaufen period some 200 years later. The Germany of the Saxon emperors shows a broad division into compact duchies and counties that still reflect the political units in which the people actually lived. The Hohenstaufen map shows a complexity and confusion unparalleled in European history before or since. We find a plethora of dominions: duchies, principalities, counties of various sorts (burgraves, landgraves, pfalzgraves, and margraves), freeholds, abbeys, bishoprics and archbishoprics, cities directly subordinate to the emperor, and so forth. Most of these dominions were not organized in continuous geographical units but were scattered among other, similarly unintegrated territories.

But the map does not tell the whole story. Because various elements of power had been detached from the land and bartered as separate entities, a single territory could be subject to any number of different authorities. Military and executive power could, for example, be in the hands of a count, while one or more other authorities held the jurisdictional rights. Title to the land could belong to still a third party who claimed all duties and taxes on the property, as well as the service and allegiance of the tenants, bondsmen, and villeins residing there. In addition, a feudal lord who was not the landholder could have a separate claim to the service of vassals in the territory. And finally, if the landholder happened to be an abbot or bishop, the administration of the property had to be transferred to a lay official, a *Vogt* or bailiff, because canon law forbid clerics to meddle in worldly disputes.

Just as a single territory could be subject to several individuals, so a single individual could have rights in several territories. A man could be a feudal lord in one district, a landowner in another, a count in still another, and an administrator of jurisdictional rights in still another yet. This multiplicity of offices held by a single man was reflected in the complex titles that many individuals bore. The same man could be duke of one place, count of another, margrave of a third, and so on. Thus, innumerable

71

fragments of power could reside in one individual or in one territory.

The administration of justice, already a separate office and function, underwent further subdivision into higher and lower jurisdiction. The higher jurisdiction was originally in the hands of the count. This was the *Hochgericht* (high court), the supreme penal court, which dealt with capital crimes. The jury was originally made up of ordinary freemen but was later restricted to the nobility. The lower jurisdiction, dealing with minor offenses and quarrels, was exercised by a delegate of the count, a *centenarius* or *Zentgraf*, later called the *Schultheiss* from *Schuld heissen*—to require satisfaction of a debt. When the counties were later divided into fiefs and ceased to be administrative units, both higher and lower jurisdiction were united in the office of the *centenarius*, and the office became an independent fief. As such, is could be ceded, traded, or usurped. Later still, jurisdiction was divided according to the status of the persons to be tried. Clerics and their servants were subject to an ecclesiastical tribunal, tradesmen and craftsmen to market law. Vassals were subject to a feudal court, peasants and bondsmen to the jurisdiction of the landed proprietor. I will not elaborate on the more subtle differentiations of local, ethnic, and professional laws or on the distinctions between various kinds of rural dependents: bondsmen, people tied to the soil, free servants, and minor freeholders. All I want to do here is to convey an idea of the multiplicity and confusion of dependencies and stations in medieval Germany.

It is hardly possible to determine the extent and nature of the powers which any individual held or to which he was subject. What was the most important authority in any given district? What was the most important office any given individual held? This varied from place to place and from person to person. It is easy to see how this state of affairs invited arbitrariness, violence, and usurpation. Anyone who had sufficient influence and power could seize rights, offices, or property with impunity because there was no universally recognized authority to restrain him.

From the twelfth century on, a fundamental change began to take place in the social structure of Germany and led to a regrouping of the population. The new classes that arose from this transformation did not reflect a unifying, national tradition be-

72

cause there was none. Also, in contrast to French social development, which was always subject to the shrewd guidance of the Capet kings, the growth of German society was beyond the control of any ruler. The classes in Germany did not take shape in accordance with any legal, philosophical, or political norms but in accordance with the kinds of property their members held or the kinds of work they performed.

Four major groups emerged. The feudal lords split into an upper and lower class of nobility. The upper class was made up of what we shall come to know as the territorial princes. The knights made up the lower class. They were impoverished noblemen whose function as soldiers and whose codes of honor had been made obsolete by new military tactics, advances in weaponry, and changes in the social order. Forced into lawlessness by their poverty, they often resorted to robbing traveling merchants and their convoys. The burghers, the tradesmen and craftsmen of the rising cities, constituted the third class. The fourth, the most miserable of all, was that of the peasants.

The transformation of the German nobility resulted in part from a phenomenon that did not occur in France or England, namely, the rise to power of the *ministeriales*, the administrators of royal or lordly estates. This development is somewhat reminiscent of the rise of the Carolingians under the Merovingian kings in the sense that a private administrative office, the office of the major-domo, provided a stepping-stone to power. But the situation of the *ministeriales* was essentially different. They were bondsmen, not free people. Like vassals, they were rewarded with land and honor; but they lacked the personal freedom of the vassals and could not claim the same privileges. They seem to have been first employed by Church dioceses as administrators of ecclesiastical estates and as armed knights. Bishops and abbots were reluctant to enfeoff their lands to free vassals in exchange for military services for fear their property might be usurped. Traditions of obedience and dependence made the *ministeriales* more tractable than vassals and less dangerous to entrust with power. Their holdings, moreover, were not true fiefs but tenures (*Dienstlehen*) over which their lords had much more control. With the growing economic activity after the period of the invasions, the *ministeriales* quickly gained importance. They achieved status distinct from the main body of servile tenants and obtained written confirmation of their rights, thus establishing their social position on a firm legal basis.

The German secular lords soon followed the example of the Church in employing *ministeriales*. In France and in England, a lord could depend on his vassals to perform military and administrative duties. In Germany, the lack of close feudal ties forced all lords, the king among them, to draw on the servile classes to fill both administrative and military posts. What the ecclesiastics had done to promote the growth of a ministerial class on Church estates, the Salian kings did on the domains of the crown.

Conrad II (1024-1039) was the first German ruler to favor the royal *ministeriales* as a class and to organize them into an administrative staff. Conrad's chief administrator, Werner, was the earliest secular minister in the history of medieval Germany. In his capacity as supervisor of the fisc, he served as a kind of controller-general. Even more remarkable was the career of Benno, who rose rapidly in Henry III's (1039-1056) service to become mayor of the imperial palace at Goslar and chief administrator of the crown lands. In 1054, he was selected for the bishopric of Osnabrück, and his appointment to an episcopal see marked the first breach in the purely aristocratic constitution of the German church. But it was under Henry IV (1056-1106) that the Salian policy of relying so heavily on *ministeriales* in the royal administration was pushed to its logical conclusion. The chroniclers of the period voiced the complaints of the aristocracy when they reported that Henry was surrounded by *vilissimi et infimi homines* (the meanest and lowest kind of people) and that he listened only to low-born counsellors, spurning the advice of high-born princes. These *ministeriales* played a role similar to that of the French legists but unlike the legists, they were not freemen. Where the legists chose to remain the faithful servants of the French monarchs, the *ministeriales*, like the feudal lords, eventually seized the power of their masters.

In the course of the dispute over investiture, the position of the *ministeriales* was greatly improved. In spite of their servile origin and still servile status, they rose to the ranks of the nobility, forming a knightly class with a place in the feudal hierarchy.

By the middle of the twelfth century, we find *ministeriales*

74

marrying into noble families and royal dynasties, succeeding to aristocratic estates and franchises, and occupying high places in church and state. The Crusades and the civil wars between the Ghibellines (Hohenstaufens) and the Guelphs (Saxons) ruined the small freemen and advanced the *ministeriales*. At the same time, the unified German aristocracy of Saxon and Salian times split into competing factions. If one family was loyal to the crown and expected rewards from the crown, then a rival family would inevitably pledge its loyalty to the pope and the anti-king recognized by the pope. Many families were even divided among themselves, with the result that some nobles found themselves holding little more than a single castle. Hardly distinguishable from the knights or *ministeriales* any more, they eventually merged with these classes.

The Hohenstaufen emperors only hastened this leveling process. In one extravagant venture after another, they squandered both the crown lands and the blood of the German nobility. While the ranks of the nobles were being weakened, the *ministeriales* were able to increase their power by administering the properties of their absentee lords. Indeed, the *ministeriales* played a key role in Hohenstaufen policy. With the help of these administrators, the Hohenstaufens hoped to transform their royal and imperial realms in Italy and Germany into a modern bureaucratic state.

It is easy enough to imagine where such a policy would lead, and its final effects became evident in the reign of Philip of Swabia (1198-1208). During his struggles with his rival, Otto IV of Brunswick, Philip urgently needed strong, loyal vassals, and he acquired them by granting large fiefs to his *ministeriales*. Other powerful lords followed his example, and when the impoverished knights saw that the princes were relying on their *ministeriales* instead of on their free vassals, the knights went over to the ministerial class themselves but retained what was left of their old property or fief as a token of their free and noble birth. This occurred with increasing frequency, and the free nobility eventually merged with the ministerial class.

As the *ministeriales* rose in rank, they assumed the title of *Ritter* (knight); and with the change of title went a change of status. They were no longer subject to the old *Dienstrecht* or *Hofrecht*. Their obligations were governed by feudal law now. This meant greater freedom and all the rights that went with a place in the feudal hierarchy: the right to enfeoff vassals, to hold courts, and, in some districts, to tax dependents.

But even though ministerial families attained these rights and sometimes even rose to princely rank, many of them, like the Erbach, Waldburg, Reuss, Liechtenstein, and Bolanden families, were still nominally bondsmen. Some of them were formally emancipated only long after they had attained the level of princes and long after their bondage had ceased to have any meaning. This anomalous state of being both prince and slave existed only in Germany.

Clearly, the *ministeriales* played a considerable role in the dissolution of the old nobility in the Frankish kingdom. Their rise to power marked a fundamental change in the values that defined the elite. Nobility was no longer based on free and noble birth but on the offices and material possessions of the ruling class.

## THE TERRITORIAL STATES

THE DISINTEGRATION of the feudal hierarchy in Germany created the basis for the growth of the territorial states. Earlier in the Middle Ages, counts had been royal officials and therefore had held the same princely titles as the major feudal lords. But when the counties became fiefs that were then divided into smaller sub-fiefs, the counts lost their high ranks and their princely titles. The supreme rank was held only by those feudal lords who held their fiefs directly from the emperor. This situation of being directly subordinate to the emperor and subordinate to him alone was called *Reichsunmittelbarkeit*, and it represented a transitional stage in the development toward the *dominium terrae*, the territorial principality.

Two merging classes were mainly responsible for the growth of the territorial principalities. One group was made up of those few families of the feudal nobility that had survived the general ruin of the aristocracy. They had retained some of their wealth and were slowly building on it. The other group consisted of *ministeriales*. Both groups gathered fiefs and landed property, and because ownership of land did not provide complete control of a territory, they also took care to accumulate all the separate rights, claims, and revenues that were connected with a specific district.

The rising princes insisted that forfeited fiefs revert immediately to the emperor. This apparent loyalty to the imperial crown only served their own ambitions, however, because the emperor could then grant these fiefs to new holders. The princes jealously guarded their acquisitions, and the emperors, preoccupied with their foreign ventures and dependent on the support of the princes, could do nothing to prevent this accumulation of power. Indeed, Frederick II expressly sanctioned it in the famous *Statutum in favorem principum* (1232). Acquiring power in this way involved chance, energy, sufficient means, and a new set of mind. This new mentality differed greatly from that of earlier leaders. Military prowess and the force of personality accounted for the greatness of Charlemagne, Otto I, and the Hohenstaufens. But the families that now took the lead and were to keep the lead for many centuries, the Hapsburgs, the Luxemburgs, the Hohenzollerns, the Württembergs, gained their position by tenacity, calculation, and efficiency. They were willing to sacrifice the splendor of the present to the building of the future, preparing that future through marriages, inheritances, and promotions rather than through conquests. They acted to improve the position of the family rather than of the individual ruler.

This family spirit and solidarity are particularly characteristic of the Hapsburgs. They held their royal and imperial positions almost uninterruptedly for 650 years, from 1273 to 1918; and from the fifteenth century on, there were only four cases of serious rivalry within the family: the disagreement between Charles V and his younger brother and successor Ferdinand I early in the sixteenth century; the quarrel between the brothers Matthias and Rudolph II at the beginning of the seventeenth century and shortly before the Thirty Years' War; the conflict of Don Carlos with his father, Philip II; and, finally, the revolt of the Crown Prince Rudolph against Francis Joseph at the end of the nineteenth century. None of these disputes led to open violence. If we compare this long and peaceful history with the violent records of all the ruling dynasties up to the fourteenth century, we can see the tremendous social and mental change that occurred in this crucial period. We shall come back to this feature of the Hapsburgs when we contrast their methods of rulership with those of the Hohenzollerns. But for now, it suffices to note that, to some degree, self-control and long-range planning characterize still other families that came to power from the thirteenth century on and that retained their positions into modern times.

Gradually, these families began to form a coherent social group. They made agreements on inheritance (*Erbvereine* or *Erbverbrüderungen*) by which the male heirs of a given family received the properties of another family that lacked heirs. This prevented the escheat of fiefs to the emperor and created a virtual monopoly of landholders among the families that were parties to these agreements.

But the establishment of the territorial states just outlined here was a long and difficult process. It met with stubborn and, for a time, successful resistance on the part of the knights and the cities. Just as the princes had exploited the feudal system to weaken the crown and secure their own power, the knightly class, which by now had merged with the *ministeriales*, did exactly the same thing within the smaller confines of the territorial principalities. The early feudal lords disrupted county organization and government. Now, in the fourteenth century, new lordships within the boundaries of the principalities threatened to destroy territorial cohesion. In addition, the growing wealth and franchises of the cities helped break down the unity of the local administrative districts and undermine the direct administrative authority of the princes.

Two important factors played into the hands of the knights and the cities. One was the princes' chronic need for money, which old sources of revenue could no longer meet in a period of rapid economic change. We shall take up these economic matters later when we study the rise of the cities. The other was that the princes still regarded their territories as private property. What had ruined the early Frankish dynasty also ruined, or at least weakened, many of these princely families. Principalities that had been fiefs of the empire until the middle of the thirteenth century and that could not be disposed of without imperial assent were treated as the private properties of their owners after the collapse of the imperial authority in the interregnum. They were divided among the sons of the deceased prince and often mortgaged, farmed out, or alienated in other ways to meet financial needs. A wasteful multiplication of courts and households resulted, adding to the financial burdens of the princes. This constant subdivision prevented the consolidation of states capable of healthy and vigorous political life. In the thirteenth century the realization of statehood in Germany seemed possible as territories took shape and borders were defined, but in the fourteenth century, this incipient cohesion was shattered, and the particularism or *Kleinstaaterei* that would plague Germany throughout her history emerged.

The territorial divisions played directly into the hands of the knights and the cities, reducing the power of the princely dynasties and involving them in internecine struggle. But the princes' need for money was the major weapon their opponents could turn against them. Since the middle of the thirteenth century, the knights and cities had resisted the princes' claimed right to levy general taxes at will and had tried to limit taxation to the traditional occasions: the ransom of the lord from captivity, the knighting of sons, and the marriage of daughters. But these regular revenues, fixed at standard rates, no longer covered the increased expenditures that accompanied the expansion of the princes' power. By the end of the thirteenth century few princes could manage on their normal income, but they were now unable to impose new taxes. Consequently, the knights and cities rose to the height of their power. The cities in particular attained unprecedented independence in the fourteenth century. In North Germany, the Hanseatic League was able to pursue its own interests without interference from the territorial princes to whom the member cities were theoretically subject. As early as 1293 the Hanseatic League showed its disregard for territorial boundaries when the two Mecklenburg cities of Rostock and Wismar joined with Lübeck and the Pomeranian towns of Greifswald and Stralsund to form a single transterritorial association. In the south, similar unions were formed to resist encroachments by the princes. Most famous of all was the Swabian-Rhenish League of 1381.

Unity of interests gave rise to similar organizations in the knightly class throughout Germany. In Austria, Brandenburg, Bavaria, Franconia, and Württemberg, leagues of knights were formed in the second half of the fourteenth century not only to oppose the princes but to maintain their position against the growing power of the cities.

Through periodic meetings and the appointment of permanent committees to watch over their concerns, both the cities and the knights consolidated their power. The princes had to negotiate and bargain with these "estates" that had, for all practical purposes, taken over the functions of government. The estates had interposed themselves as intermediate authorities between the prince and his subjects; and, except on his own domain, the prince could only contact the common people through the town authorities or through the manorial lords. It was only with the cooperation of the cities that the princes could collect taxes and only with that of the knights that they could defend their territories.

The degree of the princes' dependence is evident in the fact that they recognized associations of both knights and cities formed expressly to defend the subjects' rights and privileges against the ruler. It can also be seen in the princes' acceptance of a limited form of allegiance by which the subjects undertook fealty and obedience only on certain specified conditions and only for as long as those conditions were fulfilled. But its most remarkable expression was in the "right of resistance" (*Widerstandsrecht*), the right to take up arms against a prince who overrode established privileges or liberties. The very existence of this right presupposed that there was no final and impartial authority or tribunal in the land, and it vividly illustrates the chaos that resulted from the collapse of imperial authority and jurisdiction in Germany. Since in any given case the prince was not a disinterested party and since the emperor was without power to intervene even if he had wanted to, the subjects were authorized to take up arms in their own defense. In 1416, for example, the Bavarian knights formed a league to defend the "good old law" against "our gracious lord or any other within or without the land." The margraves of Brandenburg made a treaty with the "*ministeriales*, knights, vassals, and other subjects" of their land in 1280, expressly surrendering any right to levy extraordinary taxes; and in the same treaty, they explicitly recognized the right of "all vassals and towns" to unite in resistance if there were a breach of agreements on the part of the margraves. This permitted, in effect, a legalized, solemnly stipulated civil war. From arrangements of this kind, the concept of *Faustrecht* developed. As the word indicates, this was "law of the fist," the right to defend one's interests, by force if necessary.

The fourteenth century, too, was a period of anarchy and confusion. But its anarchy was of a different kind than that which prevailed in the thirteenth century. It was not marked by that

81

chaotic division of claims and rights that dominated the end of the feudal period but was characterized instead by the clash of the new social classes that had formed after the collapse of the German empire. The princes, the knights, the cities, and, a century later, the peasants founded organizations (*Bünde*) to defend their rights and interests against each other.

But in the long run it was the principalities that emerged as the only effective powers in Germany for centuries to come. The cities, knights, and peasants gradually lost whatever influence they had. The knights were doomed by both military and economic developments. The Hussite and the Swiss wars demonstrated the superiority of the new infantry tactics and the new technical weapons over the knights' methods of combat. When the princes began to hire mercenary troops, the knights found themselves with no alternative but to enter civil service with the princes. The knights became equally obsolete economically. As Germany became an industrial and trading country, money accumulated in the cities; but the knights grew poorer and poorer, degenerating into a kind of aristocratic proletariat. Their only share in the profits of commerce and industry derived from robbing traveling merchants. The fixed incomes from their estates decreased in value because of depreciations of the currency. At the same time, their efforts to emulate the higher standard of living set by the cities increased their need of money. This forced them to greater exploitation of the peasantry whose fixed tenures were now replaced by short-term leases at variable rates. Although the peasants were gaining personal freedom and the freedom to farm according to their own ideas, these advantages were offset by the fact that they no longer had any land of their own. They were forced to rent it from some larger proprietor on increasingly onerous terms and were subject to eviction on short notice. In addition, the destruction of the fields by the constant warfare and recklessness of the nobility made land cultivation a hazardous affair. The scene was thus set for the peasants' revolts, which began in the second half of the fifteenth century and culminated in the Peasants' War of 1524-1525.

The German cities rose to the height of their power during the fourteenth and fifteenth centuries, but eventually they, too, succumbed to the princes. The interests of the cities were purely economic; and because they lacked the political ambition of the Italian city-states, they missed the opportunity to assume national leadership. The princes made better use of their opportunities. They adopted urban administrative methods and eventually came to accept city life with all its comforts, conveniences, and cultural advantages. Because the princes were shrewd enough to learn urban ways, they were finally able to bring the cities under their own control.

# 10.

## PROVINCIALISM IN THE TERRITORIAL STATES

AFTER THE DOWNFALL of the Hohenstaufens and the chaotic period of the interregnum, the emperor never regained the supreme position he had held in the feudal empire. He had never enjoyed absolute supremacy because he was elected by peers who continued to consider themselves his equals. But as the highest feudal lord, he could still wield some real power. He commanded a following of powerful vassals, even though their number and significance steadily declined; and he determined the distribution of vacant fiefs. Also, the dignity and aura of Charlemagne and the Roman emperors were associated with his office. The people looked up to him as a legendary ruler of Christianity and the symbol of unity in the Christian world. Even in the early fourteenth century, Dante could still appeal to the emperor as the supreme arbiter and call on him to restore peace.

But the redistribution of power during the thirteenth century put an end to the authority of the imperial throne. Because feudal bonds had lost their meaning and the crown property had been depleted, the emperors had to rely on private, family property (*Hausmacht*) if they were to maintain their position among the other territorial princes. From this point on, the emperor was just one territorial power among other territorial powers, elected by virtue of his greater wealth and the influence that went with it. It was wealth and territorial possessions that enabled the Hapsburgs to attain the imperial crown. Charles V (1519-1556), the most outstanding of the Hapsburgs and the last really powerful emperor of the Holy Roman Empire, owed his election to money lent him by an Augsburg banker; and his authority derived largely from the vast dominions he controlled: Spain and her new colonies, the Netherlands, Burgundy, Austria, Bohemia,

84

and Hungary. Ever since the issuance of the Golden Bull, which had formally sanctioned the practice established by the *Kurverein* (electoral coalition) of Rhense in 1338, emperors were no longer elected by the whole assembly of feudal lords but by a group of seven electors. These three ecclesiastical and four secular princes also had the right to exercise supervision over the empire. This constitutional change clearly marks the transformation of the feudal monarchy into a huge aristocratic republic.

The German territorial princes were a cross between private landowners and rulers. As we have seen, they initially regarded their lands as mere private property. They were frequently absentee landlords who had no feeling for the provincial and ethnic coherence of their own dominions, much less of any national unit. The Hapsburgs were the richest landowners in Switzerland, but they established themselves in Austria where they saw an opportunity to amass vast territories. The Hohenzollerns, a Swabian family, became burgraves of Nürnberg, lords of Ansbach and Bayreuth, and, later, margraves of Brandenburg. The territorial princes did not represent their lands or feel any sense of responsibility for them. Their subjects were mere possessions to be exploited and even sold to serve in foreign wars. The princes retained these proprietary attitudes until the seventeenth century, long after they had reached positions comparable to those of the French, English, or Spanish kings. They, and not the powerless emperors, actually ruled in Germany. Although they succeeded in undermining the dignity and power of the emperor and although they were *de facto* sovereigns, they were still not rulers like the other European kings, because they lacked a people to represent. Theirs was indeed a *dominium terrae*, a rule over territory alone. Their "states" were patchwork conglomerations of lands, and the incoherent nature of these territorial states is reflected in the discrepancies between their names and their actual ethnic composition. Prussia, for instance, takes its name from the Pruzzi, an ancient tribe of unclear origins that has apparently been absorbed by other ethnic groups. In Bavaria, the original tribe survived intact but was then thrown together with Frankish, Swabian, and Rhenish elements, thus forming the mixture of lands and people that constitutes modern Bavaria. Lacking all organic unity of people and territory, these states could never have developed into nations. Even where the rulers represented a native popula-

85

tion or where they tried to shape a national identity, no national cohesion developed. The Wittelsbachs were an indigenous Bavarian family and in this sense did represent their people. The Hapsburgs, on the other hand, exerted so much influence that Austria came to be identified with its ruling house. But still one would hesitate to call Bavaria or even Austria a true nation, and the reason that neither of these major territorial states nor any other such state could develop as a nation was that the empire continued to lead at least a nominal existence and to promise the achievement of German unity. Indeed, during the reign of Maximilian I (1493-1519), this promise was openly expressed when the Holy Roman Empire became the Holy Roman Empire of the German Nation.

Because the territorial states were stunted in their growth and prevented from developing into nations, they were condemned to provinciality; and the courts of the territorial princes were dull and vacuous places. The princes' attempts at court life failed because they lacked not only an audience but also the means and urbanity of the western kings, whom they sought to emulate. A true court could have formed if the German nobility had been willing to gather around the imperial monarch in a central urban residence. But instead, every minor lord wanted to hold his own court, whether he was able to afford it or not. Duke Karl Eugen of Württemberg, for instance, would go to his country seat, *Solitude*, to stage ludicrous imitations of Louis XIV's *lever*. Anti-urban and anti-intellectual in the extreme, the princes did not leave their castles for the cities until the fifteenth century; and when they finally took an interest in intellectual activities, they had to learn them from the burghers. This whole state of affairs did irreparable damage to Germany's evolution, for in their formative stages the Germans lacked the civilizing influence and guidance of an urban nobility.

Vienna produced a court and society equal to those of the west, but it was the residence of an international, supranational, even anti-national dynasty that was far from German in nature. And Berlin, when it finally came to figure as a national capital, never outgrew its provincial and colonial beginnings; it was never able to symbolize and synthesize the entire German experience. It was a technical and intellectual center, but it never became a center of national culture.

It is perhaps appropriate at this point to take note of the contributions of the nobility to the development of Western culture. We live today in an age of democracy, which is probably the only suitable form of government in our technological era. Monarchy is obsolete and impossible now. The few kings who still exist have become thoroughly bourgeois and do not even try to influence the policies of their countries. (The Austrian emperor Francis Joseph was the last genuine monarch.) Dictators should not be mistaken for true monarchs. They are middle-class or proletarian upstarts who often come to power by way of the military. Whenever they gain control of technologically complex states, they are sham autocrats, unable to determine a course of action by themselves. Just as monarchy is impossible today, so class oligarchy, the rule of one social class or party, is equally obsolete in a time when all classes have gained political consciousness. We should not overlook the terrible crimes that monarchical and aristocratic regimes of the past have perpetrated, but there was a time when the guidance of an urban nobility was of great benefit to the formation of national character. What is attractive and admirable in the character of the Italians, the French, the Spaniards, and the British is largely due to the national image created by their aristocracies; and the manners and courtesy that are taken for granted in our society today originated at the courts of the past. A great deal of snobbery, hypocrisy, and ridiculous formality are, of course, associated with the existence of an aristocracy. But the fact still remains that the character of the western nations derived some lasting good from the training they received at the hands of their cultural elites.

The cultural elites of the western and southern nations would never have formed if their aristocracies had not been urbanized at an early stage in their histories. The refinement the aristocracy underwent in these countries is due in large measure to the social and intellectual influences of the city. After the intellectual monopoly of the clergy and the monasteries had been broken, the new intellectual life of Europe emerged in the cities. In France, Italy, Spain, and Britain the nobles residing at the capital city and at the king's court both practiced and patronized the arts and sciences. Noblemen were among the great thinkers and poets; and the courts of monarchs and princes became major centers of learning. Intellectual life was an integral part of the new, courtly civilization, but it was by no means the exclusive property of the nobility; indeed, it was shared by men of all ranks and classes in the society. As a result of this contact between classes, those members of the intelligentsia who were not of noble birth were able to acquire a wide social and political background and to gain an understanding of national and public affairs. The ruling class, on the other hand, learned to appreciate and value cultural life.

In Germany, the dispersion of the nobility throughout the country and the isolated, autonomous evolution of the cities produced a rift between the city and the rurally based ruling class, between intellectual and political forces. The territorial rulers were deprived of social experience. Removed from urban centers, they could take no part in developing a national culture. The cities and the rising bourgeoisie were deprived of political experience. Removed from the centers of power, they had no chance to develop a taste or aptitude for politics.

The German cities enjoyed territorial autonomy, but they never attained or even sought territorial possessions to the extent the Italian cities did. Had they done so, they would have gained political power; but they had no political ambitions. From the earliest stages of their growth, their interests and aspirations had been primarily economic. Then, in the Middle Ages, they took over the scholarly and educational functions the clergy and the monasteries had performed in earlier periods.

Because the German nobility was basically hostile to the intellectual life, the founding of universities in Germany occurred much later than in other countries; and when the German princes did establish universities, they did so only in imitation of other European rulers. While the universities of Bologna, Paris, and Oxford were founded in the twelfth century, the first German university, the University of Prague, was created some two hundred years later in 1348. The University of Heidelberg followed in 1386, the University of Leipzig in 1410. Neglected by the nobility, intellectual life became the province of the bourgeoisie; and because the middle class had no contact with the broad concerns of society and politics, bourgeois thinking remained characterized by narrow-minded parochialism on the one hand and by a bent for the utopian and the abstract on the other. The inability to grasp the realities of political life has marked the German intellegentsia ever since.

In Germany, the nobility received its intellectual training from the burghers with the result that the German noblemen became burghers themselves long before the bourgeoisie had become the dominant class in society. The only exceptions to this rule were the great Austrian, Baltic, and Silesian nobles who, for one reason or another, mingled with the high aristocracy of Europe, and the East Elbian Junkers, who never abandoned their rural provinciality.

In every respect, then, the existence of the territorial states contributed to provincialism in Germany, a provincialism produced by the antagonism and isolation of social forces that by rights should have merged to create a national life to rival that of France or England. But the factors we have just considered here—the nominal but ineffective unity of the Holy Roman Empire, the lack of human ties between the territorial princes and their lands, the animosity of country and city, of power and intellect—militated against such a development in Germany. These factors never disappeared from German life, and Germany's continuing failure to form a national unit can be ascribed in part to this persisting provincialism, the ineradicable isolation and suspicion that exist between Germany's territories and between her social classes.

# 11.

---

## THE ORIGIN OF THE GERMAN CITIES

IT WOULD BE impossible to relate the evolution of medieval Italy, France, or Spain without including the evolution of their cities as well. The role of the cities cannot be considered apart from the general development of these countries. In Germany, the cities grew as isolated enclaves within the empire, and only when we discussed the disintegration of feudalism and the formation of the different social classes in the late Middle Ages did we have to deal with the cities at all.

In the western countries, the cities existed before kingdoms and nations were formed. We have seen how the French monarchy and the French nation arose in the city of Paris. In Germany, the cities assumed importance only in the second half of the thirteenth century, long after the feudal empire was established. They did not give rise to the empire; they were by-products of it.

Long after the French and English kings had established their permanent court residences, the German emperors refused to settle in the cities of Gaul and continued to migrate from one of their *Pfalzen* to another. Under the Merovingians, these *Pfalzen* were hardly distinguishable from the dwelling places of the ordinary Frankish people. They were plain wooden houses that were gradually fortified with earthen ramparts. In Charlemagne's reign, monasteries and bishoprics served as models for new stone buildings of Roman and Byzantine design. But these structures were limited to the west at first, and only during the Crusades and the increasingly frequent campaigns in Italy did this type of architecture spread to the eastern Germanic regions. The construction of a fortified residence was originally a privilege allowed only to kings, but it was soon taken over by lesser feudal lords. Dukes and counts began to fortify their dwellings, move them up on

90

hilltops, or enlarge old Germanic *Fluchtburgen*. These structures gradually evolved into the castles or *Burgen* that served as permanent residences for the nobility.

From ancient times, cities have always formed around such castles. Examples are the Babylonian ziggurats and the sacred citadels of the Greeks, the acropoleis. The German cities too developed at the residences of secular and ecclesiastical potentates, forming around the church and cathedral castles of bishops and abbots or around the *Pfalzburgen* of kings and lords. In the early centuries of the German cities, *Burg* was the only designation for city, and the word has been retained in a number of modern names like Augsburg, Regensburg, Würzburg, and Magdeburg. The term was even added to the names of foreign cities, transforming Rome into Rûmeburg and so on.

Thus, both the German cities and the ancient ones developed around castles; but there are still some striking differences. The German cities beyond the Rhine and the Danube emerged from a void. There were no direct ties with anything that had existed before. No local, tribal, or Roman tradition linked them with a past. Even in Flanders and along the Rhine and Danube where Roman settlements had existed, the most that remained was the debris of some Roman structures. The only exception was Cologne, *Colonia Agrippinensis,* where not only the Roman walls but also remnants of Roman roads and buildings had been preserved.

But though the German cities had no apparent ties with the past, Rome still influenced their growth in an indirect way. The Church provided this tenuous link between the Roman past and the emerging German cities. One of the last expressions of Rome's urban orientation was the ruling by the councils of Laodicea and Sardica that bishops be required to maintain a permanent residence in the cities. As a result, the bishops remained at the sites of Roman towns, which then quite naturally became ecclesiastical sees. With the advance of Christian missions into Germany, however, this ruling presented difficulties because no cities had ever existed in the German interior. The English monk, Boniface, who was called the Apostle of the Germans (680-754), was forced to break the rule of city residence for bishops when he carried the Christian faith to newly conquered tribes that had never been in contact with the Romans. He founded new bishoprics in Bavaria,

Hesse, and Thuringia. The Carolingian and Saxon emperors later established settlements and bishoprics still deeper in German territory when they expanded their rule to the east and to the north.

The bishops usually built their churches, their fortified mansions, and the habitations of their clerics on hilltops. The farmhouses and farmlands were located on the flats below. These settlements were fortified with ramparts or, on the eastern plains, with canals. Because of their regular services and holiday festivals, their synods and ecclesiastical tribunals, their many gatherings and feasts, these church castles attracted traveling merchants and so developed into trade centers and eventually into cities. The German word *Messe*, which still means both "mass" and "fair," reflects the early association of trade with church rituals. But unlike the ancient Oriental, Greek, or Roman trade centers, the German ecclesiastical settlements—and the *Pfalzen* of the kings and other secular lords—were basically self-supporting estates. They did not originate trade, nor did they depend on it for a livelihood. The German cities did not grow up around permanent centers of trade but around centers that attracted trade.

Along the major rivers and the old Roman trade routes, a certain amount of commercial traffic survived from Roman times. The Syrians and Jews had originated this trade, but the Syrians disappeared from it after the Arabs took control of the Mediterranean. The Frisians, the first Germanic traders, moved into the gap the Syrians had left. Originally sheepherders, they entered commerce as wool merchants. Like all traders, the Frisians were freemen who did business on their own account. From the south they brought weapons, spices, silks, and jewels; from the north, furs and woolens. The woolen and cloth trade, and later the clothing industry, was the most prominent commercial activity in the northern countries during the Middle Ages, and it gave rise to some crucial economic changes.

The first of these changes was that the textile trade introduced growing numbers of the population to commercial activity. The traders who had initially visited the settlements only on special occasions gradually built houses and farms near the castles, carrying on their trade from these new homes. The result was that other people, particularly the landowners and *ministeriales*, developed a taste not only for buying but also for selling, bargaining, and making profits. The growing wealth of the lords and their administrators increased their desire for precious fabrics, and at the same time they became aware of the profit that could easily be made with these wares. They saw merchants come home with their bales of cloth and sell them at retail (*Gewandschnitt*) for considerable gain. Consequently, when the lords or their *ministeriales* went away campaigning or for some other purpose, they did the same thing. They purchased cloth wholesale, brought it home, and sold it retail. The landowners and administrators began to trade among themselves as a hobby. The original merchants and these amateur tradesmen from the landowning and administrative classes formed the nuclei of the new trade centers from which the German cities evolved.

The establishment of trade centers at church settlements had important legal consequences. The kings had always courted the favor of the Church and had granted it exemption of all Church property from the control or interference of royal officials. This exemption was called immunity (*immunitas*). In times of disorder, when usurpation by powerful counts and lords threatened small holdings, minor landowners turned to the Church for protection, offering their property to the saints and receiving it back as a *precarium* or *beneficium*. Because the Church enjoyed a legal status beyond the jurisdiction of the king or any of his officers, an entirely new body of law could develop in the cities that formed around ecclesiastical settlements.

The law prevailing among the rural population was still essentially the Germanic law of pagan times when peace within the tribe had been of prime importance and when a breach of that peace had been considered a breach of law. Offenses had been of two kinds: crimes against the tribe itself or crimes against a fellow tribesman or his family. Offenses against the tribe were more serious. Anything that hurt the tribe—desecration of a sacred place, an act of treason, or a breach of fidelity—was considered inexpiable. A man who committed any of these crimes was either killed in a cultic offering or expelled from the community. Those who were banned from the tribes were declared *friedlos* ("without peace"), and they could legally be killed by anyone they met.

Under Christian rule, sacral crimes fell under the jurisdiction of the Church. The Frankish king came to represent the tribal community, but now crimes committed against individuals or families became more important than crimes against the community. Just as in tribal times, murder, manslaughter, injury, rape, and robbery were not offenses against the communal order but private matters to be settled between families or clans. Peace was often restored through blood vengeance. This was the usual means of redress among peasants and noblemen until long after the Middle Ages. Duelling was the last remnant of this system to survive into modern times. An injured person or family could also sue an offender before a county tribunal, but trials of this kind were not far removed from the world of blood vengeance and duelling. They culminated either in physical combat between the contestants or in ordeals to test the innocence or guilt of the accused. In these proceedings, the judge was not a judge in the legal sense but an arbitrator who saw to it that all the rules of these ritualized trials were observed.

The Frankish kings tried to replace these primitive practices with the elements of Roman law: compulsory retribution; formal accusation and prosecution, regardless of whether a plaintiff appears or not; and adjudication of the case by a judge. They did not succeed in spreading these procedures throughout their domains; but within their own immediate spheres of influence, they introduced an entirely new and untraditional form of jurisdiction, the royal court (*Königsgericht*). Here the ruler himself administered justice according to his own personal judgment and sense of equity (*aequitas*), and cases could be appealed to him from the lower county courts. In conjunction with the king's efforts to achieve justice and to act as peacemaker among his people, the concept and practice of the *Königsfrieden* developed. This "peace of the king" was a kind of taboo that protected the king, his followers, his property, and any place where he was present. Any violation of this peace, any crime committed within this sphere of royal influence, brought instant and severe punishment.

The existence of the *Königsfrieden* came to be of great importance for the growing cities. The old Germanic law with its long, cumbersome ritual procedures was clearly unworkable in the new trade centers. There were no provisions in it for dealing with the kind of disputes that are likely to arise in commerce. A new law and a new concept of "keeping the peace" were required. The king's peace and his judgments filled these needs in the marketplaces that grew up around his *Pfalzen*. The insignia of the king

94

—cross, sword, and glove—were put up in the marketplace as symbols of the king's continuous presence. And since the churches stood under the patronage of the king, the bishops were granted a "peace of the king" for the new trading centers that were developing around them. Because canon law forbad the ecclesiastical lords to deal in worldly matters, it was the lord's advocate or *Vogt* who administered the law in the church settlements. At first he acted as a kind of policeman who made sure that the rules and regulations of commercial traffic were observed. Later, he became a *centenarius* or *Schultheiss*, a judge dealing with minor offenses. Finally, through the so-called Ottonian Privileges, jurisdiction over entire counties was conferred on bishops and abbots, and the grant of the king's peace to a marketplace henceforth became equivalent to the grant of a "market right" and "market law."

As a result of these developments, the trade centers were completely exempt from the law of the territories that surrounded them. While rural land was undergoing division into endless local, occupational, and class jurisdictions and rural law degenerating into the "law of the fist," law in the marketplaces enjoyed an autonomous growth. Unhampered by the ordinances and customs of the surrounding country, it could develop the uniformity and effectiveness that made it the first and only public law in Germany.

# 12.

## THE ASCENDANCY OF THE CRAFT GUILDS

THE NEW MARKET LAW and the exemption of the marketplaces from the counts' control brought about basic changes in the structure of medieval society. Within the pale of the trade centers, everyone was relieved of any debts or servitude owed under the feudal system. All men were free and equal in the city as long as they abided by its laws.

It is easy to see how this new freedom would appeal to the country people. The city meant escape from the taxes and tyranny of the feudal lords, and the saying *Stadtluft macht frei* (city air means freedom) became proverbial. Peasants and craftsmen who brought their goods to the market remained and settled. This angered the feudal lords who lost tenants and bondsmen to the markets, but the bishops, with the assistance of the kings, defended their newly established rights and protected their people. As the centers grew, churches were built on the market squares; market halls, court halls, city halls arose; walls and fortifications were constructed to protect the settlements. The houses of the merchants were built closer together and directly on the market square. The property connected with each house, the *Hof*, was located to the rear; and, particularly in northern cities, the houses were equipped with arcades to shelter traffic in bad weather. Outer walls or "rings" and connecting streets (*Äusserer Ring*, *Ringstrasse*) were added. Gradually the rural marketplace assumed the aspect of a city. Within the population, different ranks developed. The merchants and lower nobility separated from the craftsmen and artisans of peasant origin; but in the earliest stages of city growth, a strong sense of solidarity and community prevailed among the whole population.

The German cities developed along purely economic lines, and their lack of roots and traditions is reflected in the German word *Stadt*. Unlike the English "city," the French *cité*, the Italian *città*, and the Spanish *ciudad*, *Stadt* has no connection with the Roman word *civitas*. Nor does it recall the Roman *villa* as the French *ville* does. The German word *Burg* was retained in some place-names, but it was dropped as a general designation for city, although both French and English still use "bourg" and "borough" in this sense. *Stadt* also bears no relation to the English word "town," which is a cognate of the German *Zaun* and originally designated the fence surrounding a farm. *Stadt* derives from *coufstat*, which means simply bargaining place or marketplace. The attribute *couf* vanished from common usage, and one spoke only of the *stat ze Babenberg, stat ze Wiene, stat ze München*. The basic meaning of *Stadt* is "place," a spot where something "takes place" (*statt hat* or *stattfindet*). It is the true counterpart of the German word *Land*, territory. Neither *Stadt* nor *Land* have any ethnic, national, or local content.

The cities of the ninth and tenth centuries evolved from the trade fairs that sprang up around Church settlements. The royal *Pfalzstädte* followed, and when ambitious territorial princes saw that they could gain financially from the wealth of the cities, they too began to promote them. But the proliferation and expansion of the marketplaces did not guarantee the trade centers the autonomy they needed to develop into modern cities of a specifically German cast. Three major changes in urban government had to take place before the cities could complete their evolution. The first step was the formation of a city council and its emancipation from the control of the lord of the city, the bishop. The second was the formation of an essentially urban, purely mercantile patriciate to oppose the knightly traders and the *ministeriales*. And the third was the craft guilds' takeover of the council and therefore of city government.

In the early history of the cities, the bishops were powerful feudal lords whose administrators and bailiffs collected increasing taxes and duties for the Church and for the empire. The arrogant and corrupt administration of the bailiffs (*Vögte*) and *ministeriales* frequently alienated the city population. The first move toward liberation from the bishops was the formation of city councils. These councils gradually won the right to levy taxes for

97

the city's needs, for defense, and for municipal offices and buildings. They also appropriated police power and legal jurisdiction. In the eleventh century, during the struggle over investiture, the Church cities sided with the secular powers, stressing their ties with the king through the grant of immunity and of the king's peace. Cologne and Worms expelled their bishops in 1073 and 1074. They were the first cities to do this, and Worms later expressed its loyalty to Emperor Henry IV by granting him sanctuary when he was in danger. As a result of all these actions, the power of the bishops was shattered. In the anarchy of the thirteenth century, the cities used their wealth to acquire all the rights and titles they needed for complete territorial independence.

The bishops left the cities or were driven out by force, and with them went all the administrators, landowners, and knights who had lived within city walls. This purge of all non-mercantile elements cleared the way for the second stage of urban emancipation—the formation of a strictly merchant class. This phase was accompanied by the systematization of city law, by the organization of city administration, and by the establishment of departmental authorities and offices. From its own members, the city council appointed judges and jurors, military commanders, city builders, officials in charge of taxation and coinage, market supervisors, fire chiefs, foresters, supervisors of fisheries, mills, and roads, water commissioners, and even *Dreckmeister*, supervisors of garbage removal and sewage. In addition to one or more burgomasters, there were also commissions and delegations for special purposes and for dealing with foreign powers.

All these offices were honorary appointments, but they did entail some revenues. Gradually the city officials came to preside over a whole staff of paid subordinates, ranging from the city scribe and chronicler to the city architect, the city physician, and on down to the policemen, night watchmen, and city musicians. In this elaborate administration we see the whole world of the medieval German city unfold.

The council and the administration were in the hands of a few rich and distinguished merchant families, the council being essentially an assembly of patricians. Although the ruling families were of merchant origin and were set apart from the ordinary townsfolk only by their wealth, they considered themselves aristocrats, because, in their view, trade was superior to handicraft. They insisted on maintaining their urban status, but at the same time they did not hesitate to acquire land or to traffic with noblemen beyond the city limits. They also valued what has always been a sign of the nobility ever since ancient times: idleness. They avoided handicrafts and shopkeeping, indeed, anything that "blackens one's fingernails," preferring the honorable and leisurely occupations of holding office in the city government and carrying on trade on a large scale. In thirteenth-century Germany, trade did not include industry and banking but meant only the trade in goods that had brought prosperity to the cities and peoples of the Mediterranean, especially to the great maritime city-republics of Italy.

In Germany, the northern seaports of the Hanseatic League were foremost in this type of commerce, and they have continued in it to the present day. As a result, the mercantile aristocracy has always been able to retain an influential position in the governments of these cities. In the interior of Germany, trade in goods was only an extension of the far more abundant Italian trade, and it was soon surpassed by other kinds of economic activity more important to the flowering of the German inland towns: handicrafts, industry, and banking. In the period of the patrician mercantile councils, trade in goods—spices, silk, jewels, and cloth—also had a knightly, aristocratic character because it was conducted in an irregular and leisurely manner and because the constant danger of robber barons and thieves made it an adventurous enterprise.

The third and last step in the transformation of the cities was the takeover of municipal government by the craftsmen during the fourteenth century. The craftsmen gained uncontested predominance in many cities and a decisive influence in all but the maritime cities of the Hanseatic League. The petty bourgeois character of urban life in Germany goes back to the control the craftsmen won at this time and continued to exercise from then on.

There were guilds all over Europe, but their development and their significance varied from country to country. In the cities of Italy and southern France, the continuing influence of the nobility was strong enough to check the advance of the guild spirit.

In the towns of northern France, where the crafts were rapidly increasing in importance, the kingdom took control of the cities before the guilds could gain predominance. In the English cities, the modest ambitions of the craftsmen were quashed by aristocratic city governments under the influence of the nobles and the king. In both France and England, the guilds were nationalized from the fourteenth century on and therefore subject to the rules and regulations of the monarchy. Only in the German inland towns was there a lack of effective opposition to the rise of the craft guilds. The spirit of the craftsmen, of the petty bourgeois, took over the leadership and education of the German people and left its mark on all the other classes.

The German inland cities began as gatherings of free individuals concerned only with trade, and trade was always to remain of prime importance to them. The rise of the craftsmen was unique to the German inland cities, too, but its implications are perhaps more important than the fact itself: it led to the formation of the first true collectives and created the prototype of the modern German state.

The craftsmen joined forces against the arbitrary city governance of the merchants, and the success of their struggle was in great part due to the relative weakness of their adversaries. The German merchants lacked political experience and skill. They also lacked the wealth of their Italian counterparts. The Italian merchants had built strong castles within the cities and acquired huge estates and villas in the countryside. They maintained bodyguards to fight their family feuds for them, and if they were victorious in these feuds, they became the rulers of the city-states. Quite apart from the fact that the German merchants lacked political ambition, the volume of inland trade in Germany simply could not produce the vast fortunes the Italian mercantile families could amass.

The lack of political interest among German merchants is reflected in the limited nature of their professional associations. The essentially social character of these groups is evident in their designations as *Gilde, Zeche, Artushof,* and *Trinkstubengesellschaft.* Both *Gilde* and English "guild" go back to a Germanic root meaning sacrificial feast or gathering. *Zeche* derives from *gizehon,* to arrange or regulate. It indicates an association formed to repre-

100

sent common interests, and the purely social aspect of the term is preserved in the modern German word *zechen*, to drink in company, to take part in a drinking bout. The merchants' guilds, then, were loose social units of an informal, convivial character. Membership in such a guild was not compulsory, but because it was a mark of distinction and a source of pleasure, it was voluntarily sought. Commerce, especially in its early stages, is basically an individual occupation, and once the automony of the city and the mercantile class had been won, the only motive for maintaining these professional associations was to protect the transport of goods. The Hanseatic League was originally formed for this purpose; in Old High German, *hansa* meant "band of warriors," hence "military escort." The other major incentive for trade associations —the need to pool capital resources—had not made itself felt yet. The unlimited demand for goods precluded competition, and modern commercial procedures were both unknown and unnecessary.

The craftsmen formed guilds, too, but these associations, which were called *Zünfte*, differed greatly from the merchant guilds. There was only one merchant guild in each city, but there were several *Zünfte* because each trade was represented by its own *Zunft*. Acting and organizing as a single class, the merchants had won the autonomy of the city, and their major weapon in this struggle against the lords had been money. The craft guilds, lacking the money to buy influence, had to resort to other means in their struggle against the merchants. The only weapon they had was the refusal of their services, and if this weapon was to be effective, all the tradesmen in the city had to be subject to the control of the *Zünfte*. Just like modern labor unions, the *Zünfte* could not permit "scabs" or "strikebreakers" to destroy their solidarity and lessen their powers of collective bargaining. Membership in a craft guild and observance of its rules was therefore made compulsory for anyone who wanted to carry on a trade.

The *Zünfte* not only regulated all professional aspects of the trades but also established elaborate moral codes for their members. Strict controls over the work and general behavior of the craftsmen were imposed in order to highlight the laxity and corruption of government by the merchant class and to win the confidence of the population. This kind of discipline was essential

101

because the relatively small size of the cities at that time (20,000 to 25,000 at the most) made anonymity impossible. This concern with appearances is expressed in the word *Zunft* itself, which is related to the verb *ziemen*, to be fitting or seemly. The craft guild's assumption of responsibility for the conduct of its members established a pattern in German life that has survived to the present day. The German petty bourgeois are infamous for their insatiable curiosity about their neighbors' behavior and for their readiness to criticize it. This willingness to judge and condemn individuals by the standards of the collective has always made the German lower middle class extremely pliable in the hands of government.

As far as professional matters were concerned, the guild regulations were designed to protect both producer and consumer. The guild insisted on equal status and working conditions for all members. Raw materials and tools had to be bought either by a delegate of the guild or under the supervision of guild overseers. Clandestine purchases and sales were severely punished. The sources of supply and the amount of sales were fixed. In many cases, the products had to be tested by the guild before they were admitted to the market. Prices were set to insure a comfortable living for the master and low prices for the consumer. The use of special tools was forbidden and the number of journeymen restricted. Conspicuous advertising was prohibited. Each master was allowed only one window for the display of his products, and only a master was entitled to sell goods produced by his trade. These limitations eliminated competition for profit, but they instilled a special pride in fine workmanship. The craft guilds were much more tightly knit collectives than the modern labor unions because the wide spectrum of interests and goals their members shared produced a greater solidarity than the purely economic interests of the unions allow.

By the end of the thirteenth century, the craft guilds were strong enough to take concerted action against the merchants in the city councils. They insisted that public funds be accounted for and demanded a voice in city government. Increasing conflicts led to open revolt, and in the fourteenth century, the craft guilds took over the administration in many cities. This change had a decisive influence on the make-up of urban populations, especially in the inland cities. The merchants were either expelled, as the lords and the landed proprietors had been before them, or they were forced to join a craft guild and give up their lives of aristocratic idleness. The merchant guilds that survived could do so only by adopting the rules and outlook of the craft guilds. Through the predominance of the guilds, whole cities were transformed into work collectives. Thus, in the fourteenth century, at a time when the rest of Germany was torn by anarchy, the German cities were models of public order and discipline.

# 13.

## THE INNOVATIONS OF THE INLAND CITIES

THE COLLECTIVES that took shape in the German inland cities were to exercise a lasting influence on the social and intellectual development of the country. In them, we find the first expression of a communal spirit. The organization of the feudal empire was based on purely private relationships, and it served purely private interests. By contrast, the cities were organized to serve the public interest. For the first time, administration, finances, and defense, health, welfare, and education were not controlled by a ruling elite but by the people who bore the burdens and received the benefits of government. The guilds, with their concern for the public good, created the models of government that would later be followed by the territorial states.

But the guilds' most important contribution was a new public morality that emerged from the discipline and the professional ethics of the *Zünfte*. It was the first morality that was not based in a particular tribal, national, or religions tradition. The ideal in this morality was not the hero or the saint but the average, useful member of society. For the first time in history the model of perfection was not the extraordinary man who stands out above his fellows but the ordinary man who fits in with them and meets collective requirements. This morality arises in a community that values the individual for his contributions, economic and otherwise, to the collective. Diligence, zeal, efficiency, economy, order, decency, and docility, all these virtues of middle-class morality originated in the city of the craft guilds and represented a complete reversal of feudal values.

These middle-class values clearly reflect the Christian virtues of humility, subservience, and love; and early Christianity had

104

addressed itself primarily to people of lowly origins and station. It had, however, set up ideals toward which the individual should strive. The heroes of early Christianity were heroes of humility but heroes nonetheless: the zealot, the ascetic saint, Saint Anthony, and Saint Francis. The transformation of these "heroic" ideals into the everyday virtues of the middle class took place in the world of the craft guilds.

All ranks and classes in the medieval world felt, of course, that they based their behavior on Christian values. But each class emphasized certain virtues and interpreted them according to its own needs and inclinations. It is only natural that the knights, as military men, saw themselves as the defenders of the faith. This role does not go back to early Christianity but was created by the Church as it became increasingly secularized and more deeply involved in political adventures. By nature and training, the knights were ready to fill the Church's need for warriors; and in their capacity as soldiers of God, they also adopted the Christian virtues most in harmony with their class: self-discipline, ascetic perseverance, protection of the weak and helpless, fidelity, and promotion of the Christian faith. This code sanctioned and encouraged not only the aristocratic leanings of the knights but also their more savage tendencies. The mass killings of heretics and infidels during the Crusades, all in the name of preserving the faith, obviously had nothing to do with the teachings of Christ.

As we have seen, the craftsmen were drawn to the values of early Christianity, values which the ruling clergy, following policy laid down by Rome, had neglected in favor of cultic ritual and "holy works" that materially benefited the Church. The monks, on the other hand, had always adhered to the original Christian virtues and, through reform movements, had often tried to bring the Church and their own orders back to these virtues. The foundation of the Benedictine Order in the sixth century, the reform of the Order by Benedict of Aniane about 800, the reform of Cluny a hundred years later, of Cîteaux in 1100, and the founding of the various mendicant orders around 1200 all aimed at recovering the integrity of a Christianity that the Church had compromised time and again.

Early monastic life had been concerned only with the individual's preparation for ultimate salvation and for the blessed eternal life thereafter. This preparation consisted of meditation, prayer, and penance. Meditation included the study of the teachings of the Church fathers and other venerated and sanctioned authorities. The monks were not supposed to have anything to do with worldly affairs or to engage in worldly occupations that might divert their attention from their celestial goal. Contemplative life was valued far above active life, no matter how full of goodness the latter might be.

In the reform movements, however, a concern for the world began to appear. Worldly occupations of a humble nature, especially farming, were prescribed for the monks of the Cistercian Order, founded in the twelfth century. The monks began to turn from the contemplative to the active life. Hard labor was now considered an appropriate means to keep man away from temptations. At this point in history, only monks lived by a schedule. The hourly tolling of bells called them to prayer, spiritual exercises, and work. Max Weber has pointed out that this was the first instance of the organized workday that has become the norm in the Western world.

Eventually, the monks had to leave the monasteries if they were to accomplish the new worldly tasks of teaching the common people and attending to both their physical and spiritual needs. From the outset, the Church tried to exploit these mendicant friars for its own purposes, using them to quell the discontents and heresies that the abuses of the power-hungry clergy had evoked. The orders that had arisen in opposition to the Church hierarchy—among them the Augustinians, Dominicans, and Franciscans—were gradually won over by the popes and converted into efficient agents of the Church. The Dominicans, for example, became the masters of the Inquisition, and earned the sobriquet of *Domini canes*, the bloodhounds of the Lord. It was the popes' plan that the modest ways of the mendicants as well as their antagonism toward the official clergy should win the confidence of the common people and so enable the friars to reconcile the population with the Church.

Many friars never questioned their roles as agents of the popes, but many others went over to the people and joined them in their desire for an immediate, mystic union with God. Most of the German mystics who prepared the way for the Protestant reform were Dominicans or Franciscans, and Luther himself was an Augustinian friar. The mendicant friars were frequently sons of

106

petty burghers and craftsmen whose views they shared. In the German cities particularly, the craft guilds and the friars had a great deal in common. In contrast to the monks of the old religious orders who resided in beautifully situated monasteries surrounded by large estates, the mendicant friars settled in the cities where they lived among the craftsmen, preaching and demonstrating Christian poverty and chastity. These unpretentious clerics were the natural allies of the burghers in their struggle against the bishops and the feudal lords. Later, in the contest between the craftsmen and the merchants, the friars sided with the tradesmen, whose work was sanctioned by the teachings of Jesus Christ, and stood against the rich merchants, because, in the Christian doctrine, commerce was considered the lowest and meanest of all human occupations.

The friars and early mystics stressed the values of original Christianity, adopting them to the workaday ethic of the craft guilds and to the pride the craftsmen took in their work. It was recalled that Jesus himself had been the son of a craftsman, and in the early fourteenth century, the Dominican Johannes Tauler (1300-1361) declared that the shoemaker's work, if well done, was a higher calling than that of the priest. Here, the glorification of plain, honest work was combined with the popular longing for immediate contact with God. In Germany, mystical union with God took on a quality different from that of all previous mysticism. The absence of ecstasy and stigmata in German mystical experience suggest its abstract and thoroughly middle-class character. In every simple, humble man, it was said, Christ may arise and perform an even greater work than He did through His life and passion. Such manifestations could not be brought about by extraordinary feats or sufferings. They could not be achieved, as Tauler says, "by sleeplessness and fasting, by wearing uncomfortable clothes, or by accomplishing great and holy works. . . . Do not strive to perform great deeds. Look humbly into yourself, into the depths of your soul. Commune with yourself and with nature, and do not seek a hidden and occult God." The Dominican Eckhart (d. 1327), Tauler's teacher and the most eminent of the German mystics, advised people not to search for God in visions and inspirations but "at the hearth and in the stable." Since Christ may arise in the soul of any man and since God is present in daily life and its activities, Christian virtue and the

107

public morality of the craft guilds could merge. All that was asked of a man was that he be a good citizen of his community and that he do honest work in the station where God placed him. Union with God had become an everyday condition. Love and charity were deprived of their heroic merit and gradually reduced to standardized services to the community.

The developments we have been studying here bring us up to the Protestant Reformation, the subject of Part II in this book. But if we are to understand this crucial event properly, we must first examine two further aspects of the craft guild cities that contributed to this major transformation and had a lasting effect on the German mind.

The first of these is the social and psychological atmosphere that permeated the German inland cities and that was to determine the relationship of man and nature in modern Germany. We have already noted the rift between city and country, the sharp opposition of an increasingly regulated collective order within the city walls and a chaotic wilderness without. The existence of these two contrasting worlds—the limited, systematized world of the city and the infinite, elemental world of nature—accounts in part for the ambivalence of the German character. Germans tend, on the one hand, to be pedantic, bureaucratic, and narrow-minded. But on the other hand, they are susceptible to the irrational and the intoxicating, the fabulous and the fantastic. Their concept of nature as something utterly opposed to man, as an object of adoration and a means of escape from human restrictions underlies the Germans' incorrigible romanticism. This dual aspect of the German character, reflected in Goethe's portrayals of Faust and of Faust's assistant, Wagner, has its origins in the medieval German city. We shall explore this phenomenon at greater length in chapter fifteen, but for the moment, we shall focus on the second factor that helped prepare the way for the Reformation. This factor is the emergence of industrialism and capitalism in the craft-guild cities.

Influenced by materialistic ideology, some scholars, non-Marxists among them, have tried to prove that economic factors have been the major determinants in human activity since the very beginnings of civilization. They have gone back as far as Rome, Greece, and even Babylon in their efforts to find the origins of capitalism. But it cannot be emphasized enough that we have to

108

be extremely careful in applying modern terms to past epochs and civilizations. If we consider various human activities as isolated phenomena, we can, of course, trace them back to earliest human history. But we have to take into account the role these activities play in a civilization as a whole. When we look at history from this point of view, we find that human life has not always been primarily determined by economics and that the production of goods and the profit motive were not the decisive factors in societies prior to the end of the Middle Ages.

The one great antagonist of economy and technology is religion. Religion binds man to rituals, irrational apprehensions, and sacred concepts that prevent him from an unrestrained pursuit of material goals. In all periods when religion still exerted an effective influence on man, economic forces could not exclusively nor even decisively determine human life. The growing influence of economic motives upon human life was a symptom of secularization. This dwindling of religious power over man was the very trend we noted in the German craft-guild cities.

Curiously enough, it was the Catholic Church that supplied the crucial impulses toward economic activity in the Middle Ages. We saw how the Church promoted and encouraged trade in church settlements. It even went so far as to settle and patronize Jews in the new cities. We have already mentioned the ambivalent attitude of the Church toward trade, which, according to doctrine, was the most reprehensible of all human occupations. But because trade was indispensable to civilization and because it strengthened the position of the bishops as lords of the cities, the Church could not avoid fostering it. At first, the Church resorted to the happy expedient of diverting the ill-repute of commerce to the Jews. Later, however, when the Christian population began to relish the easy profits of commerce, the Jews were crowded out of the trade in goods and forced to bear the curse of the credit business, which was, from the Christian point of view, even more objectionable than trade itself. Finally, when the Christians took over credit transactions as well, the Jews were left with petty money-lending and its despicable usury.

The Christian rejection of the banking and credit business originated, ironically, in the old Jewish law against the charging of interest. This prohibition is frequently expressed in the Old Testament (Lev. 25:36-37, Deut. 23:20) and in the writings of the

109

rabbis. It also recurs throughout the early history of Christianity, first in the words of Jesus (Luke 6:35); then in the writings of St. Jerome, one of the Church fathers; and again as late as the Lateran Council of 1179. However, economic developments and the financial exigencies of the princes made money-lending increasingly necessary. Again it was the Church, indeed, the papacy itself, that encouraged the credit business among the Christian population when it urged its collectors of taxes and indulgences to extend loans and take interest.

The moral resistance to the credit system was very hard to overcome in the medieval mind, and it was only the pressure of circumstances that made banking and money-lending acceptable. The Jews were forced into it when they were excluded from all trade in goods. Among Christians, the political exiles from the Lombard cities were the first to enter the field of finance. As a result, the pawn and loan business was called "lombarding," the banker a "lombard," and the banking quarter in London "Lombard Street."

It was not by mere chance that European banking on a large scale first developed in the inland cities of Italy and Germany. The ports of Venice, Genoa, and Pisa (which in the Middle Ages lay close to the sea) rose to power and wealth through extensive maritime trade. As a result of the Crusades and the temporary conquest of Constantinople by the Crusaders and the Venetian fleet in 1204, the Italian cities, Venice in particular, inherited the Byzantine trade. These maritime cities provided the continent of Europe with imported goods. The inland cities, which had no access to the sea, could not compete in this kind of trade. They were compelled to look for new and more promising kinds of business, and these proved to be manufacturing and banking. Money-lending established the wealth and power of Bologna, Siena, and Florence. All the great ruling families of Florence—the Medici, the Albizzi, the Peruzzi, the Pitti, and the Strozzi—made their fortune as bankers. (The Medici began as wool-combers and later became apothecaries and physicians, hence the name Medici and the pills in their coat of arms.) In the fourteenth and fifteenth centuries, Florence was the center of the European money-lending business. The financial development of the German cities followed a similar pattern. Here too, the maritime

110

cities concentrated exclusively on trade in goods, while the inland cities engaged in industry and credit transactions.

In Venice, the most aristocratic of the Italian city-republics, an aversion to banking and a still stronger one to manufacturing persisted. The Venetian noblemen, all of whom were merchants, did not deign to engage in manufacturing, even as entrepreneurs. They regarded the handicrafts as *artes sordidae*, lowly callings, in contrast to the *bonae artes*, honorable callings. In Florence, on the other hand, the so-called craft guilds, which were in fact associations of manufacturing entrepreneurs, became very powerful in the community and played an important part in the frequent changes of rulership in the city. The guild of the bankers was one of the most prominent among these associations.

Among historians of economics, the opinion prevails that modern capitalism has its roots in Renaissance Italy. It is true that modern business terminology and institutions were created there, and modern banking techniques derive chiefly from the shrewd tricks of Italian money-lenders attempting to disguise the infamous practice of taking interest. Bookkeeping and accounting were introduced by the administrations of the Italian cities, and they were first systematized by the Italian mathematician, Luca Pacioli.

However, if we look at Renaissance life as a whole, we still find a fundamental difference between the mentality prevalent in the Italian cities and the mentality of modern businessmen. Like most businessmen, the Italian merchants and bankers were shrewd and efficient, but their main ambitions were political rather than economic. They all wanted to assume the rule of their city-republics, and they all spent money lavishly not only to gain political power but also to live in a style commensurate with their aspirations. Money-making and economic production were not goals in themselves but means for attaining political power and enjoying life. Today, we do not think of the Medici or of other illustrious Italian families as businessmen but as brilliant princes and patrons of the arts. Thus, it is not to the Italian city-republics but to the German inland cities that we must turn if we are to locate the origins of the capitalistic mentality.

# 12.

## THE BEGINNINGS OF CAPITALISM

AT THE END of the last chapter, I tried to suggest some reasons why the term capitalism can be properly applied only to commercial development in Germany, even though by the end of the Middle Ages money-lending and banking were beginning to play an increasingly important role everywhere in Europe. Rulers in Italy, France, and England, competing with each other for power and prestige, were in constant need of money to maintain their lavish courts and their armies of mercenaries. Since mercenaries and the new weapons they employed were extremely expensive, the French and English kings required just as large sums as the German emperors and princes. But nowhere were financial pressures as telling as they were in Germany; nowhere else did independent financiers have government so completely at their mercy.

In other countries, financial power was counterbalanced by political power. In Italy, the businessmen themselves were the rulers; and in France and England, firmly entrenched kings knew how to exploit and cheat the money-lenders. After the conclusion of the Hundred Years War, the authority of the traditional dynasty in France emerged stronger than ever in the reign of Louis XI. The French kings were able to impose taxes and forced loans at will. In addition, they sold offices and robbed the Jews, whose wealth they had originally promoted by extending them privileges. Philip IV (Philippe le Bel) increased the royal treasure vastly in 1308 when he confiscated the property of the Knights Templars. They had become the richest, most powerful bankers of that period; and in order to have a pretext for taking their money, Philip accused them of numerous heresies and crimes. In times of emergency, the French kings usually relied on foreign business-

112

men, at first Florentines, then Germans. The kings mortgaged their revenues to these financiers but rarely kept the terms of the agreements. If they borrowed from their own countrymen, they usually victimized their closest associates and most faithful ministers, exploiting them only to abandon them to ruin later. Charles VII's treatment of Jacques Coeur is a typical example. But despite the fact that the French kings continued to conduct futile wars and to indulge in boundless extravagance, they were still able to extract money from foreign businessmen, particularly from Germans, even after the financial collapse of 1557.

In England, Parliament was becoming more and more influential, and the estates were gaining independence enough to remind their monarch that, as far as taxes were concerned, their good will had its limits. But the kings found ways to circumvent Parliament and obtain money by means other than taxation. From the thirteenth century on, the English kings took forced loans from Florentine businessmen who consequently suffered major losses through their dealings with these unscrupulous kings. The English kings also derived vast sums from imposing surcharges on duties. Any trader who refused to pay these charges was refused a license to do business. Edward IV (1461-1470) raised extra revenues, again without authorization from Parliament, by means of confiscations, by his personal trade in goods, and by means of outright gifts (so-called "benevolences"), some of which he took by force, some in exchange for privileges. Through similar yet even more devious practices, Henry VII (1485-1509) amassed such a great fortune that his son, Henry VIII, after his confiscations of the monasteries, was in a strong enough financial position to be able to carry on a successful credit business.

However reprehensible the methods were that both the French and English kings used to obtain money, the fact remains that the money so obtained was turned to the purposes of the crown and therefore contributed to the further consolidation of these countries. Germany at the end of the fifteenth century presents a very different picture. The territorial rulers had the same ambitions as the French and English kings but lacked the resources and the latitude of power to raise revenues by the arbitrary methods of the western monarchs. The emperor had long since been stripped of imperial property, and he was completely dependent on the princes for financial support. When an imperial tax was once levied, the so-called "common penny" (*gemeiner Pfennig*), the lack of a reliable bureaucracy and of popular support made it impossible to collect. Chronically plagued by poverty, the emperors were always in debt to one element of the population or another. Frederick III became a fugitive in his own empire because of his effort to levy a special tax against the rich merchants. He was forced to travel through his own lands in an ox cart and to seek asylum in friendly monasteries and cities. Even in the reigns of seemingly powerful emperors, financial difficulties constantly endangered the dignity of the imperial crown. On one occasion, Maximilian I was unable to leave the city of Augsburg, because the butchers and bakers to whom he owed money had locked up his horses. After hours of negotiations, he was forced to put up objects of gold and silver for security. The king of England promised Maximilian subsidies for the conduct of his Italian campaign, but when these subsidies did not arrive in time, it was only with the aid of the English ambassador that Maximilian could convince his own subject, Jacob Fugger, to guarantee the money required. Charles V, "on whose dominions the sun never set," found himself in similarly embarrassing situations. In 1552, in flight from Prince Maurice of Saxony, Charles had to appeal to Anton Fugger for funds he could not obtain from any other source. But nothing illustrates the demeaning circumstances of the imperial crown better than Charles's own election in 1519. As the German historian Leopold von Ranke commented, one can read of this incident in German history "only with shame and disgust." This election amounted to an outright auction of the imperial title. The competition between King Charles of Spain (later Charles V) and King Francis of France hinged entirely on the amounts they could offer as bribes to the electoral princes. These princes raised their demands from day to day as the time of the election grew nearer, and they insisted on a guarantee of payment from Germany's most reliable bankers, the Fuggers. Thus, the election depended ultimately on these German moneylenders who were guided purely by their own financial interests rather than by national concerns. Jacob Fugger did not exaggerate when he later remarked to Charles V: "Without me, Your Imperial Majesty would never have obtained the Roman crown."

Secular politics was not the only area in which the Fuggers wielded extraordinary influence. This banking family also financed

114

the purchase of ecclesiastical offices for the German clerics, whose greed for power and money was practically unlimited. As banker for the clergy, and even for the pope himself, Jacob Fugger could rightly boast that it was he who filled the German bishoprics.

All this indicates the degree of power the money trade had acquired in Germany. In no other country at this time could a banker control major political events. Only in Germany did the money trade, indeed, trade in general, win unlimited freedom to operate according to its own rationale. Trade and finance did not remain just contributing factors in the course of political events but became autonomous forces to which all else was subordinated. This ascendency of financial interests was an early and crucial step in the development of the modern capitalistic mentality.

Another premise for the development of a purely economic mentality was the unique situation prevailing in the German craft-guild cities. Here the two great antagonistic yet intimately connected movements of the modern social and economic world took shape: capitalism and socialism, individualism and collectivism. We have already mentioned that the craft guilds represent the first true collectives in human history and that they served as the prototype for modern labor unions. But the working conditions and social position of the craftsmen were still very different from those of the modern worker. Although guild regulations enforced uniformity, they still left the medieval craftsman a large degree of independence in the conduct of his own work. In the craft guilds, collectivistic and individualistic tendencies balanced each other, but in the course of the fifteenth century the antinomy between these two tendencies began to make itself felt and foreshadowed the peculiar ambivalence that characterizes the mentality of the middle class, the inner conflict between collective morality and individual freedom, between collective responsibility and individual initiative.

In the cities dominated by the craft guilds, the merchants were forced to adopt the ways of the craftsmen, but the trading class did not die out. On the contrary, it remained strong enough to exert its influence on the craft guilds. An exchange between the two groups took place, a blending of the trade and craft mentalities. New methods of manufacture and marketing were introduced, and the inland cities entered a phase of unprecedented prosperity.

**115**

This development had two major causes. One was the increased trade of the Italian city-republics. This trade drew the German inland cities, especially Augsburg and Nürnberg, into its orbit and enriched the merchants of these cities. The other was the decline of the craft guilds. Influential master craftsmen succeeded in securing special privileges for themselves. They were able to purchase larger shares of raw materials, expand their workshops, and increase the number of their journeymen beyond the fixed limits. In addition to practicing their craft, they began to carry on independent trade. In this way, they managed to gain advantages over other masters in the same craft.

A new class formed between the traders and craftsmen. These "craft merchants" made poorer masters dependent on their distribution systems and credit arrangements. A merchant would withdraw from his mercantile guild, join a *Zunft*, and gradually transform his role as a mere supplier of raw materials into that of both supplier and distributor for a given craft. Or, conversely, a master would leave his craft guild, join a mercantile guild, and move from the production of goods to large-scale production involving other masters. Some of these new middlemen even belonged to both craft and merchant guilds, a practice that had been forbidden when the craft guilds were at the height of their power. But regardless of whether these craft merchants or merchant craftsmen came to their new position from trade or from the crafts, they all became *mercatores* who controlled the supply of raw materials, employed increasingly large numbers of masters as their *laboratores*, and reserved the right of distribution and sale for themselves. In appropriating all these functions, they became prototypes of the modern industrial entrepreneur.

The craft guilds, of course, resisted these developments. They were prepared to accept a vertical division of labor, a division of guilds according to the raw materials used or the finished goods produced; but they opposed the creation of new guilds that would divide the work process, prevent masters from turning out the finished product themselves, and so cut them off from immediate access to the market. The craftsmen would not object to separate guilds for, let us say, shoemakers and bootmakers; but they would oppose a division into sole-makers, heel-makers, buckle-makers, and so on. The unsuccessful resistance of the craft guilds to the horizontal division of labor was an early skirmish in the workingman's long and futile struggle to defend the integrity of his work and his life against the growing tyranny of things. The next and perhaps most dramatic phase in this struggle was the desperate revolt of the workers against the machine at the end of the eighteenth century.

In Nürnberg, and especially in Augsburg, some of the new entrepreneurs accumulated such large fortunes that they could engage in banking and credit operations, branches of economic activity that had not been carried on in Germany to any appreciable extent during the Middle Ages. But from the fifteenth century on, the German credit business grew rapidly and extended throughout Europe. Augsburg became a banking center that exceeded even the Italian cities in importance. As we noted before, Florence had produced both international bankers and craft merchants who carried on trade with the craft products of dependent masters. What is unique to Germany—apart from the great influence that the credit business gained in the empire—is how German bankers like Jacob Fugger utilized their opportunities and became the first to develop large-scale industry. We are only too aware today of the impact these early industrialists would have. They created the first industrial proletariat with all its characteristic social ills: insecurity, lack of proper housing, migrations, the truck system, child labor, and so on. Journeymen who could no longer become masters initiated the first organized labor movements, and later industrial workers would resort to revolts and strikes in an effort to improve their conditions. But the most disastrous effect industrialization would have was the transformation and dehumanization of man by the capitalistic mentality.

# 15.

## THE GERMAN CITY AND THE
## GERMAN CHARACTER

THE SECOND ASPECT of life in the German inland cities that was to leave a permanent mark on the German mentality was their social and psychological atmosphere, that curious blend of rigorous public morality, narrowness, and pedantry on the one hand and a taste for the infinite and elemental on the other.

The most important social innovation of the inland cities was the creation of a public spirit. This spirit failed to develop in the rest of medieval Germany because nowhere else in the empire did large masses of people live together closely and permanently. Public life is a by-product of urban life. In the Latin countries, urban life formed around a court. That was not the case in Germany, and public life was consequently very different in the German cities. This difference becomes apparent if we compare the plan of an Italian city with that of a typical German one. In the center of Florence, for instance, we find the *Piazza della Signoria*. *Signoria* means the house of the ruling lords. The Italian piazza is a spacious square (or sometimes a circle, as in Siena) with a floor of smooth, polished stones. It is framed by *palazzi* and imposing houses. Each building stands separately and has a symmetry of its own. The Italian piazza, like the Greek *agora* and the Roman *forum*, was a place for public assemblies, a place that invited *parlamenti* and *trionfi*, public feasts, pageants, and parades. Public life was ever present here. Trade was relegated to a subordinate role in this main square, or it took place in a different location altogether.

By contrast, the *Markt* is the center of the German city. The German *Markt* usually has an asymmetrical, irregular shape, as

118

arbitrary and casual as the contours of a territory. Its rough cobblestone pavement is suitable only for carts and trucks. Where the focal point of the piazza is the open space at its center, the *Markt* has no single point of focus. Attention is not naturally drawn to its center but to the arcades, shops, and stands surrounding it. If we compare a medieval German street with an Italian street of the same period, we will notice a similar phenomenon. The German street displays great variety. One house stands high; the next is low and squat. Stone buildings alternate with wooden ones. One has a steep gable astride its facade; another shows its roof broadside, its lines broken by attic dormers. One house or floor protrudes; another recedes. Facades are covered with little towers, bay windows, moldings, and woodcarvings. Where each house in an Italian city is a symmetrical unit in itself, each house here is unbalanced and incomplete. Each one needs its neighbor, each depends on the other for support. Because each building is fragmentary and unable to stand alone, the entire street—the *Zeile* or "row," as it is often called—is the architectural unit, not the individual house. The overall impression of a medieval German town is one of variety, complexity, and interdependence. The narrow, winding streets with their interlocking buildings suggest the closely knit structure of the society that trafficked in them.

In the Italian cities, public life took the form of a public spectacle. Everyone could observe the gatherings and festivals that took place in the piazza and so participate in the public life of the city. But because this kind of forum and arena was lacking in the German cities, the citizens did not enter into an open, shared public life. On the contrary, public life assumed the form of a public morality that penetrated into the homes of the citizens and dominated their private lives.

What were the values this public morality of the craft-guild cities imposed? Logically enough, work was held in the highest esteem in a society of working men. Anyone who has lived in Germany will know how important work is to the Germans, but this was not always so for all Germans. The medieval craftsmen were the first group in history to value work as the highest good. The nobility in medieval Germany—like the nobility in all countries at all times before and after—held just the opposite view: idleness, not work, was to be treasured. We must also remember

119

that in early Christianity work was not something to be sought but something to be endured. Work was the punishment man had to undergo as the result of the fall: "In the sweat of thy face shalt thou eat bread." In the early church, people who performed hard work were considered more susceptible to Christianity than the idle, but it was not their work as such that made them so. They were deemed more open to the message of the gospel simply because their poverty and misery exposed them less to the temptations and vices of the world. And in the ascetic movement of the early monastics, the emphasis was not on work but on leisure, because only leisure made the contemplative life possible.

The German mystics exalted the humble work of the craftsmen, and we find Luther doing the same thing. For him, a man's occupation or profession (*Beruf*) was not merely a "job" but had the significance of a sacred mission (*Berufung*) as well. This view goes back to the essentially Catholic idea that a man should accept his station in life as his God-given role. He should not try to change his position but should try to do his best in it. Because the body of Christian believers was regarded as the body of Christ (*corpus mysticum Christi*), it was essential that every individual fulfill his task in order to maintain the health of the entire organism. Even the heretic Wycliffe subscribed to this view: "The Church is divided in these three parts: preachers, defenders and ... laborers. ... As she is our mother, so she is a body, and the health of the body consists in this: that one part of her answer to another, after the same measure that Jesus Christ has ordained it. ... Kindly man's hand helps his head, and his eye helps his foot, and his foot his body ... and thus should it be in the Church. ..."

Luther attributed special significance to the role of the crafts in Christian society, emphasizing the need for the craftsman to accept the conditions and satisfactions of his humble station. "Shoes and boots are the works of your calling. Your life acquires meaning through them alone, and you must not attempt to go beyond this goal that has been set for you." ("Die Stiefel oder Schuhe sind die Werke des Berufs, bei den man bleiben und gestehen muss, nicht weiterfahren noch herausbrechen über das gesetzte Ziel.") In the centuries after the Reformation, this attitude persisted as a major element in the middle-class mentality. Gradually, it lost its religious significance until all that remained

was the modern German's devotion to work and his docile acceptance of his position in society.

The predominance of the work ethic in the German middle
class would have a telling and detrimental influence on the development of German educational institutions. Because the model for
education was established in the craft-guild cities, the emphasis
lay on the acquiring of technical skills needed to progress from
apprentice to journeyman and ultimately to master. Education
was not a process of enlivening and enlightening the whole man
but one of developing the skills required for performing a single,
highly specialized task. Only in the latter half of the eighteenth
century would German writers like Goethe, Schiller, and Hölderlin oppose this narrow educational concept with that of *Bildung*,
the humanistic ideal of promoting the growth of the entire personality.

Since work was the dominant concern of the craft-guild cities,
it is not surprising that the social patterns and attitudes pertain-
ing to work would spread into other areas of human activity.
Clear evidence of this can be found in the conduct of marriage
and family life in the cities. Here, for the first time in history,
women enter into a partnership with their husbands and begin
to achieve equality in society. Prior to this time, both in antiquity
and in the Christian world, the role of women had always been
subordinate. But in the craft guild cities, a *Meisterin*, the wife
of a master, shared her husband's work and status. She often
worked in her husband's shop as his equal, not as his subordinate.
Perhaps the most striking proof of her equality was the fact that
a widowed *Meisterin* was entitled to carry on her husband's
business.

The control the guild exerted over the working life of a couple
also extended to their private life. Guild regulations forbid extra-
marital sexual relations and demanded proof of legitimate birth
before anyone could be admitted to membership. If a craftsman
knowingly took a wife of illegitimate birth, he was automatically
expelled from his guild. Neither in the upper nor lower class was
illegitimacy ever a serious stigma. The illegitimate children of
kings, popes, and lords never suffered because of their birth. In
France, Royal Bastard was even an official title. But among medieval craftsmen, no such violations of the sanctity of marriage were
permitted. The result was greater freedom and status for women

but at the same time an invasion of public standards and morality into the private lives of citizens.

As we have seen, the physical shape of the craft-guild cities reflected not only the comforting warmth and coherence of the society that inhabited them but also its restricting and confining nature. The world outside the city walls was in direct contrast to the one within. In medieval Germany, the natural world was still relatively untamed, and anyone outside the protective walls of the city was exposed to the dangers and discomforts of the northern wilderness: harsh climate, impenetrable forests and marshes, wild animals. The perils of life outside the city were real enough, but they assumed exaggerated proportions in the medieval mind because belief in the demonic forces of nature still survived from early tribal times. For medieval man, the elements were inhabited by evil powers in league with the devil himself. But as nature posed a physical and moral threat to man, it also presented a great temptation. It offered escape from the confinement of regulated, ordered life in the city. For those who were bold enough to risk their lives and their souls, it offered the possibility of delving into the deepest secrets of creation.

It was at this point in the Middle Ages that what we might call romantic attitudes formed in the German mind. The taste for the elemental and the infinite ran counter to the ethic of the craft-guild cities, but was also a product of that ethic. The sharp opposition of city and country, civilization and wilderness led to a close, if hidden, relationship between the two. The very stringency of the moral code the city imposed acted as an incentive to violate that code. Because traffic with the chaotic and demonic elements in nature and in one's own being was so strictly forbidden, the desire for such contact grew all the more. Similarly, the more menacing the forces of nature were felt to be, the more appealing and adventuresome the prospect of encountering them seemed. The rigorous order the cities created indirectly encouraged a taste for the chaos they hoped to lock outside their gates.

The image of the knight has persisted as an embodiment of the adventurer, a man willing to travel to distant lands and do battle with devils and demons alike. Although the knights were an obsolete class by the late Middle Ages, this image of them still persisted in the popular mind. We should note, however, that the image of the adventurer underwent an important change in this

122

same period. The knight, the adventurer in the physical realm, gradually gave way to the figure of the intellectual adventurer. Not the knight but another medieval figure has become the heroic prototype for modern man. That figure is Dr. Faustus, a scholar so committed to his quest for knowledge that he joins forces with the devil in the hope of penetrating nature's deepest mysteries. The emphasis changes from the physical to the intellectual realm. The prototype of the adventurer is no longer the warrior who explores unknown lands and conquers by virtue of his physical prowess and courage. Instead, it is the sorcerer and scientist who explores the unknown of nature's secrets by virtue of his intellect and at the risk of his soul. But despite this change in emphasis, both figures reflect an impulse that first made itself felt in the inland cities of medieval Germany, the impulse to break free from ordered life within the city walls and to lose oneself in the infinite chaos beyond them.

# Part Two

---

## THE REFORMATION

# 16.

## THE DECLINE OF THE CATHOLIC CHURCH

Now that we have a fairly adequate idea of the social, intellectual, and cultural state of Germany at the end of the Middle Ages, we may proceed to a study of the Reformation. It is impossible to consider the German Reformation without also considering the Italian Renaissance at the same time. Historians have come to see these phenomena as the two great sea changes that brought medieval Europe into the modern era, and the innumerable university courses that bear the title "Renaissance and Reformation" suggest how closely related these events are in traditional historiography. In the period between the world wars, it became fashionable among historians and theorists of history to declare the traditional division of history into antiquity, the Middle Ages, and the modern period as obsolete. Spengler originated this notion, and it was later advocated by his ideological successors and disciples, Toynbee and Sorokin among them. Also, more detailed historical studies have helped to controvert this traditional division. We are perhaps more aware of the fact today that changes do not take place suddenly but by a slow, evolutionary process.

The beginnings of any given development can, of course, be traced as far back as we care to trace them. If we want to be accurate, we cannot place the beginnings of the Italian Renaissance in the fourteenth century, as nineteenth-century historians did. Initial signs of it occur much earlier, and in modern historical writing, we find several renaissances. I have already mentioned two: the Carolingian and the Ottonian.

The Carolingian Renaissance occurred in the eighth and ninth centuries, the Ottonian in the tenth. Then, too, we have a very real renaissance in the twelfth century, and the Italian Renaissance itself actually began in the thirteenth century. We seem to have renaissances all through the Middle Ages. The same is true of religious reforms. The careless use of terms and of new historical information can destroy the structure and coherence of human history. Our knowledge does not expand gradually but erratically, in rapid advances that tend to exaggerate the importance of new data and concepts. Instead of trying to integrate the new findings with the old ones, the changing fashions of scholarship simply cast aside or ignore those parts in the general picture which would in any way temper or tone down the new findings or reduce them to their proper proportions within the whole. In this way the whole concept of human evolution and of human history is disrupted.

The discovery of early renaissance or reform movements does not in any way invalidate the significance of what we have traditionally called Renaissance and Reformation. The early movements were limited in scope. They faded away without altering the spiritual landscape of Europe in any decisive way. The Renaissance and Reformation ushered in sweeping and permanent changes, bringing Europe out of the Middle Ages and into the modern period. For Germany, the Reformation meant the beginning of a national consciousness and of a specifically German character. For central Europe, it meant that the dominance of the Catholic Church had come to an end. The power of the Church had been declining for some time, but the Reformation put an end to her position as the sole spiritual authority in Europe. The Catholic Church was no longer catholic. It became a party among other parties, a creed among other creeds. Secular activities were now emancipated from the control of the Church; politics, the sciences, and the arts all began to develop autonomously. It was no accident that the Renaissance and Reformation occurred in the same period. They had common sources and led to a common goal: the secularization of Europe.

Four main factors brought about the Reformation: first, the decline, especially the moral decline, of the Church and the papacy; second, the anarchical condition of the empire; third, the increasing number of heresies and popular mystical movements toward the end of the Middle Ages; and fourth, the personal disposition and destiny of Martin Luther.

As we have seen, the fates of the empire and the papacy were inextricably linked to each other. In their efforts to usurp the power of the other, they finally destroyed themselves. In Germany, the struggle of the emperors with the popes brought about the dissolution of the feudal empire into a multitude of territorial powers. In Italy, the same struggle encouraged the growth of the Italian city-republics and the secularized mentality of Renaissance Humanism.

Now to understand the conflicts that arose between the Church and the secular powers, one has to realize that the Church of the early Middle Ages was an entity in itself. It was free from the interference of secular rulers and enjoyed many liberties and immunities. It owned considerable property throughout Europe, and its income and expenditures were very large. Its income— the tithes of the parish priests, the feudal dues of the bishops, the rents of the monasteries, the annates, and the judicial fees of the popes—frequently had to be extorted from unwilling debtors. The administration of Church funds required so much attention from the clergy that it deeply troubled the conscience of many of the best men in the Church. As Edward Cheyney points out in his *Dawn of a New Era, 1250-1453*, ecclesiastical correspondence and official records of the thirteenth, fourteenth, and fifteenth centuries show that churchmen devoted more time and attention to matters of finance and organization than to anything else. All the worldly possessions the Church had accumulated made it vulnerable to internal corruption and to the moral censure of pious Christians.

The decay of the Church's power began with the struggle over investiture in the eleventh century. The conflict between Church and empire reached its high point during the reign of Frederick II (1215-1250), who took it upon himself to reassert the divine authority the imperial crown had possessed under Caesar. But what was intended as a revival of the crown's spiritual authority instead gave rise to the secular mentality of the Renaissance. Frederick's governors in the Italian cities, his vicar-generals and podestas, already displayed the same ruthless qualities that would later characterize the Renaissance princes.

In 1245, Frederick II was formally deposed by Pope Innocent IV, and it is significant that this deposition was proclaimed in France during the Council of Lyons. In order to get rid of the Hohenstaufen family, the pope cast himself upon the mercy of

France, the mightiest of the rising territorial powers. He delivered Sicily to Charles of Anjou, the brother of the French king Louis IX (Saint Louis). Charles, however, proved to be a greater danger to the papacy than the Hohenstaufens. Ironically, the victory of the popes over the emperors spelt disaster for the papacy itself; for in seeking aid from the rising national states, Rome acknowledged that a universal empire no longer existed. Her admission that there was no longer any political unity in Europe served to undermine her own claim to universal spiritual authority.

From this point on, the western kings became the pope's most dangerous rivals. Edward I of England and Philip the Fair of France made nearly simultaneous attacks on the immunities of the Church and attempted to tax its property. Pope Boniface VIII issued one bull after another, declaring it unlawful, under pain of excommunication, for lay governments to tax Church property and for tithing clergymen to pay such impositions. At the jubilee of 1300 and before 200,000 pilgrims, he reaffirmed his supremacy in Christendom; but the power of the western countries was already too firmly established. The pope's own clergy deserted him. As a body, the English clergy could not admit to violating the pope's commands; but as individuals, they willingly paid taxes to the king. In an assembly convoked by order of the king, the French clergy acknowledged that in times of national emergency —in this case, war against England—they were obliged to contribute to the national treasury. The pope threatened to excommunicate Philip and to lay all France under an interdict. Philip responded with open violence. Not only did he set out to depose Boniface by declaring his election to the papacy illegal and by appealing to a general council of the Church to provide for the election of a new pope, but he also seized the pope and his cardinals at the little town of Anagni in the Appenines and made the eighty-six year old man his prisoner.

A similar conflict with Boniface's successor resulted in the famous "Babylonian captivity" of the papacy in Avignon for a period of seventy years (1305-1378). During this period, the French monarchs secured the election of Frenchmen as popes and thus made the papacy an instrument of French national policy. A marked moral decline of the papacy accompanied this loss of power and autonomy. Petrarch, who spent much of his lifetime in Avignon during this period, left a description of the popes' life there. "Here reign the successors of the poor fisherman in Galilee. They have strangely forgotten their origin. [Avignon is] Babylon, the home of all vices and all misery. . . . I know by experience that no piety exists here, no charity, no faith, no reverence, no fear of God, nothing holy, nothing just, nothing sacred. . . ."

The Babylonian captivity was followed by the Great Schism of 1378-1417. At the papal election of 1378, a contingent of thirteen French cardinals declared the election of Urban VI null and void. They claimed the election had not been free but had been conducted in fear of the Roman population's violent demands for an Italian, and preferably a Roman, pope. The French cardinals consequently elected Robert of Geneva to the papacy as Clement VII. For the next thirty-nine years, there were two popes, neither of whom enjoyed universal recognition. Indeed, from 1409 on there were three claimants to the papacy.

The Council of Constance was convoked in 1414 with the express purpose of putting an end to the Great Schism. The Council finally did elect a pope, Martin V, and bring about at least a formal reunification of the Church. But it was too late to rescue the universal authority the Church had once been able to claim. The pressures for reform were too great, and the Church's prestige had suffered irreparable damage fom the Babylonian captivity and the Great Schism. From this point on, the popes could claim universality in name only. In reality, the papacy had been reduced to an Italian principate, and the behavior of the popes soon became indistinguishable from that of other Renaissance princes. The life the Renaissance popes led at their opulent courts in Rome is too well known to require further elaboration here. There was no crime, no abuse, no libertinage that was unknown to the brilliant but ruthless popes of this epoch. Innocent VIII earned the sobriquet "Father of Rome" because he sired so many children, and this same pope founded a "bank of indulgence" where absolution from murder and manslaughter was sold at high prices.

The courts of all these popes, both in Avignon and later in Rome again, were exceedingly expensive, and the popes availed themselves of every possible opportunity to increase their income. The famous letters of indulgence, originally designed to finance the Crusades by taxing persons who did not participate in them,

131

were just one of the many means the popes employed to raise money. Another was the sale of "reservations" and "provisions." These were agreements by which the buyer was guaranteed election or appointment to a Church office immediately after the death of the incumbent. Resentment of this practice ran particularly high in England because the most valuable English benefices fell into the hands of courtiers who had obtained them in Rome or Avignon by means of such "provisions."

These papal encroachments on local authority alienated the national churches, prompting them to break with Rome and to reorganize on a purely national basis. The expulsion of the British from France at the end of the Hundred Years War laid the foundation for the policy of "Gallicanism," the demand for an autonomous French church; and in England, the Anglican Church arose from a similar national impulse in the English church.

Moral corruption within the Church resulted from excessive concern with material power. The decay of spiritual authority led to a loss of material power, and this loss of material power contributed in turn to even greater spiritual degeneration. The collapse of the universal Church, then, was the result of a long process in which failures of moral, spiritual, and material strength interacted to destroy the entire structure. The Catholic Church did, of course, rally again during the Counter-Reformation; but it was never again to regain the universal position it had held before the Babylonian captivity and the Great Schism.

# 17.

## HERESY AND MYSTICISM

SINCE WE HAVE already dealt in Part I with the anarchical condition of the empire in the late Middle Ages, we need not devote further attention to it here. But it is perhaps worth noting again how sharp the contrast was between the empire and the western nations at this point in history. France and England had already achieved a fairly high degree of national coherence and independence. The French and English kings were strong enough to ward off any papal encroachments on their authority and to prevent the Church from taxing their populations. In Germany, the political structures of Church and empire were still hopelessly entangled with each other. A large number of the territorial princes and clerical electors shared in the proceeds of papal taxation and of the indulgence trade. As a result, the German territorial rulers were all too willing to align themselves with the popes. The abuses that arose from this collusion prompted Luther to launch his first attacks on the Church.

But Luther's work of reformation was far more than a response to corrupt financial practices in the Church. It was also the final phase of a religious and spiritual revolution that had begun to take shape in the heresies and popular mystical movements of the Middle Ages. These heretical movements originated primarily in two segments of the population: the learned clerics who dwelt earnestly upon their faith, and the plain people who rejected the mediation of the Church and felt a need for direct communication with God. These emotional and intellectual currents were all connected with each other, and all of them drew on pre-Christian, pagan sources. We can distinguish three basic tendencies among them.

133

The first is a rationalistic one best exemplified by Scholastic philosophy. Plato and Aristotle were the major ancestors of Scholasticism, and Aristotle's *Logic* exerted a particularly strong influence over the clerical schoolmen. Christian doctrine had to deal with the same human problems that Greek philosophy had speculated about before it: the creation, death and the afterlife, ethical and epistemological questions. The Church provided answers to these problems in its dogma and in the teachings of the Church fathers. Although the Greek philosophers and the Church may often have arrived at very similar solutions, the Greek approach was very different from the Church's; and this difference of approach accounts for the rise of a rationalistic, heretical movement in the Middle Ages. The Church answered the great questions with dogma, faith, and authority. The clerics who studied the ancient authors saw, however, that the Greek philosophers sought to deal with the same questions by means of speculation, knowledge, and reason. The eventual outcome of this conflict would be the emancipation of reason during the Renaissance and the consequent flourishing of modern science and philosophy.

In our discussion of Charlemagne, we noted that for all the piety that characterized the man there was also a strong rationalistic impulse alive in him and in his time. The life of the mind was important to him, and he sought the company and instruction of learned men. The beginnings of rationalistic revolt against the Church go back as far as Charlemagne. But the first major conflict between dogma and reason did not come to a head until the eleventh century. The dispute centered around the question of transubstantiation. Church dogma asserted that Christ was physically present in the bread and wine of the Holy Communion, that the bread and wine were in fact His body and blood. The rationalistic position was that the bread and wine could only be symbolic representations of Christ's body and blood because their accidental properties—their color, taste, and texture—remained, despite the sacramental consecration that presumably transformed them into the body and blood of Christ. Berengar (ca. 1000-1088), headmaster of the Cathedral School of St. Martin at Tours, stood by the rationalistic position, maintaining that even God was powerless to contradict a logical conclusion. Berengar was anathematized for his courageous stance, becoming one of the first in a long series of reasoning men who would suffer for their defiance of Church authority.

In the eleventh and twelfth centuries, Scholastic debate centered around the conflict between the realists and nominalists. Their disagreement over "universals" was first voiced in a dispute on the problem of the Holy Trinity. Roscelin from Compiègne in France and Anselm from Aosta in Italy were the leaders in this controversy. The nominalists, Roscelin and his school, contended that "universals" and general qualities do not exist in reality but are merely names for abstractions of the human intellect. Only individual beings and individual attributes are real. If the three personalities of the Holy Trinity formed one entity, as the realists and Church doctrine maintained, then not only the Son but God the Father and the Holy Ghost would also have been incarnated and died on the Cross. But since God the Father and the Holy Ghost did not in fact become flesh and suffer crucifixion, they must be separate deities. Consequently, there can be no Holy Trinity. We can see here how the implications of logic gradually undermined the central dogmas of the Church.

One of the leading nominalists of the fourteenth century was the British theologian William of Occam (1280-1349), called the *doctor invincibilis.* He was a Franciscan friar whose major work was done in Paris and in Germany. At the University of Paris, he came into contact with two other revolutionary thinkers of the age, Marsilius of Padua and Jean de Jaudun. All three men shared the ideal of absolute poverty, and they defended this ideal vigorously in the controversy over "evangelical poverty." This dispute between two factions of the Franciscans threatened to split not only the order but the Church itself. It was the teaching of the "Spiritual Franciscans" that since Christ and the apostles had lived entirely without property, they had established poverty as an ideal for the Church to follow. This view was, of course, immediately condemned by the pope, who seized Occam and the general of the Franciscan Order, Michael of Cesena, imprisoning them as heretics at Avignon. Some four years later they escaped to Italy and then went to Germany where they lived in Munich under the protection of the emperor Louis the Bavarian.

From the Franciscan convent in Munich Occam poured out a succession of works on philosophical and political questions. Un-

135

der his influence, Marsilius of Padua wrote his great work *Defensor pacis* (*The Defender of Peace*), a bold assertion of the supremacy of the state over the Church and of the equality of all members of the Church, indeed, of all Christians, before God. In Luther's time considerable attention was given to Occam in the German schools, and the English theologian's thinking had great influence on Luther himself.

A second challenge to the authority of the Church was "intellectual mysticism." This movement goes back to Neoplatonic teachings that entered Christianity through the Apocrypha and came down to the Middle Ages in this form. According to these half-philosophical, half-mystical teachings which had a great influence on the formation of the Christian dogma, God manifests himself through a hierarchy of beings that bridge the gap between God and man. Man becomes one with God by ascending to Him by means of ecstatic and ascetic exercises. Dionysius Areopagita, a Christian Neoplatonist of the fifth century, writes: "We recognize God by ascending from the order of all that is—an order determined by Him and containing, as it were, images . . . of divine prototypes—to that which is supreme over all. We ascend, as far as we are able, by the true way that . . . leads to the origin of everything. The most divine recognition of God is accomplished through ignorance, in that union beyond the reaches of mind where the mind, relinquishing everything that is, surrenders itself and merges with an ecstasy of light. . . ."

The tendency to transform a personal, individualized deity into a pantheistic god inherent in all of creation is clearly evident here, and this intellectual mysticism merged easily with a corresponding movement outside the monasteries, a popular movement of "emotional mysticism" that rejected the mediating role of the clergy and sought direct union with God.

Even a relatively modest survey of all the popular sects and cults that arose from this mystical impulse would extend far beyond the scope of this chapter. All we can hope to do here is mention a few of the more important precursors of the mystical movement I mentioned in our discussion of the craft-guild cities.

In these popular movements, we find the same return to pagan sources that characterized Scholasticism and intellectual mysticism. Here, Mithraism was particularly influential. Mithras was the Persian god of light who warred against the powers of darkness. In the doctrine developed by the Bulgarian sect of the Bogomiles ("Friends of God"), Mithraistic and Christian elements merged. According to Bogomile dogma, the god of light was opposed by the prince of darkness. Lucifer, the son of the prince of darkness, had drawn spiritual beings into the abject life of the material world; but salvation could be achieved through Jesus Christ, an angel of the god of light. Through a pure, ascetic life and through union with the savior, man could gradually ascend to higher levels and eventually win salvation. In this doctrine, union with the savior was direct; there was no place for the mediation of the clergy, the authority of the pope, or the Church's "power of the key."

Bogomile dogma spread into Italy and southern France where it was embraced by the Albigenses, a sect that originated in the French city of Albi and that became so powerful in the twelfth century that the Church launched a crusade against its adherents in 1209 and annihilated them.

Direct, unmediated union with Christ was a central element in the Waldensian movement, too. This movement was founded around 1200 by Peter Waldo, a French merchant from Lyons, who, on reading the Gospels after the death of a close friend, felt inspired to a prophetic calling. He practiced and preached poverty, chastity, penitence, and charity in an effort to emulate the purity of Christ's life. Hoping to bring the people into direct contact with the example of Christ, he translated parts of the Gospels into the vernacular and read them in public assemblies. Luther would do the same thing on a much greater scale with his translation of the entire Bible; but in both cases, for Waldo and for Luther, the motivation was the same: to make Scripture directly available to the common man and so to dispense with the mediation of the clergy.

The great threat that the Church saw in all these movements was the attack on the "power of the key." If any man could achieve mystical union with God entirely by his own efforts, then both Church and priest no longer served any mediating function at all; they both forfeited the power they had once held over the population. Perhaps no other figure in the early heretical movements did more to undermine the Church's authority than Joachim de Floris (ca. 1130-1202). He seems to have come from a noble family in Calabria. During a visit to the Holy Land

137

sometime around 1175, he had visions in which, he claimed, God granted him prophetic powers and enjoined him both to interpret Scripture and to write of things to come. He returned to Italy, was ordained a priest, and took the vows of the Cistercian Order. Appointed abbot of the monastery of Curazzo against his will, he left this office to devote himself to preaching and writing. In his view, the history of the world was divided into three periods: the period of the Law, or of the Father; the period of the Gospel, or of the Son; and the period of the Holy Spirit. He believed that the world of his time was in the second period, a time marred by avarice, lust, and impiety among churchmen and misery among the laity. He prophesied that this period would end in 1260. By then, the Church would be purified. The hierarchy would disappear from it, and a new order of monks would emerge as true spiritual guides for a far happier human race.

In 1255, Joachim's writings appeared as a single work, the *Everlasting Gospel.* The thirteenth and fourteenth centuries were even more receptive to him than his own time had been, and his teachings spread rapidly. Bitterly critical of the Church and prophesying a new era of religious ecstasy in which the Church would have no part, Joachim's teachings eroded the authority of the Church throughout Europe. It is only natural that the Church tried to suppress his works. As early as 1213, his essay on the Trinity was declared heretical and in 1260, a council in Arles condemned the entire body of his writings.

In the fourteenth century, all the mystical currents of the early Middle Ages flowed together in the work of Johannes Eckhart (ca. 1260-1327) and his two followers, Johannes Tauler and Heinrich Seuse. With their desire for immediate union with God, their reliance on the Bible as a source of knowledge, their distaste for the empty ceremonies of the Church, and their emphasis on the simple faith of the medieval craftsmen, these mystics did more to prepare the way for the Reformation than anyone before them. Like their predecessors, they too came into conflict with the authority of the Church. Eckhart was accused of the heresy of pantheism, but he died before the Church could bring action against him. But despite the fact that Eckhart and his predecessors represented a threat to the Church, they still conceived of their teachings as legitimate attempts at reform within the framework of the Church. Luther himself did not set out to split the

138

Church but to reform it. Only in looking back on the gradual process that culminated in the Reformation proper can we see that the Church's authority had crumbled significantly during Eckhart's lifetime and even long before it. Wycliffe and Hus would undermine that authority still further, leaving the Church vulnerable to the blow that would finally shatter it.

# 18.

## WYCLIFFE AND HUS

THE WORK of the English clergyman John Wycliffe (1324-1384) and of the Czech priest Jan Hus (1370-1415) represents a new phase in the developments leading up to the Reformation. Wycliffe and Hus both attempted a fundamental reform of the Church, and they both exerted a greater influence on the religious life of Europe than any of their predecessors. They were not purely speculative men, like the Scholastics and mystics; nor were they simply reformers of ecclesiastical abuses, like many of the ascetic monastics. Active and contemplative at once, they gained almost complete control of the reform movement and of religious life in their respective countries. When we consider the impact these men had, we might well wonder why they did not precipitate the Reformation themselves and why history would have to wait for Luther before the great change that had been in the making for so long could actually be accomplished. Personality was one decisive factor; another was the different political and social framework within which each man had to work. Milton realized how close Wycliffe had come to accomplishing the major work of the Reformation, but he also realized how circumstances in England had militated against Wycliffe's success. He wrote in his *Areopagetica*: "Had it not bin the obstinat perverseness of our prelats against the divine and admirable spirit of Wicklef, to suppresse him as a schismatic and innovator . . . the glory of reforming all our neighbors had bin compleatly ours."

England has always been somewhat remote and isolated from the European continent. Because of this isolation, she had been able to function as the mainstay of Christian studies and piety at the beginning of the Middle Ages and to train the emissaries and

140

missionaries who Christianized central and eastern Europe. Another result of this isolation was that none of the continental heresies reached the British Isles before the fourteenth century. The only English heretic, William of Occam, worked on the continent; his influence came to England indirectly and was not immediately felt there. It is difficult to imagine that long preparation did not precede religious reform in England just as it had on the continent, but since we have scant record of such preparation, we have to assume that John Wycliffe initiated the English reform movement virtually by himself.

Wycliffe led a rather peaceful life despite his revolutionary activities. His life was centered at the University of Oxford where he took a degree in divinity. He began lecturing there about 1360 and seldom left Oxford until 1378, six years before his death. He preached occasionally in London and elsewhere, and in 1374 he became rector of Lutterworth in Leistershire but did not give up teaching at Oxford. He was primarily a scholar, a bold and independent thinker, and a subtle debater. He was described as "the most eminent doctor of theology in his days" and as "the flower of Oxford scholarship." Even those at Oxford who disapproved of his doctrines were proud of him as "a great clerk." Like Occam, he too became embroiled in disputes over the temporal claims of the papacy. At the request of King Edward III, he wrote and spoke in opposition to papal provisions and went as an envoy to a conference with papal representatives at Bruges in 1374. He also wrote, for the use of Parliament, an argument against the feudal payments claimed from England by the pope. Thus, his first major role was that of an official advocate defending English national independence against the claims of Rome.

The development of Wycliffe's heretical ideas is difficult to trace, but we do know that his disregard for the teachings of the Church and his reliance on the Bible as the true source of faith dated from an early period. Because of his constant references to the Scriptures, his students called him "the evangelical doctor." Neither the tradition of the Church nor the authority of the pope, he thought, carried any weight compared with the words of the Bible. His critical view of the Church enhanced this conviction. He wrote and spoke against the clergy's holding property or receiving income. Christ and his apostles had lived as poor men and "it belongeth not to Christ's vicar nor to priests of the holy

Church to have rents here on earth." Wycliffe also condemned the mendicant orders that had settled into comfortable residences and lucrative appointments. "These irreligious that have possessions, they have commonly red and fat cheeks and great bellies." The prelates were "horned fiends to be damned in hell." Wycliffe's opponents countered with equally forceful language, calling him "Mahomet" and the "Devil's instrument" and transforming his name into "Wicked-life." The pope charged him with "vomiting forth from the recesses of his body false and heretical propositions."

From criticism of corruption in the Church, Wycliffe proceeded to develop more fundamental and constructive views. Referring back to Augustine's theory of predestination, he anticipated Calvinistic dogma and defined the role of the Church in thoroughly Calvinistic terms. He advocated an evangelical, national church without temporal authority and subject to the king. This church would consist of all those predestined to salvation, and any good man might act as a priest. Ceremony and symbolism; confession, penance, and absolution; pilgrimages to the shrines of the saints; the use of holy water; the veneration of relics; prayers for the intercession of the saints and of the Blessed Virgin—all this should be abolished for "Jesus Christ and his apostles used them not." Wycliffe denied the pope's power to excommunicate unless Christ Himself had condemned the sinner. He questioned the primacy of Peter, ridiculed the claims of such a wicked man as Urban VI to infallibility, and declared the pope's practice of granting indulgences by dispensing the accumulated merits of the saints a "fond blasphemie." The Church maintained that Jesus Christ and the saints had accumulated such a vast treasure of merits that the Church could use this treasure to expiate the sins of the living and to ransom the dead from purgatory. This was the theoretical basis for the "holy trade" in indulgences.

The pope called Wycliffe's teachings *lolii* or weeds, and under the name of Lollardy, they spread throughout English society, not only among the clergy, the poor priests, and the common people, but also among the nobility. Queen Anne was probably one of Wycliffe's adherents, and his confessed followers included the Duke of Lancaster as well as the Earls of Salisbury and Northumberland. His influence in the House of Commons was so great that proposals were introduced again and again to the effect that the lands and temporal possessions of the Church should be confiscated. In Wycliffe's lifetime, the efforts to silence him were conspicuously slight, tardy, and ineffective. Few heretics fared so well. His academic superiors were indisposed to interfere with his teaching, and despite one papal bull after another urging the archbishop of Canterbury, the bishop of London, the king, and the university to arrest Wycliffe and his supporters, he had to answer personally for his questionable views only twice, both times to reluctant ecclesiastical authorities and without serious consequences for him. At the second inquiry, held in 1378, the archbishop admonished him to stop promulgating doctrines condemned by the pope. Wycliffe accordingly withdrew from public preaching and devoted the remaining six years of his life to writing his major Latin works.

Despite the spread of Lollardy in England, Wycliffe's reform efforts there could not achieve the momentum that Luther's would in Germany. The peasants' revolt of 1381 caused a consolidation of reactionary forces and thus helped the Church stem the tide of heresy. Since religious heresy and social revolt were closely linked with each other, conservative fears of further violence led to the suppression of all deviations from political and religious norms. Archbishop Sudbury, a man of the people, was sympathetic to Wycliffe's ideas; but after his death during the insurrection, the archbishop's office fell into the hands of two conservative successors. From this point on, vigorous action was taken against all dissidents. The Church courts wrote and enforced rules for securing conformity to orthodox doctrine. Wycliffe's books were burned in the marketplace of Oxford, and in 1401, the clergy pressured Parliament to enact the so-called Lollard Statute. This law required that convicted heretics be turned over to secular authorities and be burnt alive "before the people . . . so that punishment may strike fear into the minds of others." Still, it took a full half century to suppress Lollardy, and even then its effects could still be felt in England and abroad. The Church in England could never regain the position it had held before Wycliffe, and its victory over him was won at the high price of increased dependence on the national government, indeed, of complete subjection to royal supremacy.

But more important than Wycliffe's influence at home was his impact on the continent, particularly in Bohemia. Here too re-

143

ligious reform was closely connected with an awakening of strong national feeling. The Czechs, whose territory extended like a great wedge into the center of Europe, had long been subject to the overwhelming influence of the Germans, who had assumed control of state, church, and commerce in Bohemia.

From the middle of the fourteenth century on, a great change began to take place. Charles IV, the Luxemburg king and emperor who ruled in Bohemia from 1333 to 1378, was the son and grandson of Bohemian kings. He encouraged Czech nationality in every possible way and made Prague a great European capital. The Bohemian nobles were urged to follow local customs, and the Czech language, like other vernacular tongues of the period, was adopted for use in official documents. In 1344, the bishopric of Prague was separated from the province of Mainz and became an independent archdiocese. In 1348, a university was established on the model of Paris, Oxford, and Bologna. At first, it was a German university because Germans dominated it. But soon it became a center of the Czech national movement, rivaling the older institutions in size, accomplishments, and attractiveness for foreign students.

This national awakening was accompanied by a movement for ecclesiastical and moral reform. Ecclesiastics of local birth were placed at the head of local churches, and new regulations of a reformatory nature were issued. Popular preachers spread this religious revival throughout the country, just as Wycliffe and his followers had done in England. And just as the English preachers had used Latin or English according to the character of their congregations, so the Bohemian preachers spoke in Latin, in German, or in Czech, as their audiences required. This movement was independent of the Church, and in Prague two rich merchants even built and endowed a chapel for this kind of preaching, stipulating that the speaker always had to be of the secular clergy and had to preach to the people in the Czech language.

The exchange of students among the universities of Europe brought English students to Prague and Czechs to Oxford. Adalbert Ranconis, who had taken a degree in Prague and had probably studied at Oxford as well, encouraged this practice by establishing fellowships for Czech students devoting themselves to the liberal arts or theology at Paris or Oxford. Recipients of these

144

fellowships were no doubt mainly responsible for bringing Wycliffe's writings to Prague.

Wycliffe's ideas found a ready reception in Bohemia. About 1380, the popular preacher Matthias of Janov had written a book entitled *Rules of the New and Old Testament,* in which he declared as positively as Wycliffe that the Bible alone is the standard of faith and that salvation is by faith alone. Belief in Christ, not baptism or confirmation, makes a Christian. The Gospels and the Psalter were already known to the Czech people in their own language; and before the fourteenth century was over, the entire Bible had been translated into Czech.

The national and religious revival in Bohemia and the critical attitude toward the Church encouraged the immediate spread of Wycliffe's writings. His influence on the great Czech reformer Jan Hus was so great that Hus can almost be considered a disciple of Wycliffe. Hus was born in 1370 in a remote part of Bohemia. Of humble parentage, he grew up in poverty and worked his way through the University of Prague. He began lecturing there in 1398, becoming dean of the faculty of philosophy in 1401 and rector in 1403. He was also a canon of the cathedral and confessor to the queen. Ordained a priest in 1400, he gained great popularity as a preacher, and was appointed chaplain of Bethlehem Chapel. Of Wycliffe he said in a letter: "I am drawn to him by his writings, in which he seeks to bring back all men to the law of Christ, and especially the clergy, to the end that they may dismiss the splendor and glory of the world and, with the apostles, live after the life of Christ." For some years, Hus was regularly appointed to preach the semi-annual Latin sermon to the assembled clergy at the cathedral; but as he diverged more widely from accepted doctrine and became more outspoken in his criticism of the clergy, the archbishop and several of the canons turned against him. In 1409, they appealed to the pope. The necessary bull was soon issued. In accordance with its provisions, the archbishop ordered that all persons having copies of Wycliffe's writings should surrender them and that all preaching outside the cathedral and the parish churches should cease. More than 200 manuscripts were turned in, and there was a holocaust of Wycliffe's writings in the courtyard of the archbishop's palace. While the cathedral bells tolled and the clergy sang the

145

Te Deum, the university, now purely Czech and largely Hussite, protested against the destruction. Disregarding the archbishop's order, Hus continued to preach to thousands in Bethlehem Chapel. The pope ordered Hus to appear for trial in Rome. Hus refused to go, and a few days later, the archbishop excommunicated him and all others who had disobeyed orders to bring in heretical books and to cease popular preaching.

Riot and tumult spread through the city. In a sermon Hus appealed to the people. "I know not," he said, "whether the pope [John XXIII] who has just died, the one who has issued orders to burn the books of Master John Wycliffe, . . . is in heaven or in hell, but I have appealed against him. Will you support me?" His listeners shouted their assent. Hus urged them to stand firm and not to fear excommunication: "Let us gird ourselves and stand for the law of God after the example of the old covenant."

In the years 1410 to 1412, religious conflict spread through Prague and much of Bohemia. An interdict laid upon the city turned some townsmen against reform, and they attacked Bethlehem Chapel. On the other hand, indulgences sold to pay for Pope John's crusade against the king of Naples aroused the usual opposition that the sale of indulgences evoked. The pope's messengers were driven out of the city, the pardons piled on a cart, carried through the streets, and burned in the marketplace.

Alarmed at the rapidly spreading disorder, the king appealed to Hus to suspend his preachings. Like Wycliffe before him, Hus complied with the request. He left Prague at the end of 1412 and took refuge at the castle of a friendly nobleman. Here and in other retreats he wrote books and pamphlets while his doctrines continued to gain support throughout the country.

In 1414, the emperor summoned him to appear at the Council of Constance and granted him an imperial safe-conduct. This council, which had been convened to end the papal schism, now undertook the definition and extirpation of heresy, focusing on the teachings of Wycliffe and Hus. It ordered the destruction of Wycliffe's writings and further decreed that Wycliffe's body be dug up and cast out from consecrated ground, a decree that the bishop of Wycliffe's diocese actually carried out twelve years later.

When Hus arrived at Constance on November 3, 1414, great numbers of people received him with affection and reverence.

146

For a few weeks, his lodgings were a center of religious discussion. This, of course, was distasteful to the pope and the cardinals; and late in November, Hus was formally accused of heresy, arrested, and confined in a convent on a small island in the lake. He was then subjected to harsh treatment and an inquisitorial investigation of his religious views. His friends, and even the emperor, protested against his imprisonment; but the pope insisted on the established rule of the Church that deprived a person charged with heresy of all civil rights until the charges were disproved. Betraying the trust Hus had placed in him, the emperor failed to enforce the safe-conduct and later acquiesced to all the proceedings against Hus.

Hus was kept in prison for seven months and chained to a post for much of that time. Finally, he was allowed to appear before the council. He angered emperor and clergy alike by denying the right of those in mortal sin to govern either the state or the Church. He also insisted on his right to accept or refuse the judgment of the council as he saw fit. This alone was enough to condemn him in the eyes of the Church. Various formulas of abjuration were offered him, but all of them offended either his reason or his conscience. After four weeks of negotiation, he was brought before the whole council, formally declared guilty of heresy, deposed from the priesthood, and divested of his ecclesiastical robes. A fool's cap painted with devils was placed on his head; and, in accordance with Church practice, the council turned him over to the secular authorities for punishment, thus relieving the Church of direct responsibility for inflicting the death penalty. He was then led to a meadow outside the city walls and burned at the stake. He died with serenity. His ashes were thrown into the Rhine so that no relics of his martyrdom would remain. A year later, Hus's friend Jerome of Prague suffered the same fate.

We cannot study all the consequences of Hus's life and martyrdom, but two major developments demand our attention. The first of these is the outbreak of the Hussite Wars, which raged in much of eastern and central Europe for almost twenty years. Like the Hundred Years War in France, the Hussite Wars were both civil and foreign wars; but they were unique in being religious as well. In this respect, they anticipated the Thirty Years' War. The Hussite armies were inspired by a fierce national and

147

religious enthusiasm. At first, they were almost purely Bohemian; but they gradually assimilated large mercenary and foreign elements and ultimately became a veteran professional army against which few opponents could stand. They developed novel tactics entirely their own. Following the old eastern practice, they arranged their baggage wagons into a square or circular fortification. They then used field cannons and handguns to repulse attacking forces repeatedly until the enemy was annihilated.

The pope declared five successive crusades against this heretic nation. The crusading armies were usually made up of German feudal or mercenary troops and were led by German princes. In 1428, the Hussites began to stage invasions into Moravia, Silesia, and Hungary, then into Germany. They penetrated into Saxony in the north and almost to the Rhine in the west, virtually unopposed by the powerless Germans. These invasions prompted a series of stormy meetings in the German Reichstag from 1422 to 1434. Attempts were made to introduce financial, military, and constitutional reforms in Germany. It was proposed that a permanent tax be levied to support a standing imperial army, but the territorial powers resisted centralization of any kind. Nothing came of the proposed reforms, and the German armies remained the same ill-organized and poorly paid troops that had always fled from the Hussites.

The second most important consequence of Hus's work was that the Hussites were finally able to win unprecedented concessions from the Church, concessions that represented the first real threat to the Church's unity and universal authority. At the Council of Basel (1431-1449), the Hussite delegates did not appear as culprits before their judges, as Hus and Jerome had in Constance. They had gained such strength that the Church was forced to receive them as equals and to compromise with them. In the so-called Compacts of Prague, formulated during the Basel negotiations, the Church granted Bohemia what amounted to ecclesiastical autonomy. From that point on, archbishops and bishops of the Bohemian church were to be elected by the Bohemian clergy. No foreigner could grant benefices in Bohemia or Moravia, nor could a native of these countries be called before a foreign ecclesiastical tribunal. In addition to these rights granted to the Bohemian church, religious rights were also granted to the Bohemian people. The Hussite demand that any member of the

148

laity be able to receive both bread and wine in communion was conceded to all Bohemians and Moravians, and punishment for mortal sin was to be administered to clergyman and layman alike. All these concessions ran counter to Catholic doctrine and went far beyond English anti-papal legislation or the Gallican Liberties won by the French church.

Under the pressures of the Hussite movement and of discontent throughout the Church, the Council of Basel made an attempt at Church reform from within. But the pope refused to yield final authority to the council; internal reform could not be achieved; and the Church, like the empire, remained divided against itself. Indeed, whatever reform efforts the council made were beside the point. There was no universal Church left to reform, because the Compacts of Prague granted official recognition of a national heresy and sanctioned the existence of a national church. The Hussite movement had made it patently clear that the unity of both Church and empire was destroyed and could never be restored.

# 19.

## LUTHER'S EARLY YEARS

WYCLIFFE and Hus did not accomplish their work in a vacuum. And they probably would not have been able to effect the reforms they did if other pervasive forces had not been at work at the same time, forces that not only played a role in the success of the Hussite movement but also continued to exert their influence throughout the fifteenth century, making all of Europe more receptive to Luther's message.

In the last half of the fourteenth century, the Black Death raged in Europe. One of its effects was a further secularization of the Church. The monastics had already lost considerable influence by the time the plague decimated their ranks and weakened them even more. But the plague killed large numbers of the secular clergy as well, reducing the presence of any kind of clerics among the population. Since reformers had already broken down the sanctity of the priest's office and since the numbers of ordained priests had been drastically reduced, it was only natural that laymen began to take over the duties of the priesthood. Deacons gained the authority to administer the sacraments, and the faithful were encouraged to hear confession for each other.

The plague also generated fear throughout the entire population of Europe, a fear that was further aggravated by the possibility of Turkish invasions. Death was in the air, breeding anxiety and restlessness. The image of Christ the Savior retreated behind the image of an avenging deity come to punish the sinful with sword or pestilence. Pilgrims thronged from one shrine to another, hoping to find deliverance from their fear and pardon for their sins; but the Church was unable to give them the comfort they sought, and a large number of religious associations of a dis-

150

tinctly lay character developed. Their members gathered for religious purposes and created a religious regimen apart from that of the Church.

The profound malaise occasioned by fear of both the plague and the Turks continued through the fifteenth century, heightening growing dissatisfaction with the Church, dissatisfaction fed by ever increasing attacks from Humanistic critics on the one hand and by the popular mystical impulse on the other. But these factors alone do not account for the fact that Luther was able to complete the work of reformation where Wycliffe and Hus could not. The force of Luther's personality played an important part in his success but by no means a decisive one. Hus too had been a remarkably strong person who won a huge following and who refused to compromise his faith, even when faced with death at the stake. But circumstances militated against his achieving the reform that would change the course of European history.

As we noted before, the work of Wycliffe and Hus was closely linked with national movements. Their teachings radiated out all over Europe, but their full impact was felt only within the confines of their respective nations. Luther's impact, by contrast, was not limited to a national arena because there was no German nation to enclose it. The chaotic state of the empire served to spread Luther's message rather than confine it to a certain area. Like the force of an explosion on an open plain, the shock wave of Luther's teachings could roll out in all directions. But more important still, the chaos of the empire accounts for Luther's very survival. If the emperor had had any clear authority and had not been completely absorbed in questions of succession, election, and foreign affairs, then Luther might well have suffered the martyrdom of Hus and Jerome. He did, of course, have a powerful friend and protector in Frederick the Wise, the elector of Saxony; but it was only the constantly shifting power constellation among the territorial princes, and especially among the electors, that made Frederick a key figure in the calculations of both the pope and the emperor and so enabled him to protect Luther. Thus, it was the disarray of the empire that was responsible to a great extent both for Luther's survival and for the ultimate triumph of his cause.

Before embarking on the extensive study of Luther's life and work that will take up the rest of Part II, we would do well to remind ourselves that we are concerned in this book with the characterological history of the German people. Luther is a central figure in German history not only because he is the central figure of the Reformation but because he is the prototype of the modern German. He embodied the society that produced him and at the same time created the society that came after him. This cannot be said of his predecessors in the reform movement. Both Wycliffe and Hus were essentially scholars and clerics who rose to high positions in the service of their universities, their cathedrals, and their nations. Hus was of peasant stock, but he left his origins behind him. Just the contrary is true of Luther. He clung to his origins as he assimilated the characteristics of other social classes. The result was that he became a composite of four major classes in medieval society: the peasant, the craftsman, the monk, and the scholar. Incorporating all these classes in his own personality, he was able to speak to them all and provide a model for them all. By force of his character as well as his actions, he formed modern Germany and the modern German.

Luther's great-grandfather and grandfather lived as peasants in Möhra, a little Thuringian hamlet near Eisenach. His father, Hans Luther, married Margarete Ziegler of Eisenach. By peasant custom, the older sons were sent out into the world to make their way while the youngest inherited the farm; and as an elder son, Hans Luther was forced to take his wife away from home. He was attracted to the county of Mansfeld, about sixty miles northeast of Eisenach, a mining district where he hoped to make a good living. On November 10, 1483, while the couple was traveling to Mansfeld, their first son was born in Eisleben. The parish priest baptized the child Martin after the saint whose day it was.

Hans Luther was a frugal, hard-working man. Beginning as a stranger and a common miner, he gradually won the respect of his fellow citizens and was eventually elected to the highest office in the town of Mansfeld. He was ambitious to give his boy the education he himself lacked, and Luther always recognized and appreciated what he owed his father. His mother was a quiet woman, bowed by long poverty and toil. Both parents were very strict. "My father," Luther said many years later, "once whipped me so severely that I fled from him, and it was hard for him to win me back. . . . When I once stole a miserable nut, my mother beat me until the blood flowed. My parents meant well, but their

152

strict discipline finally drove me into the monastery." Luther had at least one brother and three sisters. He rarely saw them and never wrote to them after he left home at the age of thirteen.

At home, he was taught the orthodox religion of the Catholic Church. God the Father and Jesus were represented to him as stern, cruel judges whose wrath had to be appeased through the intercession of the saints. Another of these early teachings that never left him was the belief in witches and kobolds, a belief that had survived in the minds of the people from primitive Germanic times. "In my native country," he once said, "there is a hill called the Pubelsberg. On top of it is a lake; and if a stone is thrown into the water, a great tempest will arise over the whole region; for the lake is inhabited by captive devils. Prussia is full of these devils, and Lapland is full of witches."

The boy first went to the village school where he was taught to read and speak Latin under poor and brutal tutelage. At thirteen he was sent to the school of the Brothers of the Common Life (*Nullbrüder*) at Magdeburg where he contributed to his own support by begging. In those days, begging was one of the recognized means by which the poor could get an education, and it was no more a disgrace than the acceptance of a scholarship is today. Thirty-five years later in his "Defense before Duke George," Luther wrote of his experience in this school: "When in my fourteenth year I went to school in Magdeburg, I saw with my own eyes a prince of Anhalt who went in a friar's cowl and begged bread on the highways. He carried a sack so heavy that he bent under it. . . . They had so stunned him that he did all the work of the cloister like any other brother, and he had so fasted and mortified his flesh that he looked like a death's head, mere skin and bones. . . ." After one year at Magdeburg, Luther went to Eisenach to attend the school of St. George.

About May 1501, he matriculated at the University of Erfurt, where he lived together with other students and studied a slightly modernized version of the old Scholastic trivium and quadrivium (logic, grammar, and rhetoric—arithmetic, natural sciences, ethics, and metaphysics). Medieval instruction had hardly progressed beyond Aristotle, who was still regarded as an infallible authority. Study of the natural sciences was conducted without any visual experience or original research and drew exclusively on Aristotle's works. In philosophy, however, nominalism was the dominant school and "the new learning," the Humanistic revival of classical antiquity, had also reached Erfurt. Some students devoted themselves to the humanities, but Luther kept to a Scholastic curriculum.

After taking a bachelor of arts degree in 1502 and a master's in 1505, he started to study jurisprudence; but he had worked in law only two months when he abruptly decided to enter a monastery. There has been much conjecture about the motives behind this decision. The basic cause was probably his overpowering sense of sinfulness. The training of his early youth—both at home and in the monastic schools—had no doubt encouraged such a tendency in the young Luther. But external circumstances seem to have had some bearing on his decision as well. We know that the plague broke out in Erfurt in the spring of 1505. Some students died, and most of the others left the town, Luther among them. How far Luther had progressed toward his decision at this time and what effect the epidemic had on his thinking is uncertain. The decisive event occurred a short time later when Luther was on his way back to Erfurt after a visit at home. On July 2, Luther was caught in a violent thunderstorm at Stottherheim, not far from Erfurt. In terror of the storm, he vowed to St. Anna that he would become a monk. For Luther, of course, a thunderstorm was not simply a natural phenomenon but an eruption of the demonic forces in nature and a sign that the devil himself was at hand.

Luther entered the Augustinian Order at the cloister of the Black Friars in Erfurt. In September 1506, he took the irrevocable vows of poverty, chastity, and obedience; and in February 1507, he was ordained a priest. The celebration of his first mass was a great occasion to which he invited his father and the parish priest of Eisenach, Johann Braun, with whom he had formed a close friendship while he was at school there. Luther's earliest extant letter is his invitation to this friend to attend the mass. The opening sentences of this letter are particularly characteristic of Luther: "God, glorious and holy in all His works, has deigned to exalt me, wretched and unworthy sinner, and to call me into His sublime ministry only for His mercy's sake. I ought to be thankful for the glory of such divine goodness (as much as dust may be) and to fulfill the duty laid upon me."

Once a monk, he continued the study of philosophy and took

154

up theology as well. About a year and a half after his first mass, he was called to the recently founded University of Wittenberg to teach Aristotle's *Ethics*. He spent a year in this position, continuing his own studies at the same time. But in the fall of 1509, he was sent back to Erfurt "because he had not satisfied the Wittenberg faculty," as the dean's book indicates. Luther claimed he was dismissed because he had no money and Wittenberg was unwilling to support him, but it is very likely that there was some trouble about the lectures he was to give. He wanted to discontinue philosophy and take up the Bible. It was the academic rule that a young professor had to devote three semesters to expounding Peter Lombard's *Sentences*, the common textbook in theology, before he was permitted to lecture on the Scriptures. Luther fulfilled this requirement in Erfurt, remaining there nearly two years. During this time, however, he left Erfurt long enough to make a pilgrimage to Rome. Then, with his academic apprenticeship completed, he was called to a permanent position at Wittenberg in the summer of 1511.

These are the external events of Luther's youth. Much more interesting and important is his inner development. He did not arrive at his revolutionary conviction by means of an intellectual process. His motivation arose instead from personal and emotional sources, from an awareness of his own sinful condition. This sense of ineradicable sinfulness—the belief that man is incapable of extricating himself from the sinful state into which he is born—is the basic experience of Luther's life. The anxiety and despair it engendered gave rise in turn to Luther's desperate search for spiritual peace

The contemplative and ascetic life of the monastic did not grant him this peace. On the contrary, it only increased his doubt. He felt he could never do enough to win God's favor and deserve God's pardon. In the monastery, Luther carried out all his duties conscientiously and mortified the flesh to the extreme, freezing in his unheated cell and starving himself until he fainted from lack of nourishment. He was so conscious of his own sinfulness and so thorough in documenting it that he was known to confess as long as six hours at a time, wearying his confessors with his endless recounting of minor sins. But none of this brought him relief. His excesses of devotion were only followed by renewed attacks of despair.

155

Luther's experience in the monastery illustrates the irreconcil-able conflict he felt in his life and demonstrates why it was essen-tial for him to find an alternative form of faith. Medieval Catholic doctrine maintained that man achieved salvation by works alone, that man earned his right to salvation by purging himself of sin and acting in accordance with the will of God. This doctrine doomed Luther to perpetual torment. Because he felt himself to be incorrigibly sinful, all the good works he performed were in vain. God was not a God of love for Luther but a harsh, cruel judge who could never be appeased.

The history of Luther's inner development, then, is the history of his liberation from the doctrine of justification by works. A number of factors helped Luther achieve this liberation, but the crucial one was his experience of the Bible. It was from the Bible that Luther drew his first assurance of spiritual peace for himself and the first inklings of what would become the central tenet of his life and of the Reformation itself. While reading Paul's Epis-tle to the Romans sometime in 1508 or 1509, Luther came on the line in 1:17: "The just shall live by faith." As he pondered this verse, Luther began to realize that the Church's teachings had been wrong. Man was not redeemed by his own works but by faith in God. Justification by faith is the cardinal doctrine of Luther's theology and the cornerstone of his religious reform. He had endured many years of torment before he arrived at it; and in the years that followed, he would build on it, consolidating his thinking and preparing himself for the great controversy his ninety-five theses would initiate in 1517.

# 20.

## THE NINETY-FIVE THESES

THE STRUGGLES of conscience Luther went through in his early career had no "revolutionary" implications whatsoever. They were of a personal nature and did not impinge on his loyalty to the Church at all. Only after his journey to Rome, which he seems to have made between October 1510 and February 1511, do we find him expressing any dissatisfaction with the Church as an institution.

Regulations of the Augustinians required that monks always travel in pairs, and Luther was sent to Rome as the *socius itinerarius* of Johann von Mecheln, an Augustinian friar who often traveled on official business of the order. Luther once said that his main purpose in going to Rome had been to make a general confession of all his sins and to receive absolution. Clearly, he set out on this journey as a faithful pilgrim, ready to see the glories, not the failings of the Holy City. Once there, Luther gave some attention to the sights of the ancient city, but most of his time was spent wandering from church to church, collecting all the indulgences available to the pious worshipper. He was still so thoroughly under the spell of the Church that he even wished his parents dead so that he could take advantage of the many opportunities to free their souls from purgatory. "I was a foolish pilgrim," he said later, "and believed all I was told." Still, despite this unquestioning faith in the Church, he could not help being shocked by many things he saw in Rome. "Rome is a harlot," he said. "I would not have missed seeing it for 1,000 gulden, for I never would have believed what other people might have told me of conditions there had I not seen them myself. The Italians mocked us for being pious monks, for they think Christians fools.

They say six or seven masses in the time it takes me to say one, because they take money for it, and I do not. The only crime Italians condemn is poverty. They still feel obliged to punish homicide and theft a little, but no other sin is too gross for them. . . ."

After Luther had returned to Erfurt in February 1511, his friend Johann Staupitz, dean of the theological faculty at Wittenberg, offered him a professorship of divinity. Wittenberg was a rapidly growing city at that time. In 1485, the family of Wettin had divided its lands into two parts. The elder brother, Ernest, elector of Saxony, received the electoral district of which Wittenberg was the center. When Frederick the Wise became elector in 1486, he chose Wittenberg as the capital of this district and immediately began to develop the town, adding a castle, a church, and various public buildings. In 1502, he founded the university, appointing Staupitz the first dean of the theological faculty. Both Staupitz and Frederick would become crucial figures in Luther's later career.

After taking the degree of doctor of divinity in October 1512, Luther assumed his professorship and began to lecture on the Bible. In his lectures given in the years 1513 to 1517, he developed his new religious ideas, particularly the theory of justification by faith. He was mainly interested in the relevance of the Bible to his own times, and his lectures were full of references to Pope Julius II and the bishop of Brandenburg. He also brought his former Erfurt professors, Trutvetter and Usingen, under attack: "It is mere madness for them to say that a man of his own powers is able to love God above all things and to do the works of the law . . . without grace. Fools!" Here we see the determinist element emerging in Luther's thinking. Man's faith must be answered by God's grace.

Luther also joined Erasmus and other Humanists in their effort to break Aristotle's hold on all branches of learning. "His [Aristotle's] propositions are so absurd," Luther wrote to Johann Lang, "that an ass or a stone would cry out at them. My soul longs for nothing so ardently as to expose and publicly shame that Greek buffoon, who, like a specter, has befooled the Church." On September 4, 1517, Luther published ninety-seven theses against Aristotle, demanding the elimination of his works as textbooks. Everyone is familiar with the ninety-five theses against indulgences, published the following month; but few people know of these theses against Scholastic philosophy. Yet Luther, who did not think the theses on indulgences worth publishing, printed this protest against Aristotle and his followers and sent it around to numerous friends and other public figures, including his old professors in Erfurt.

Toward the end of 1515 or early in 1516, Luther began to study the German mystics. He edited an anonymous mystical treatise which he called "Theologia Teutsch" and said of it in his preface: "There is no better book, after the Bible and St. Augustine." What attracted Luther most to the mystics was their confirmation of his own experience in their doctrine of the necessity of spiritual rebirth. Man had to pass through anguish and despair to achieve this rebirth and to make himself worthy of union with God.

Besides writing, studying, and lecturing, Luther began to preach in this period. His attacks on the many abuses of the Church and of the secular powers consequently reached a wider audience. His opinion on the case of the Humanist Johann Reuchlin indicates what his views on the Church were at that time. Reuchlin was on trial for heresy because he had refused to participate in the scheme of a converted Jew named Pfefferkorn to burn all Hebrew books except the Old Testament. This refusal prompted the Dominicans of Cologne to take action against Reuchlin. In this trial, which lasted from 1510 to 1516, the monks and obscurantists sided with the inquisitors, the Humanists with Reuchlin. The case became a *cause célèbre* all over Europe and gave rise to a famous satire, the *Epistles of Obscure Men* (*Epistolae obscurorum virorum*), written by the Humanists Crotus Rubianus and Ulrich von Hutten. The *Epistles* ridiculed the bad Latin, ignorance, gullibility, and superstition of the old theologians. Luther, though a monk himself, sided with the Humanists against the inquisitors. His views on the Reuchlin controversy are most amply expressed in his correspondence with Spalatin, the closest, most faithful, and most valuable friend Luther had.

Luther and Spalatin were of the same age and had come to know each other in 1512 when Spalatin was a tutor to the Wittenberg princes. About 1514, Spalatin was appointed chaplain and private secretary to the elector, Frederick the Wise. In this position, he was able to win essential support for Luther at the elector's court, support that would later mean the difference between

159

life and death for Luther. To be sure, the elector was well disposed toward Luther. He was a man of genuine piety, but his piety expressed itself in a somewhat grotesque fashion. He had made a pilgrimage to the Holy Land and brought back a large collection of relics to which he kept adding periodically. He built the Castle Church at Wittenberg to house these sacred objects. By 1505, he had accumulated 5,005 items which were graced with enormous indulgences equivalent to 1,443 years of purgatory. In addition to this provision for his future life, he had 10,000 masses said in Saxon churches each year for the benefit of his soul. Luther did not hesitate to criticize this folly; and, in general, he was very outspoken in his relations with the elector. Luther wrote to Spalatin: "Many things please your elector and appear glorious in his eyes, which displease God and are base. I do not deny that the prince is of all most wise in worldly matters, but in those which pertain to God and salvation I think he is seven times blind, as is your friend Pfeffinger [treasurer and collector of taxes]. I do not say this privately, as a slanderer, nor do I wish that you should in any way conceal it; when the opportunity comes I am ready to say it to both of them." In a letter of November 1517 addressed to the elector himself, we see how openly Luther criticized his prince; but at the same time we see how careful he was to soften his criticism with flattery: "Most gracious Lord and Prince! As your Grace promised me a gown some time ago, I beg to remind your Grace of the same. Please let Pfeffinger settle it with a deed and not with promises. He can spin mighty good yarns, but no cloth comes from them. . . . My gracious Lord, let me now show my devotion to you and deserve my new gown. I have heard that at the expiration of the present impost Your Grace intends to collect another and perhaps a heavier one. If you will not despise the prayer of a poor beggar, I ask you for God's sake not to do this. For it heartily distresses me and many who love you that this tax has of late robbed you of much good fame and favor. God has blessed you with high intelligence in these matters, . . . but it may well be God's will that a great mind sometimes be directed by a lesser one so that no one may trust himself but only God our Lord. . . ."

We come now to the turning point of Luther's career. His convictions were formed, but a stimulus was needed to bring them into the open. The famous indulgence controversy of 1517 to

1519 provided this stimulus. Up to this time, Luther had remained a true son of the Church despite severe criticism he had leveled at it. And even now, in attacking the flagrant abuse of the indulgence trade, he did not intend to start a fundamental revolt; nor did he consider himself basically at odds with the Church until ecclesiastical authorities forced him into irreconcilable opposition.

We have already touched on the nature and origin of the indulgence trade. According to the theory of the Roman Church, a penitent is freed from eternal punishment in hell if he confesses his sins and is absolved from them; but he still remains liable to the milder punishments of penance in this life or of purgatory thereafter. The early Church instituted the practice of commuting penance (but not time in purgatory) in recognition of good works, such as a pilgrimage or a contribution to the Church. The Crusades were responsible for the growth and the corruption of the indulgence trade. Mohammed promised his followers paradise if they fell in battle against unbelievers; and as early as 855, Pope Leo IV promised heaven to the Franks who died fighting the Moslems. A quarter of a century later, John VIII proclaimed absolution from all sins and remission of all penalties for soldiers who participated in the holy war. From this time on, the "crusade indulgence" became a regular means of recruiting; and indulgences came to include remission of time in purgatory as well as of penance. Later, about 1145, pardon was also assured to those who gave enough money to equip one soldier. After the Crusades, the practice remained; but now an indulgence was simply a pardon sold by the Church. Agents sent out to sell these pardons were given the power to confess and absolve. Eventually, they were even granted the power to deliver the souls of the dead from purgatory.

The existence of this latter power was first confirmed by Pope Calixtus III in 1457, but full use of it was not made until twenty years later when indulgences of this kind became the most profitable of the entire indulgence trade. It is important to note that at this time in Church history dogma could not be established by papal proclamation. A powerful party in the Church held that a council was the supreme authority in matters of faith. Therefore, Luther's opposition to indulgences for the dead did not leave him open to charges of heresy.

161

It was not the theory of the Church that excited Luther's indignation but the practices of her agents. The common man was encouraged to believe that the purchase of a papal indulgence alone, without genuine repentance, would assure remission of punishment. Furthermore, the "holy trade" had become so thoroughly commercialized that the Fuggers, in return for their services in forwarding the pope's bulls and in hiring sellers of pardons, could make a secret agreement with the Church in 1507 by which they received one third of the total profits of the trade. In 1514, they took over complete management of the business in return for the modest commission of one half the net receipts. The Church was, of course, extremely careful to keep any knowledge of this agreement from the people.

The incident that provoked Luther's attack and thereby launched the Reformation was a particularly blatant example of corruption in the indulgence trade. Albrecht of Brandenburg, a Hohenzollern prince, had, through political influence, risen to the highest ecclesiastical position in Germany. In 1513, at the age of twenty-three, he was elected archbishop of Magdeburg and administrator of the bishopric of Halberstadt—an accumulation of sees that canon law prohibited but that the pope nonetheless confirmed in return for a large payment. Albrecht was then elected archbishop of Mainz and primate of Germany on March 9, 1514. As he was not yet of canonical age to possess even one bishopric, much less three of the greatest in the empire, the pope demanded an enormous sum to confirm the election. The pope first asked 12,000 ducats for the twelve apostles; Albrecht offered 7,000 for the seven deadly sins. Finally, the average between apostles and sins was struck at 10,000 ducats, a sum equal in purchasing power to nearly a million dollars today. Albrecht borrowed this amount from the Fuggers and was confirmed on August 15, 1514. In order to give the new prelate a chance to recover his losses, Leo X obligingly declared an indulgence for the benefit of St. Peter's Church. Albrecht did not realize as much from this sale as he expected, because a number of princes, including the rulers of both Saxonys, forbade the trade in their dominions. Sales were further diminished by Luther's unexpected attack. Albrecht's principal agent was the Dominican Tetzel, a bold, popular preacher already expert in the indulgence business. He did everything in his power to impress the people with the value of his commodities. In his sermons he described the agonies of purgatory in great detail and emphasized how easy it was for anyone to spare himself or his dead relations these tortures for the modest price of one gulden.

Though forbidden to enter Saxony, Tetzel approached sufficiently near her borders to attract a number of her people. In January 1517, he was in Eisleben; and in the spring he came to Jüterbog, so near Wittenberg that Luther could see the bad effects in his own parish. Luther decided to bring matters to a head by holding a debate on the subject. He announced his intention in a very dramatic way. On All Saints Day, November 1, the relics kept in the Castle Church at Wittenberg were displayed and the special graces attached to them publicly announced. This festival always drew great crowds to Wittenberg. On October 31, 1517, Luther posted his ninety-five theses on the door of the church to announce to all these visitors his intention of holding a debate on the value of indulgences. Each thesis, or topic for debate, struck a blow at some popular error or flagrant abuse:

1. When our Lord and Master Jesus Christ said "Penitentiam agite," he meant that the whole life of the faithful should be repentance [not penance].

32. Those who believe themselves saved by papal letters will be eternally damned along with their teachers.

36. Every truly repentant Christian has full remission of guilt and penalty even without letters of pardon.

82. Why is the pope not moved by charity to empty purgatory?

On the same day Luther wrote a letter to Archbishop Albrecht, imploring him to prohibit the sale of indulgences. Albrecht immediately began an "inhibitory process" against the "presumptuous monk" and sent an account of the matter to Rome along with several of Luther's works.

The attack on indulgences was like a match touched to gunpowder. Everyone had been thinking what Luther alone was bold enough to say, and almost everyone applauded him. Many people wrote to him, congratulating him on what he had done and exhorting him to stand fast. The theses gained immediate and enormous popularity. Luther was astonished at their reception, and before he knew it they were printed at Nürnberg in both Latin and German. The Humanists there greeted them enthusiastically, and Albrecht Dürer sent Luther a present of his woodcuts as a token of appreciation. Indeed, Luther was even alarmed by the impact his theses had made. "Now that my theses are printed and have circulated far beyond my expectation," he wrote in a letter, "I feel anxious about what they may bring forth. . . . I have doubts about them myself and should have spoken differently . . . had I known what was going to happen. . . . I have felt moved to write a defense of my theses . . . and if the Lord give me leisure, I should like to publish in German a work on the virtue of indulgences that would supersede my desultory theses. For I have no doubt that people are deceived not by indulgences but by the use made of them. . . ."

Luther printed the defense of his ninety-five theses under the title *Resolutiones*. In a letter to Leo X, written toward the end of May 1518, he dedicates this defense to the pope; and though still speaking as a submissive son of the Church, he suggests that the attacks of his enemies have only confirmed the correctness of his views. The letter is well adapted to the man to whom it is addressed, a Humanist who would be more likely to despise the writer as an uncultured German than to condemn him as a heretic. The pope had read the theses, and had judged them clever but animated by envy. On another occasion he expressed the opinion that they had been composed by a drunken German who would see the error of his ways when sober. In any case, he did not take the affair very seriously and simply ordered Gabriel della Volta, general of the Augustinians, "to quiet that man, for newly kindled flames are easily quenched." Volta instructed Staupitz, the provincial vicar, to force the presumptuous brother to recant. The matter was brought before the Augustinian chapter of Saxony, which met at Heidelberg in April and May 1518. This was the first of Luther's famous disputations and public defenses. Augsburg, Altenburg, Leipzig, and Worms were to follow. Luther refused to recant and even expounded his fundamental ideas in a public debate on free will and justification by faith. "The doctors," he wrote to Spalatin, "willingly heard my disputation and rebutted it with such moderation that I felt much obliged to them. . . ."

Meanwhile, however, the usual procedures against heretics and reformers had been initiated. The enraged Dominicans had denounced Luther to the fiscal procurator of the Curia Romana, and when it was learned that the efforts of the general of the Augustinians had failed, Leo authorized the procurator to begin formal action "for suspicion of heresy." The general auditor, Ghinnucci, obtained an expert opinion on Luther's theses from Silvester Prierias, a Dominican and Thomist, then summoned Luther to appear in Rome within sixty days, sending him the citation and Prierias' memorial. Luther answered Prierias with a pamphlet in which he asserted that both pope and council could err.

But before Luther had time to decide whether to obey the summons or not, the Curia suddenly altered its method of procedure. On August 23, the pope wrote Cardinal Cajetan, his nuncio to the Diet of Augsburg, to cite Luther to Augsburg at once, to hear him, and, if he did not recant, to send him bound to Rome or, failing that, to put him and his followers under the ban. These measures had been suggested by Cajetan himself, who, on his arrival in Germany, had seen the general commotion Luther's acts had caused. Cajetan was still further alarmed by a sermon Luther had published on the subject of bans. Bans, Luther said in this pamphlet, flew about like bats and deserved no more attention than those blind little pests. Cajetan, determined to teach Luther what a terrible thing a ban really was, urged Rome to take action. In this matter, Cajetan had the support of Emperor Maximilian, who disliked and feared both Luther and the elector of Saxony. At the same time, Hecker, the provincial of the Augustinians in southern Germany, was urged to cooperate in securing Luther's arrest.

Luther's powerful friends did not desert him at this critical juncture. The elector of Saxony refused to let Luther appear in Augsburg without a safe-conduct from the emperor. Also, Staupitz went to the hearing at Augsburg to insure that the safe-conduct was not violated.

Luther had three interviews with Cajetan on three consecutive days, October 12, 13, and 14, 1518. At the opening of the first interview, Luther demonstrated his humility by prostrating himself before the cardinal. Pleased by this gesture, the nuncio complimented Luther on his learning and bade him recant his errors. When Luther asked what errors the cardinal meant, Cajetan cited two. The first was Luther's denial, in the theses, that the merits of Christ are a treasure of indulgences. The second was Luther's assertion in the *Resolutiones* that the efficacy of the sacrament depended on the faith of the recipient. Luther did not recant, and the discussion with his judge often became heated. Despite all the precautions that had been taken to insure Luther's safety, it was clear that he was in considerable danger at this point. As we have seen, safe-conducts for heretics had been broken before; but Luther stood firm against the threats of his foes and the supplications of his friends, resolved to do nothing against his conscience.

While he waited in Augsburg to see if he would be called before the cardinal again, he wrote a letter to Cajetan: "Most reverend Father in Christ, I confess, as I have before confessed, that I was assuredly unwise and too bitter and that I was too irreverent toward the name of the pope. And although I had the greatest provocation, I know I should have acted with more moderation and humility and not answered a fool according to his folly. For so doing I am most sincerely sorry and ask pardon. . . ." These few sentences show how Luther was torn between the demands of his conscience on the one hand and his genuine desire to submit to authority on the other. Here, at this crucial moment in Luther's life, we see once again that curious combination of rebellion and submission that is such a basic element of the German character.

Luther waited three days for a reply to his letter. When none came, he slipped out of Augsburg at night and returned to Wittenberg.

# 21.

## THE DEBATE AT LEIPZIG

IMMEDIATELY after his return to Wittenberg Luther wrote an account of his interviews in Augsburg and published it under the title of *Acta Augustana*. Cajetan, for his part, wrote the elector Frederick asking that Luther be arrested and sent to Rome. The elector summoned his counsellors. One of them, Fabian von Feilitzsch, related the fable of the sheep who, on the advice of the wolves, sent away the watchdogs. If we turn Luther over to the Church authorities, he said, we shall have no one to write in our defense, and they will accuse us all of being heretics. It is unlikely that Frederick even considered surrendering Luther. At this point, Frederick was more inclined to hide him, as he would later at the Wartburg. On December 18, 1518, the elector wrote a diplomatic letter to the cardinal, saying he was not convinced that the accused monk was a heretic. Learned men had informed him that Luther's doctrines were objectionable only to those whose pecuniary interests were involved. Frederick emphasized that he wanted to act as a Christian prince should but that he could not compromise his university by sending an uncondemned man to Rome.

Cajetan had been convinced by the Augsburg interviews that it would be difficult to convict Luther of heresy. He therefore requested the pope to settle the points in dispute once and for all. The pope responded with a bull issued on November 9, 1518. He mentioned no names in this bull, but he did condemn the errors that certain monks had spread concerning indulgences and other points. It was impossible to claim now that the matters in question had not been authoritatively decided. At the same time the pope appointed Karl von Miltitz as a special nuncio to Ger-

167

many and instructed him to arrest Luther. In an effort to win Frederick's good will, Leo had Miltitz award Frederick the Golden Rose, the highest decoration the Church could grant for services rendered her and a distinction Frederick had long coveted. If Frederick remained uncooperative, however, Miltitz was also furnished with a ban against Luther and with the authority to declare an interdict on Saxony.

Frederick's resistance and Miltitz's bungling account for the failure of the pope's plan. Miltitz, a Saxon by birth and a vain, frivolous man, acted counter to his instructions and tried to set everything right by diplomatic means. He arranged for a personal interview with Luther, whom he expected to cajole into recantation. This interview took place at Altenburg, the residence of the elector, early in January 1519. Luther handled Miltitz shrewdly, making minor concessions that did not affect his fundamental points; and the two men were able to reach an agreement. Both sides were to refrain from preaching, writing, and acting further on the points in question; and Miltitz was to write the pope at once, asking him to recommend the matter to some learned bishop who would hear Luther and point out the errors he should recant. "When I learn my mistakes," Luther wrote in his report to the elector, "I will gladly withdraw them and do nothing to impair the honor and power of the Roman Church."

Miltitz, too easily satisfied with his achievement, reported to the pope that Luther was ready to recant everything. Leo X was so pleased with this news that, in March 1519, he sent a friendly letter to Luther, inviting him to Rome to make his confession and even offering him money for the journey. However, the political situation prevented Leo from taking any further action. In January 1519, Emperor Maximilian had died. The candidates for the imperial crown were King Charles of Spain, King Francis I of France, and the elector of Saxony. Since the pope had grievances against both kings, he was forced to favor the elector. The interest of the papacy in this election overshadowed all other matters for a time and precluded any effort to force Frederick into a decision against Luther. As a result, the process for heresy was suspended for fourteen months.

If Miltitz was satisfied with his interview, Luther was not. When they parted with the kiss of peace, Luther felt that the kiss was a Judas kiss and that the envoy's tears were crocodile's tears. Still, Luther tried to live up to the agreement. He published an "Instruction on Certain Articles," in which he clarified his position on a number of points. Prayers for the dead in purgatory, he wrote, are allowable. Of indulgences, it is enough for the common man to know that an indulgence partially relieves him of sin but is a much smaller thing than a work of charity. The Church's commands, he said, are to be obeyed, but one should place God's commands higher. "Of good works," he continued, "I have said and still say that no man is good nor can he do right unless God's grace first makes him just; wherefore no one is justified by works, but works come naturally from him who is just." In conclusion he added that there is no doubt that God has honored the Roman Church above all others. We see an old pattern recurring here: Luther tries hard to control himself and preserve Church discipline, but no matter how hard he tries, his fundamental tenets still break through and nullify any concessions he has made.

The first article of the agreement, stipulating that both sides should maintain silence, came to naught because neither party observed the truce. On the contrary, the whole controversy soon gained even wider publicity through Luther's debate with Johann Eck in Leipzig, the fourth of Luther's disputations. This debate was the decisive one that made reconciliation with the Church impossible.

Johann Eck, doctor of theology, chancellor of the University of Ingolstadt, canon of Eichstätt, and preacher at Augsburg, was the ablest and most persistent opponent Luther ever had. From 1517 to 1543 this champion of the Church fought Luther at every turn and did everything in his power to checkmate him. Like Luther, he was of peasant origin and a monk by profession, a theologian of extraordinary ability and a man of great energy and resources. He had distinguished himself in a number of debates before 1517, and he was eager for still greater fame. Just before launching his attacks on Luther, Eck had charged Erasmus, the foremost scholar of the day, with something akin to heresy, because Erasmus had said the Greek of the New Testament was not as good as that of Demosthenes.

The publication of the ninety-five theses gave Eck a more substantial object to attack, and he assailed them in a pamphlet called *Obelisks*, that is, dagger symbols ( † ) used as marks of reference. Besides calling Luther a fanatic Hussite, Eck also labeled him heretical, seditious, insolent, and rash, adding for good measure that he was clumsy, unlearned, and a despiser of the pope. Luther said of Eck's attack: "It is nothing less than the malice and envy of a maniac. I would have swallowed this sop for Cerberus, but my friends compelled me to answer it." Luther responded in a pamphlet called *Asterisks*. But before the altercation progressed any further, it was taken out of Luther's hands by another Wittenberg professor, Andreas Bodenstein of Carlstadt (called Carlstadt), a man destined to play an important part in the Protestant revolt. He was a revolutionary by nature and longed to out-Luther Luther. While Luther had been away at Heidelberg in the spring of 1518, Carlstadt had come forward with a set of theses on free will and the authority of the Bible. Eck responded with some countertheses exalting the supremacy of the pope. Carlstadt, who held a benefice directly from the pope, was reluctant to debate this point; but Luther had no such scruples, and toward the end of 1518 he published twelve propositions directed against Eck. Of these, the twelfth was the most significant: "The assertion that the Roman Church is superior to all other Churches is proved only by weak and insipid papal decrees of the last 400 years, against which stand the accredited history of 1,100 years, the Bible, and the decree of the Nicene Council, the holiest of all councils."

This attack on the power of the Roman See caused a sensation. Eck sought a debate with both Wittenberg professors. Luther wrote him on February 18, 1519: "I wish you salutation and that you may stop seducing Christian souls. . . . You boast that you seek God's glory, the truth, the salvation of souls, the increase of the faith, and that you teach of indulgences and pardons for the same reasons. You have such a thick head and cloudy brain that, as the apostle says, you know not what you say. . . . / I wish you would fix the date of the disputation or tell me if you wish me to fix it. More then. Farewell."

Leipzig was finally chosen as the place for the debate. During the next six months, Luther's principal occupation was preparing for this encounter. He plunged eagerly into the study of Church history and especially of canon law. The research Luther conducted at this time only strengthened his convictions. To his friend Spalatin, who was worried about him, he wrote in February 1519:

> For the sake of the elector and the university, I repress much which otherwise I should pour out against Rome, Babylon rather, that spoiler of the Bible and of the Church. For the truth of the Scriptures and of the Church cannot be spoken, dear Spalatin, without offending that beast. Do not therefore hope that I shall be quiet or safe in the future, unless you wish me to give up theology altogether. Let my friends think me mad. For the thing will not be ended (if it be of God), even should all my friends desert me, as all Christ's disciples and friends deserted him, and the truth be left alone to save herself by her own might, not by mine, nor by yours, nor by any man's. I have expected this hour from the first.
>
> My twelfth proposition was extorted from me by Eck, but since the pope has so many defenders, I do not think they ought to take it ill, unless they forget that it was expressed in the freedom of debate. At all events, even should I perish, nothing will be lost to the world. For my friends at Wittenberg have now progressed so far, by God's grace, that they do not need me at all. . . . I fear I am not worthy to suffer and die for such a cause. That will be the blessed lot of better men, not of so foul a sinner. . . .

The debate in Leipzig was held from June 27 to July 18 in a richly decorated hall of the Pleissenburg, a castle that was preserved until the beginning of our century. A large and distinguished audience had gathered, including Duke George of Saxony, later one of the most determined opponents of the new doctrine.

In the first week, Eck debated with Carlstadt about free will. But the crucial battle came in the second week when Eck and Luther took up the question of papal primacy. In his report to Spalatin, Luther wrote: "Indulgences were quickly disposed of. Eck agreed to almost all I said, and the use of indulgences was turned to scorn and mockery. . . . He is said to have granted that, had I not disputed the power of the pope, he would have agreed with me easily on all points. He even confessed to Carl-stadt: 'If I could only agree with Luther as much as I do with you, I would go home with him at once.' The man is fickle and subtle, ready to do anything. . . . He asserts one thing in the academy and another in the church to the people. Asked by Carlstadt why he did this, the man shamelessly replied that the people ought not to be taught points on which there was doubt. . . . In the last days of his debate with Carlstadt, he agreed to everything and yielded every point: that spontaneous action is sin; that there is sin in every natural good work; that it is only grace which enables a man to do what he can for the Disposer of Grace—all of which the schoolmen deny.

"So in the whole debate he treated nothing as it deserved except my twelfth proposition [denying the supremacy of the pope]."

Eck's goal in the debate had been to make Luther's opinions appear identical with those of Hus. Luther took up this challenge and boldly asserted: "It is certain that among the articles of Hus and the Bohemians there are many which are most Christian and evangelic and which the universal Church is not able to condemn." These words sent a thrill through the audience. Duke George shook his head and said loudly: "That's the plague!" Eck had thus accomplished his aim of forcing Luther to acknowledge his heretical position.

At Leipzig, the line of combat was drawn; the camps were formed throughout Germany. Whatever Luther did from now on moved him into an increasingly radical position. The course of events reacted on him, propelling him on to assume leadership of all the revolutionary forces of the time. Every occurrence carried him on like a wave and left him far in advance of his previous position. Each book he read, each friend he made offered a powerful stimulus to his development. It was one of those very rare moments in history when all the various trends of an age seem not only to be expressed by a single personality, but to form that personality in such a way that we can hardly distinguish what belongs to the individual alone and what to the changing world that avails itself of him, both shaping and assimilating him. In these few years from 1519 to 1523, we see a major transformation in European history pass through the narrow de-

172

file of a single man and his inner career. This transformation would soon transcend the man, gathering its own momentum and eventually escaping the control and guidance of the individual who had set it in motion.

How external events affected Luther's inner development becomes clear in his relation to Hussite doctrine. When Eck repeatedly accused Luther of being a Hussite, Luther often interrupted him, shouting "This is false" or "He lies impudently." Although Luther cautiously defended certain Hussite propositions at Leipzig, he was still reluctant to identify himself with Hus's doctrine. During his early years in the cloister, he had read one of Hus's works and had wondered how a heretic could speak in such a timely Christian manner, but he had also assumed that this particular book must have been written before Hus's apostasy. In preparing for the Leipzig debate, Luther had read enough of the history of the Council of Constance to be convinced that many of Hus's tenets were evangelic, and this prompted him to speak in favor of Hus at the debate. But only in the beginning of 1520, after he had found time to read more widely in Hus's writings, did he fully recognize that Hus had been his predecessor. Now he did not hesitate to proclaim himself the condemned heretic's disciple. He first gave notice of this decisive and dangerous step in a memorable letter to Spalatin:

> I have an idea that a revolution is about to take place unless God withhold Satan. I have seen the devil's artful plans for my perdition and for that of many. . . . The Word of God can never be advanced without whirlwind, tumult, and danger. The Word is of infinite majesty; it is wonderful in the heights and in the depths. . . . One must either despair of peace and tranquillity or else deny the Word. War is of the Lord who did not come to send peace. Do not hope that the cause of Christ can be advanced in the world peacefully and sweetly, for you see that the battle has been waged with His own blood and that of the martyrs. I have hitherto taught and held all the opinions of Jan Hus unawares. So did Johann Staupitz; in short, we are all Hussites without knowing it. Paul and Augustine are Hussites to a word. Behold the horror I have discovered without the aid of any Bohemian teacher or leader. I know not what to think

for astonishment when I see such terrible judgments of God on mankind, when I see that the plain gospel truth has been publicly burnt and considered damnable for 100 years, and no one comes forward to assert it! Woe to the land!

Hus was not the only writer who had exposed the iniquities of Rome. Another was the brilliant fifteenth-century Humanist Laurentius Valla, who wrote a treatise proving that the *Donation of Constantine* was a forgery. This celebrated document, composed sometime in the ninth century, purported to be a deed drawn up by the emperor Constantine in the fourth century. It presented the pope with central Italy and, more important still, gave him general overlordship of the western world. For six centuries this forgery had been accepted as authentic, and it had become the cornerstone of papal pretensions and of canon law.

But Luther did not have to rely on books alone for support. Talented, energetic men were ready to assist him, too. Ulrich von Hutten, whom Luther had first known as the editor of the German edition of Valla's book, offered himself and his powerful group of knightly patriots as allies in the fight against Rome. Hutten came from an old Franconian family and was one of the first or the last, if you will, to combine old knightly ideals with the new Humanistic erudition. He is one of the many transitional figures in which the age of Luther abounds. Of weak constitution and plagued by sickness (syphilis) most of his life, he lent his ardent ambition and fiery temperament to a number of ill-defined idealistic causes which all aimed at ending the predominance of Rome. He wanted to free scientific and Humanistic studies from the fetters of Scholasticism, to liberate Germany from the ecclesiastical influence and interference of Rome, and to establish a new, reformed German empire under the leadership of a regenerated knightly class. His great hope was his friend Franz von Sickingen, a different kind of transitional figure, who combined the qualities of a knightly condottiere with those of a businessman. Through clever administration of his family property and shrewd commercial dealings, Franz von Sickingen had assembled a considerable fortune. He used this fortune to raise mercenary armies which he then hired out at exorbitant prices. With his large resources and his political connections, he constituted a considerable threat to even the most powerful princes. He and

174

Hutten played an important if short-lived part in the stormy events of the period.

By 1520 these knightly patriots could see what their cause and the cause of German freedom could gain by uniting with the cause of religious emancipation. Hutten's one great fear was that Luther would compromise or be crushed by his foreign oppressor. Hutten wrote to Luther, urging him to stand fast and promising him support. Shortly after the arrival of this letter, Luther received another similar one, this time from Sylvester von Schaumburg, another leader of the knightly class, who offered Luther protection if he should need it. Luther felt this support to be timely indeed. Hutten had been correctly informed that a bull against the heretic had been drawn up at Rome. Cardinal Riario, a friend of Erasmus and a moderate, had written the elector on May 20, 1520, urging him, if he valued his safety, to "make that man recant." The elector forwarded the letter to Wittenberg, and Luther's prompt reply to Spalatin amounted to an open challenge:

> I am sending the letter of the Franconian knight, Sylvester von Schaumburg, and unless it is too much trouble I wish the elector would communicate its contents to Cardinal Riario so that they may know in Rome that even if they thrust me out of Wittenberg with their furies they will only make matters worse. . . . In this lies their danger; for were I saved by those protectors [the knights] I should grow more terrible to the Romanists than I am now while publicly teaching under the elector's government. . . . For hitherto I have given in on many points, even when enraged, out of respect to my sovereign, but then there would be no need to consult his wishes. The fact that I have proceeded no further against the Romanists cannot be attributed to my moderation or to the success of their own tyranny but to the name and authority of the elector and to my respect for the University of Wittenberg.
>
> The die is cast; I despise the fury and favor of Rome; I will never be reconciled to them nor commune with them. Let them condemn and burn my books. For my part, unless all the fire goes out, I will condemn and publicly burn the whole papal law, that slough of heresies. The humility I have hitherto shown, all in vain, shall have an end, lest it still further puff up the enemies of the gospel.—I see they write with cowardly

fear and a bad conscience, trying to put on a ferocious mien with their last gasp. They try to protect their folly by force, but they fear they will not succeed as happily as they have in times past.

This is open revolt. No heretic had ever spoken to Rome this way before. Both the pressure of external events and the evolution of his own thinking gradually but inevitably forced Luther to make this final break with the Church.

The many students and young teachers who flocked to Luther in Wittenberg offered him continuing encouragement and support. Among these young men was Philip Schwarzerd, better known as Melanchthon, the Grecized version of his name. Luther first met Melanchthon in the summer of 1518, and the young scholar soon became Luther's most able helper. This precocious youth entered Heidelberg at thirteen and took his bachelor's degree at fifteen. He completed a master's degree a year later and had not reached twenty-one when he was called to teach Greek at the University of Wittenberg. Although he was destined to win his fame in the field of divinity, his major interest was in classical studies. He was unlike Luther in character but a perfect complement to him, a scholar and pedagogue rather than a man of action, a pacifier rather than a fighter. It was he who developed, clarified, and systematized Luther's ideas, thus becoming the actual founder of Lutheran theology. To be sure, disagreements between Luther and Melanchthon arose in the later years of their relationship. In important negotiations on articles of faith, Melanchthon was often too weak and kindly to withstand the pressure of his opponents if Luther was not present to keep him firm. But Luther never allowed these differences to impair their friendship and cooperation.

In addition to all the human, political, and social factors that furthered the Reformation, we must also note a technological one that was of tremendous importance: the invention of printing with movable type. It can safely be said that the printing press did as much to spread Luther's ideas among the people as the radio did to spread Nazi propaganda in our time.

The printing press gave Luther a tremendous advantage that previous reformers, plagued by isolation and slow communications, had not enjoyed. Luther was the first man to make full use

176

of the press as an instrument for influencing public opinion. There were, of course, no newspapers as we know them today; but innumerable short pamphlets—and even letters—poured forth from the printing houses, and were eagerly bought and read. Luther was a genuine pamphleteer. Nearly everything he wrote, even his most important treatises, first appeared as pamphlets. The pamphlet provided his activist's mind with its most adequate form of expression; and since Luther wrote in the vernacular he may even be said to have created the German book trade. Before he started publishing, the majority of books printed in Germany were in Latin; but soon after his first writings appeared, works in German began to predominate. In 1518, there were only 150 German works published; in 1524, there were almost 1,000. Luther himself was an extremely prolific author. His works, numbering more than 400, fill more than 100 volumes. He wrote in a powerful, direct style that made him immediately popular. In 1519 a famous Basel publisher wrote him that his works had already been exported to France, Spain, Italy, the Low Countries, England, and to all parts of the empire. This was all before he had written the three pamphlets of 1520 which, apart from the translation of the Bible, are the most important works of Luther's entire production.

# 22.

## THE THREE MAJOR TREATISES AND THE EDICT OF WORMS

THE EXPERIENCES of the period following the Leipzig debate had only confirmed Luther in his radical position, and he spoke now in the most rebellious tone he would ever adopt. In a reply to a new attack by Prierias, Luther wrote: "Verily, it seems to me that the only remedy is for the emperor, the kings, and the princes to take up arms and attack this plague of our earth. . . . Why don't we strike with force of arms at these cardinals, these popes, this whole rabble of the Roman Sodom that continuously desecrates the Church of God? Why don't we wash our hands in their blood?"

This same tone characterized the language of Hutten's revolutionary knights. The wealth and influence Sickingen commanded made the support of the knights invaluable to Luther, but this support was soon taken away. Sickingen and his followers suffered total defeat in 1523 when they attacked the ecclesiastical princes of the Rhine. Sickingen was killed in battle, and Hutten died later as a fugitive in Zurich. This defeat marked the end of the knights as a force in German history.

We find evidence of Luther's alliance with the knights in the first of his three great reformatory pamphlets written in 1520. This pamphlet, *An den christlichen Adel deutscher Nation* (*To the Christian Nobility of the German Nation*), is the most revolutionary of Luther's works. The pamphlet draws on the writings of Hutten and Crotus Rubianus as well as on Erasmus' *Dialogue of St. Peter and Julius II*. Many details in it were taken from the private letters and personal conversation of friends who had been in Rome. Another important source was the *Gravamina Nationis*

178

*Germanicae* (*Grievances of the German Nation*), presented by Erhard von der Mark at the Diet of Augsburg in 1518. In the preface to his pamphlet, Luther wrote: "The time of silence is past, and the time to speak has come. . . . I do not excuse myself; let him blame me who will. Perhaps I owe my God and the world some folly which I have now undertaken to pay honestly and as best I can, even if it be to become court fool. . . . I must fulfill the proverb that whenever the world has some work to be done, a monk must do it, even if he be ground to pieces by it. In times past, fools have often spoken wisely, and the wise have often been great fools. As St. Paul says: If any man would be wise, let him become a fool. . . . May those of moderate understanding forgive me. I do not seek the favor of those who are wise beyond measure; I have tried often and diligently to win their approval, but from henceforth I will not try, nor will I care what they think. . . ."

The pamphlet begins with a compliment to Charles V and an appeal to him to redress the grievances that weigh so heavily on all men. Luther did not know how futile this appeal was. The Hapsburg emperor was not only allied with the Church politically but also devoted to it by nature and training. As a true Hapsburg he had little interest in the German nation and did not even speak the language. He dreaded all national and popular movements and regarded the slightest deviations from established rules and forms as revolutionary acts.

Luther argues that the Church had surrounded itself with three walls. The first of these is the claim that civil government has no power over the Church. The second is that no one but the pope has the right to interpret the Bible. And the third is that only the pope has the right to summon a council. The Romanists had thus made themselves immune to punishment and had "entrenched themselves in these three walls to commit all manner of rascality and evil. . . . May God now give us one of those trumpets with which the walls of Jericho were brought down."

The tearing down of these "walls" represented a total revolution in religious life, and Luther spells out the practical implications of this revolution, implications that constitute the basic elements of the Protestant reform. "All Christians are really of the spiritual estate and there is no difference except of office . . . for we are all made priests by baptism. . . . Each one should help

179

his neighbor's body and soul as the members of the body serve one another. To say . . . that the temporal authority has no right to punish the spiritual . . . is as much as to say that when the eye is suffering, the hand should do nothing for it. . . . Wherefore the temporal powers of Christendom should freely exercise their office, not regarding whether it is pope, bishop, or priest that they punish, but only that the guilty suffer." Luther is following Wycliffe here and at the same time putting a secular interpretation on the medieval concept of Christendom as a *corpus mysticum Christi.* But the truly revolutionary ideas suggested here are the establishment of an evangelical community and the supremacy of secular government, even in matters of religion. These ideas meant the abolishment of the Church's power of the key and the end of the Church's significance both as a secular and ecclesiastical body.

Most of the practical reforms Luther suggests are directly or indirectly related to these basic ideas:

1. The reduction of the monastic orders: "The begging friars are a curse. . . . Many monasteries should be suppressed and no more founded. It would be an excellent thing if the inmates were allowed to leave when they pleased 'as in the times of the apostles and long after.'"

2. The abolishment of celibacy: "We see how it has happened that many a poor priest is burdened with wife and child and wounded in his conscience, and yet no one does anything to help him. . . . I advise that it be left free to every man to marry or not as he chooses."

3. The abolishment of canon law and the adoption of the Bible as the foundation of law: ". . . it were good if canon law, from the first to the last letter, . . . were eradicated. More than enough law is to be found in the Bible. In the schools of divinity the Bible should be supreme and other works be duly subordinated. Each city should have schools for boys and girls, where the gospel should be read to them either in Latin or German."

4. The abolishment of saints' days and all holidays except Sundays.

In addition the treatise includes a host of propositions concerning church and civil reforms, such as:

—the reduction of the papal court and the number of cardinals ("or else that the pope support them from his own purse").

—the abolishment of the interdict ("Is it not the devil's work to mend a sin by doing greater sin?")

—the abolishment of annates, provisions, plurality of offices, appeals to Rome, papal reservations, pilgrimages, and private masses.

—the recognition that Hus and Jerome of Prague were burned unjustly.

—the elimination of Aristotle from the universities. ("A potter has more natural science than is contained in all his books.")

—the precedence of state law over imperial law.

In many other propositions, such as those against extravagance in dress and against commerce, Luther is no longer the religious reformer but expresses the feeling and prejudices of a medieval peasant or craftsman.

Where the pamphlet *To the Christian Nobility of the German Nation* was primarily concerned with the practical abuses of the Church, Luther's second major treatise, *On the Babylonian Captivity of the Church of God,* focused on questions of dogma. Using the Bible again as his authority, Luther attacked the sacramental doctrines of the Church, maintaining that only three sacraments are documented in the Bible: baptism, penance, and holy communion. And even these three are only "sacramental signs" for the one true sacrament, the Word of God itself. The Church had added confirmation, marriage, ordination of priests, and extreme unction to the original sacraments, and there was no authorization for these additions in the Scriptures. Furthermore, the original three sacraments had been so abused by the Church that they had lost their meaning. Luther argued that the sacramental procedures were utterly pointless if faith were lacking. If a communicant did not believe in the Word of God, then the ritual of communion would be void of religions significance for him. Luther's argument was revolutionary, because it implied that the services of priests and the entire ritual of the Church were superfluous.

The third of these three crucial treatises, a little pamphlet of thirty pages published in November 1520 in both German and

Latin, was entitled *On the Liberty of a Christian Man*. This treatise is perhaps the most important of all because it shows for the first time a turn of mind which would have dangerous consequences for German evolution. It begins with a paradox: "A Christian is a free man, subject to none. A Christian is a dutiful servant, subject to all." These statements, Luther suggests, seem to contradict each other; but if we can reconcile them, they will edify us. "Both are contained in that saying of Paul's (1 Cor. 9:19) 'For though I be free from all men, yet have I made myself servant unto all.' Paul also says in Romans 13:8, 'Owe no man any thing, but to love one another.' True love, by its nature, is dutiful and obedient to what it loves. And in Galatians 4:4 we read of Christ: 'God sent forth his son, made of a woman, made under the law.'"

This linking of freedom and obedience, this interpretation of freedom as submission, is a characteristically German interpretation, and we shall come on it time and again as a pervading motif in German thought and history. But the truly pernicious aspect of Luther's theory is not evident in this conceivable, though highly questionable, interpretation of the relationship between freedom and obedience. In the course of his argument, Luther implies that man's nature is divided, that he is both spiritual and corporeal, and that these two elements are in constant combat, the spirit fighting the flesh, and the flesh fighting the spirit. From this he concludes: "But it is clear that external things have no effect on Christian liberty. . . . For what can it profit the soul if the body is well, free, and lively, eats, drinks, and does what it pleases, since even the wickedest slaves of all vice often have these advantages? Again, how can ill health or captivity or hunger or thirst hurt the soul, since the best men and those of the purest conscience often suffer these things?" Here is the fallacy. From the fact that the body is often able to conquer the spirit or the spirit is often able to conquer the body, Luther concludes that spirit and body are entirely separate and have nothing to do with each other. Luther's human being is divided into two different parts, and the mischief of this false division is further compounded by Luther's emphasis on faith as opposed to good works. "Good works," he says "do not make a good man, but a good man produces good works." It is certainly true that the mind and spirit are crucial factors in the total make-up of a man, but they

182

are by no means the only crucial factors. By performing good works one develops a taste for the good and for the beauty of goodness.

If people are taught that justification is by faith alone, they will come to disregard the importance of action altogether. This is exactly what happened to large segments of the German people. We first see this tendency in the Antinomians, and it persists to the time of Pastor Niemoeller, who let Nazi atrocities go unchallenged, finally opposing the Nazis only when they attacked the Protestant faith.

These three pamphlets had an immediate and widespread impact, and shortly after their appearance the struggle between Luther and the Church neared its climax. After Charles of Spain had been elected emperor and the Leipzig debate had brought Luther's heresy into the open, the proceedings against him were renewed. Another effort was made to induce Frederick to surrender Luther. The elector's importance for the pope had diminished now, and Saxony was threatened with an interdict in case Frederick did not comply. Later events showed, however, that the pope probably would not have resorted to such drastic measures. Again the threat did not work. Frederick replied in his usual courteous and procrastinating manner. The pope immediately appointed a commission to draw up a bull against the heretic. Eck's arrival in Rome precipitated the publication of this bull. After the Leipzig debate, Eck had visited several universities, urging them to support him and condemn Luther. Two of them, Cologne and Louvain, did so. Eck then went to Rome, and at his promptings, the pope issued the bull *Exsurge Domine* on June 15, 1520. Canon law provided that a heretic must be given a warning before he is condemned. Consequently, this bull did not excommunicate Luther, but only threatened excommunication in case he did not recant within sixty days after publication of the bull in Germany. The bull begins with the words: "Arise, Lord, plead Thine own cause, arise and protect Thy vineyard from the wild beast who is devouring it." Eck, who had been instrumental in drawing up the bull, was commissioned to post it in Germany. Before he could do so, however, Hutten published the document there, thinking it would do more harm to the Church than to Luther. Eck officially posted the bull at Meissen, Merseburg, and Brandenburg toward the end of September. He also tried to force it on the universities of Germany, but he had little success. At Erfurt the students seized all the printed copies and threw them into the river.

Hoping to secure an imperial condemnation of Luther, Leo X dispatched Aleander and Caracciolo as his nuncios to Charles and to the Reichstag. Charles was to be crowned emperor in October 1520 and to preside at his first diet in Worms in early 1521. After posting the bull *Exsurge Domine* in Cologne, Aleander met with the emperor-elect and persuaded him to issue a condemnation of Luther effective in the Netherlands.

Charles was crowned at Aachen on October 23. The plague broke out in the overcrowded city, and the royal suite, including the nuncio, was forced to leave. They went to Cologne, where the elector Frederick, while traveling to the coronation, had been detained by an attack of gout. Frederick had posted an "Offer and Protestation" by Luther, and he carried with him a humble appeal from Luther to the emperor. The elector was hard pressed to deliver the heretic. Frederick consulted with Erasmus, who was also in Cologne at the time, and asked him if Luther had erred. The answer he received quickly spread all over Germany: "Yes, Luther has erred in two points, in attacking the crown of the pope and the bellies of the monks." Erasmus recommended that Luther's case be submitted to a tribunal of learned and impartial men. In a second interview with the nuncios, Frederick refused their requests and insisted on such a court as Erasmus had suggested.

The sixty days allowed for Luther's recantation expired at the end of November. Instead of recanting, however, he struck back at his enemies, publishing two manifestoes against the bull, then publicly burning both it and the canon law. A notice to the students, drawn up and posted by Melanchthon on the morning of December 10, read as follows: "Let whosoever adheres to the truth of the gospel be present at nine o'clock at the Church of the Holy Cross outside the city walls where the impious books of papal decrees and Scholastic theology will be burnt according to ancient and apostolic usage, inasmuch as the boldness of the enemies of the gospel has grown so great that they daily burn the evangelic books of Luther. Come, pious and zealous youth, to this pious and religious spectacle, for now is the time when the antichrist must be revealed!" At the set time, a large crowd gathered just outside the Elster gate near the Black Cloister. The students built a pyre; a "certain master," probably Melanchthon, lit it; and Luther threw the whole canon law into the flames, then added the bull of Leo X, whom he apostrophized in these solemn words: "Because thou hast brought down the truth of God, He also brings thee down unto this fire today. Amen." After the professors had left, the students sang dirges and diverted themselves at the pope's expense.

Excommunication was inevitable now. The "holy curse" was signed in Rome on January 3, 1521, and sent to Aleander. Not only did it ban both Luther and his followers, such as Hutten and Pirckheimer, but it also denounced the elector Frederick. The nuncio to the Diet of Worms rightly feared that the document would militate against the cause of the Church rather than further it. He therefore returned the bull to Rome for revision. This proved extremely fortunate, because the revised bull, excommunicating Luther alone, was not published at Worms until May 6, three weeks after Luther had appeared before the Reichstag.

The main tasks for this meeting of the Reichstag were the drafting of a constitution for the empire and the formulation of grievances against the tyranny of the Roman hierarchy. The Reichstag could hardly overlook the religious controversy that was raging throughout Germany, but the unprecedented decision to summon the heretic before the diet of the empire was not reached until the Reichstag had been in session for a month. Luther himself did not expect to be called before the diet. He hoped instead to be allowed to defend his doctrines before a specially appointed tribunal of able and impartial theologians. Erasmus continued to advocate this plan.

The Curia Romana opposed this solution violently. They saw no reason for giving Luther a chance to defend his convictions and wished only to punish the condemned man. Aleander advocated the policy of the Curia, and he enjoyed the full support of the emperor. Two camps began to form. One sided with the Church, the other with Luther. Frederick, "that fox and basilisk," as Aleander called him, was foremost among Luther's sympathizers; and the elector Palatinate also favored the heretic. The common people, too, were strongly behind Luther. "Nine tenths of the Germans," wrote Aleander, "shout 'Long live Luther' and the other tenth 'Death to Rome.'" During the proceedings, Hut-

185

ten and his followers gathered near Worms and threatened to destroy the papists if any harm should come to Luther.

Aleander addressed the diet on February 18, 1521, condemning the new heresy in the strongest language he could summon and demanding that proper steps be taken to extirpate the impending schism and its author. After a stormy debate the Reichstag decided to summon Luther to recant his heresies and to be questioned on points concerning the power of the pope and the grievances of the German nation. The emperor drew up a formal summons, addressing the excommunicated man as "honorable, dear, and pious"; giving as the purpose of the citation "to obtain information about certain doctrines originating with you and about certain books written by you"; and assuring a safe-conduct to and from the diet. Even at this late date mediators were hoping to settle the matter amicably by asking Luther to repudiate only a few objectionable articles. When these articles were forwarded by Spalatin, Luther answered: "I shall recant nothing. . . . I shall answer the emperor that if I am summoned solely for the sake of recantation, I shall not come. . . . I could recant just as well here if that is their only business. But if he wishes to summon me to death, holding me an enemy of the empire, I shall offer to go. With Christ's aid I will not flee, nor will I abandon His word in the battle. I am convinced that those bloody men will never rest until they slay me. But if it were possible, I would want the pope's followers alone to be guilty of my blood."

The expected summons and safe-conduct reached Luther on March 26. On April 2 he set out, accompanied by his colleague Amsdorf, a brother monk, and a young student. The town provided a wagon and horses, and the university voted twenty gulden to cover the expenses. The journey was a triumphal one for Luther. He preached at Erfurt and was given a hero's welcome there. But despite all the popular support he enjoyed and despite the imperial safe-conduct, Luther was still in considerable danger. Spalatin warned him of this, but he answered: "I am coming . . . and I shall enter Worms though I must pass through the gates of hell and defy the princes of the air."

He arrived in Worms on the morning of April 16 and was greeted by a vast throng of people. At four o'clock the next day he was summoned to the Reichstag, but he was not actually admitted until nearly six. This appearance before the emperor, the princes, and the representatives of the free cities of the empire was one of the high points in Luther's career. The proceedings were brief and to the point. An officer warned Luther that he must say nothing except in answer to the questions he would be asked. Then an official of the archbishop of Trier asked him whether the books lying on the table were his and whether he wished to stand by all that he had said in them or to recant some part. Luther answered that the books were indeed his. As to the second question, he asked that time be granted him for deliberation. He had expected that certain articles would be questioned and that he would have an opportunity to defend them in debate, but he was not ready to recant without a chance to present his case. The session was adjourned, and Luther was ordered to appear the next day at the same time.

The following day the same question was put to Luther again. He answered with a major oration, first in German and then in Latin, citing canon law to the effect that the doctrines of the pope are to be held erroneous if they ran counter to the Bible; and he asked that he be proved wrong with evidence from the Gospels or the Prophets, "for I am most ready to be instructed and when convinced will be the first to throw my books into the fire." "Let us take care," he added, "that the rule of this excellent youth, Prince Charles . . . does not begin inauspiciously. For I could show by many examples drawn from the Scriptures that when Pharaoh and the king of Babylon and the kings of Israel thought to pacify and strengthen their kingdoms by their own wisdom, they really only ruined themselves. . . ."

The interrogating official replied: "Luther, you have not answered to the point. You ought not to call in question what has been decided and condemned by councils. Therefore, I beg you to give a simple, unsophisticated answer without horns. Will you recant or not?"

Luther answered: "Since your Majesty and your Lordships ask for a plain answer, I will give you one without either horns or teeth. Unless I am convicted by the Scriptures or by right reason —for I trust neither in popes nor in councils, since they have often erred and contradicted themselves—unless I am thus convinced, I am bound by the texts of the Bible. My conscience is captive to the Word of God. I cannot and will not recant anything, since it is neither right nor safe to act against conscience. God help me. Amen."

The Spaniards in the audience broke into groans and hisses, the Germans into applause. Luther left the hall amid growing tumult. When he reached his lodgings, he joyfully exclaimed: "It is done!" He had held his ground.

On April 26 he left Worms. About a week later, while traveling toward Schloss Altenstein, he was taken captive by masked riders who rode with him to the Wartburg, the castle where Luther's protectors had decided to keep him.

In the meantime, decisive steps had been taken at Worms. Charles V had been sincerely shocked by the audacity of the heretic. He wrote a statement, which he later read to the electors and to some princes, affirming that he would stake all to uphold the Catholic faith of his fathers. After waiting until the elector of Saxony and other of Luther's allies had left Worms, the emperor drafted an edict which he submitted to four electors and to a few remaining members of the diet for approval. This Edict of Worms, signed on May 26, described Luther's doctrine as a cesspool of heresies and prohibited the printing and circulation of his works. In addition, it placed Luther under the ban of the empire, forbade anyone to shelter him, and demanded that he be turned over to the authorities.

After the Diet of Worms, the reform movement assumed again the independent existence it had led in its early stages. For a short time, the history of the Reformation, indeed, the history of Germany and of Europe, had merged with the personal history of Martin Luther. But now all the currents of thought and feeling that Luther had drawn together rushed ahead, no longer subject to his control, and evolved into a vast movement that affected men of all classes and callings and that impinged on all fields of human activity. The political and cultural transformations that Europe underwent in the course of this evolution pointed the way that history would take in the modern era.

# 23.

## THE SPREAD OF PROTESTANTISM

FROM THE Wartburg Luther was unable to exert any direct influence on public life. Indeed, during this year of his retreat, the movement he had initiated developed an impetus of its own. As a result, Luther's personal career can no longer be our primary concern. We shall focus instead on the social and political changes his religious revolution effected throughout Europe.

Of these changes, perhaps none is more crucial than the shift that took place in the power structure of the empire itself. The broad political and cultural divisions of modern Germany can in part be traced back to the Diet of Worms, for it was there that the territorial princes first gravitated into two camps formed on the basis of lasting convictions rather than of particularistic interests or political expediency. A group sympathetic toward evangelical reform stood out openly against a staunchly Catholic group. Among those whom Luther won to his cause at Worms was Philip, landgrave of Hesse, an energetic and ambitious young prince who became the leading figure and ablest champion of Lutheranism after the death of Frederick of Saxony. The outspokenly evangelical group was still a small minority at Worms, but its influence should not be underestimated. Charles V obviously did not take its presence lightly, because he cautiously waited until the Lutheran sympathizers had left the diet before he issued his edict condemning Luther. From this point on, the evangelical forces gained strength rapidly, and the conflict between the two groups became increasingly sharp.

Political circumstances contributed a great deal to the spread of the Reformation and, therefore, to the ever widening rift between orthodox Catholics and the reform movement. After the

189

Diet of Worms, the emperor returned to Spain and became involved in a series of wars with the French king, Francis I, for domination of Italy. The first war in this twenty-year dispute lasted from 1521 to 1526, a crucial period for the development of the Reformation. With the leader of the Catholic party absent from Germany, the Reichstag met at Nürnberg in 1522. Influenced by Frederick of Saxony, it declared the Edict of Worms impracticable and demanded the convocation of a general council of the Church. Thousands of people—among them many members of the diet and even a sister of the emperor—defied the pope and his nuncio, Campeggi, by taking communion in both kinds from the hands of the Lutheran pastor Osiander. In 1525, the grand master of the order of Teutonic Knights in Prussia, Albrecht von Brandenburg, dissolved the order and adopted Lutheranism for himself as well as for his territory. In 1526, Philip of Hesse, the princes of Lüneburg, Prussia, and Magdeburg, and Frederick's successor, Johann of Saxony, formed the League of Torgau, the first organization of princes sympathetic to Luther. At the Diet of Speyer held in this same year, the league was able to procure an enactment that favored Lutheran doctrine by leaving decisions relating to faith in the hands of the estates. In the Catholic camp, the dukes of Bavaria and several bishops of southern Germany closed forces with Ferdinand of Austria, Charles's younger brother, in the Convention of Regensburg.

During this time, however, Charles had been victorious in his war against Francis and had concluded this struggle with the Peace of Madrid in 1526. In 1529, he won a second war against Francis. The successes of the emperor strengthened the position of Ferdinand and the Catholic party in Germany; accordingly, in 1529, a second Diet at Speyer reaffirmed the Edict of Worms and resolved to enforce it strictly. The Lutheran sympathizers among the princes protested. Hence, Luther's followers came to be called Protestants. In the following year, at the Reichstag of Augsburg, where the emperor again presided in person, the Protestants presented their *Confessio Augustana*, the Augsburg Confession, written by Melanchthon. Eck attacked the confession with a "Confutatio" that was countered in turn by a Protestant "Apology." The Protestant effort proved unsuccessful, however, and the diet voted to abolish all reforms.

In response to this challenge, the Protestant princes and cities drew even closer together, forming the League of Schmalkalden at the end of the year 1530. By that time, Protestantism had spread throughout Germany, branching out from Saxony and Hesse to Ansbach-Bayreuth, Braunschweig-Lüneburg, Mecklenburg, Anhalt, Mansfeld, Eastern Frisia, Schleswig-Holstein, Prussia, parts of Silesia, and to many cities, such as Magdeburg, Nürnberg, Ulm, Reutlingen, Constance, Strassburg, Hamburg, Lübeck, and Rostock. In all these cities and principalities, the supreme ecclesiastical power had been transferred to the secular authorities, thus providing the basis for the development of the territorial churches (*Landeskirchen*).

Charles V was not able to give his full attention to resolving religious strife in Germany until 1546. Before that he had been obliged to devote his energies to innumerable campaigns from Tunis and Algeria to the Provence, Flanders, and Hungary. Only after the successful conclusion of these campaigns and after the final, decisive defeat of his archenemy, Francis I, could Charles turn to Germany and her problems. But by then it was too late. Sweden, Norway, and Denmark had become Protestant. The reform movements of Zwingli and Calvin were well established in Switzerland. Calvin had published his *Christianae Religionis Institutio* in 1535 and had founded his theocratic state in Geneva in 1541. Calvinism had taken root in Scotland, and in France and Hungary the Calvinists formed important minorities. In Holland they were soon the dominant Protestant group. Other Protestant sects like the Anabaptists and the Bohemian Brethren sprang up, and nearly all of northern Germany had joined the Lutheran movement.

The Reformation had taken a firm hold all over Europe by the time Charles V finally decided to eliminate it in Germany and to restore the unity of the Church. Even if he had been able to achieve these goals, his success would have been temporary. The movement had become much too strong for him to control. The Catholic Church had realized this and had already assembled its forces for the Counter-Reformation, an effort to reestablish the authority of the Catholic Church throughout Europe. At this late date Charles V started his local war against the German Protestants, a war that was also intended as a last, decisive test of strength between the emperor and the territorial principalities, a last attempt to bring the German princes under imperial rule. Charles had been able to subdue the Spanish princes, but Ger-

191

many was not Spain, and the outcome of Charles's Schmalkaldian War (1546-1547) illustrates how powerless the emperor had become in Germany. Although Charles's forces won a military victory, Charles was ultimately defeated in his purpose because of the intrigues of Duke Maurice of Saxony.

The Schmalkaldian War began when the Protestant princes refused to attend or recognize the Council of Trent. In response, Charles placed the leaders of the League of Schmalkalden—the elector John Frederick of Saxony and the landgrave Philip of Hesse—under the ban of the empire. Duke Maurice of Saxony, the nephew of Luther's old enemy Duke George, concluded a secret alliance with the emperor, although he was nominally a Protestant himself. Maurice then invaded the territory of his cousin, the elector John Frederick, while Charles's Spanish and Italian troops were conquering the Protestants of southern Germany. Charles defeated the elector of Saxony in the battle of Mühlberg, occupied all of Saxony, and entered Wittenberg as a conqueror. Having taken the elector of Saxony and the landgrave of Hesse prisoner, Charles transferred to Maurice the title of elector and the electoral lands while leaving to John Frederick, the former elector, only Thuringia and the ducal title.

The emperor assumed that he had achieved his goals, and at a diet in Augsburg in 1548, he imposed an "interim" on the Protestants, commissioning Maurice to enforce its terms. The "interim" permitted Protestant forms of communion and the marriage of priests but required complete submission to the Catholic Church. Maurice, however, had changed his loyalties. He had attained what he wanted, and now he was concerned with preserving his independence and the independence of the territorial princes as a group. He was also incensed because the emperor had refused his request to free his father-in-law, Philip of Hesse. Consequently, Maurice entered into an alliance with Henry II, king of France, who, at Maurice's instigation, invaded Lorraine and occupied Metz, Toul, and Verdun. At the same time, Maurice attempted to capture the emperor, who was on his way to Trent, and nearly succeeded in seizing him at Innsbruck. After this narrow escape, the emperor found himself stranded at Villach in Carinthia without troops, funds, or followers. Once again it was a Fugger, this time Jacob's nephew, Anton, who lent an emperor money and rescued him from an embarrassing situation.

192

Charles's victory in the Schmalkaldian War had turned into defeat. With Ferdinand as his mediator, he was forced to negotiate new and, for him, disastrous terms with the princes of the Schmalkaldian League. Philip of Hesse and John Frederick of Saxony were liberated, the "interim" was abolished, and free exercise of religion was granted to the adherents of the Augsburg Confession until the next diet, which took place in 1555. In that year, the religious Peace of Augsburg was concluded. The territorial princes and the free cities that had adopted the Augsburg Confession were granted freedom of worship, the right to introduce the Reformation within their territories (*jus reformandi*), and equal rights with the Catholic states. The principle of *Cujus regio ejus religio*, the right of the princes to determine the religion of their subjects, was thus established. Dissenters in any territory were allowed to emigrate.

Charles never returned to Germany, nor was he ever able to recover the cities of Toul, Metz, and Verdun from France. Having lost on all fronts, he abdicated and retired to the Spanish monastery of San Yuste, where he died in 1558.

The German territorial princes had won their independence, and Protestantism had established itself as a legally acknowledged rival to Catholicism. Religious struggle continued throughout the sixteenth century. The Inquisition terrorized Spain and Italy; France was torn by the Huguenot Wars; and in Germany tension between the rival camps continued to mount well into the seventeenth century when it finally broke out in the Thirty Years' War. In this major conflict, as in the history of the Reformation itself, political ambition as well as religious conviction played a central role. Predominantly religious motives characterized the first two phases of the Thirty Years' War, the Bohemian and Danish periods, and even the beginning of the third, or Swedish, period. In northern and central Europe, the cause of religious revolution overshadowed any other concern; and the Catholic faction, too, was much more sincere in its defense of the faith now than it had been in the Renaissance. But despite the religious fervor generated in the early stages of the war, it gradually became clear that the real issue at stake was whether France or the House of Hapsburg would gain political control of Europe. The rivalry that had begun in the struggles between Charles V and Francis I was now being fought out on German soil. The insignificance of

193

religious conviction in the later years of the war is demonstrated by the fact that the French, who persecuted the Huguenots in their own territory, did not hesitate to ally themselves with Protestant princes in Germany and Scandinavia in order to achieve their political ends.

After the Thirty Years' War, the religious antagonism between Catholicism and Protestantism expressed itself in rival modes of life. The Austrians and Bavarians developed a distinctly Catholic mentality and character. The pleasures of life could be enjoyed as long as one accepted the dogma of the Church, observed its rites, and sought absolution for sin through confession. In the course of increasing secularization in the modern period, this attitude resulted in a separation of religion from everyday life. Both spheres became autonomous; neither interfered with the other. In Prussia, on the other hand, a distinctly Protestant mentality developed, shaping society and state. Here, no separation of religion and life took place. Religious obligations assumed the role of a moral code in everyday life, and in the course of secularization, religion and its precepts were transformed into service to the state and community. The old Roman Limes marked the dividing line between Protestant and Catholic Germany, and a similar division ran throughout Europe. The Counter-Reformation had succeeded in Italy, Spain, and France. Scandinavia and the Netherlands, however, could not be won back to the Catholic Church.

In the territory of the Holy Roman Empire, the conflict between Prussia and Austria, beginning with the Seven Years' War and ending with Bismarck's victory over Austria in 1866, perpetuated the underlying division between the Protestant North and Catholic South. In this struggle, Austria was doomed from the start. Under the conditions of the modern era, the disciplined, industrious Protestant mentality was destined to acquire and wield power. If we survey European history from the Diet of Worms to the late nineteenth century, we can readily see how the course of that history was foreshadowed at Worms in 1521. Luther's refusal to recant signaled the end of Catholic domination in Europe. His act prompted the coalescence of the religious and political forces that would dominate German and European history thoughout modern times.

194

# 24.

## MÜNZER AND THE ANABAPTISTS

THE REFORMATION could not help but effect major changes in the lives of the masses as well as in the politics and policies of kings, princes, and emperors. One such change was the end of the knights as an independent social class. Led by Hutten and Sickingen, they had hoped to utilize their alliance with the forces of the Reformation to regain their former position. But their campaign of 1523 against the ecclesiastical princes of the Rhine valley ended in defeat, and they were never able to rally again.

In this conflict, too, religious conviction sometimes gave way to political expedience. Philip of Hesse, for example, joined the ecclesiastical princes in putting down the knights even though he was a champion of the Protestant cause himself and should, by rights, have sided with the knights in their attack on the Catholic princes. But he was a prince before he was a Protestant, and it was more important to him to uphold the authority of his class than to defend his faith.

Though not particularly laudable, Philip's behavior in this case is not completely surprising. It is not astonishing that a prince would let political considerations take precedence over religious ones. But that Luther himself, the figurehead of the Protestant cause, would turn against the Protestant knights is astonishing, if not shocking. He had previously accepted the aid of Hutten and Sickingen at a critical point in his career when Frederick of Saxony and the knights were the only support he could count on. But now, after the Diet of Worms, he deserted his former allies and denounced their attack on the ecclesiastical princes. In this action we can see the moral consequences of the division between soul

195

and body that Luther made in his treatise *On the Liberty of a Christian Man*. Although Luther had attacked the religious abuses and worldly power of the ecclesiastical princes, he could not condone actual revolt against them. They were, after all, princes as well as ecclesiastics, that is, they were secular authorities to whom the population owed unquestioning obedience.

What Luther had done was to take the medieval concept of a division between soul and body and adapt this concept to a new era, laying the foundations of German middle-class morality and dividing the human being into a creature whose spirit and soul were totally free but whose body was totally subject to the demands of state and society. Luther himself could be utterly consistent and intrepid in matters of faith, risking martyrdom if need be; but at the same time his doctrine of justification by faith encouraged indifference toward active, political life, because salvation depended wholly on faith and individual penance, not on good works. In Part I of this study we saw how German history, from its very beginnings, prepared the way for the Lutheran doctrine. The desire for freedom and subjection was present in the Germanic chieftains who conquered Rome; later, feudalism and the craft-guild cities encouraged this tendency in the German character. As we go ahead to study German history after Luther, we shall see how this Lutheran division of soul and body remained a constant and decisive factor in modern Germany. Indeed, the course of the Reformation during Luther's own lifetime —the ideological conflicts and the Peasants' War of 1524-1525— already illustrates the grave consequences Luther's doctrine had, and would continue to have, for German society. The Peasants' War was the only true revolution that Germany ever experienced, and its failure was to have a permanently inhibiting effect on the German revolutionary spirit.

The events leading up to the Peasants' War go back to the year when Luther was in hiding at the Wartburg. During Luther's absence from Wittenberg, his disciples Carlstadt, Zwilling, and Melanchthon assumed control of the reform movement. Since Melanchthon, who was the closest of the three to Luther, was primarily a scholar, he left the practical matters of leadership to his more active and revolutionary colleagues who now began to put some of Luther's reform proposals into practice. Under their influence the town council passed ordinances diverting the income from the property of twenty-one resident brotherhoods and from endowed masses to a common fund for the city. This money was to provide for orphans, help students at the schools and the university, supply poor girls with dowries, and loan capital to craftsmen. The town fathers were charged with the surveillance of morals, particularly with the suppression of brothels. In the churches all pictures and superfluous altars were to be removed, and communion was to be administered in both kinds.

Social reforms went hand in hand with religious ones and were often accompanied by violence. Zwilling's sermons against the mass and the canonical hours incited the population to riot. Zwilling also campaigned against the monasteries, threatening and insulting the monks in an attempt to drive them away from the monastic life. Carlstadt attacked the mass with such success that the priests celebrating it in the parish church were stoned.

Disorder spread. Monks at Erfurt left the cloister, and plans were made to stop all masses on January 1, 1522, not only in Wittenberg but in the surrounding country as well. A rectory was plundered, and the citizens of Wittenberg demonstrated in force against the presence of relics in the Castle Church.

Much disturbed by all this turmoil, Luther secretly visited Wittenberg early in December 1521. On leaving, he issued a "Warning to all Christians to keep from Uproar and Sedition." In this document he argued that tumult is the work of the devil and that all Christians should shun it, working for their goals by peaceful means only.

Luther's admonition might have checked the violent mood if the party of revolution had not received new support from the so-called prophets of Zwickau. Thomas Münzer, a religious and social radical, had brought the weavers of this small Saxon town together in a sect bent on reforming both state and church. This remarkable man, who was later to play a leading role in the Peasants' War, was born in 1498 in Stolberg in the Harz Mountains. His father is said to have died on the gallows, executed by the despotic counts of Stolberg. Unusually talented in theology, Thomas quickly earned a doctor's degree and a chaplainship in Halle. Under the influence of the German mystics and the writings of Joachim de Flores, he treated the dogma and rites of the Catholic Church with conspicuous contempt, prophesying the millennium as well as imminent punishment for a degenerate Church

197

and a wicked world. He interpreted Luther's Reformation and the general upheavals of the times as omens of the great chiliastic event predicted by Joachim de Flores.

In 1520 Münzer went to Zwickau as the first Protestant pastor of that community. Here he encountered the Anabaptists, a sect that had developed independently of the Reformation. The Anabaptist movement went back to the mystics, to Wycliffe and Hus, and possibly as far back as the Waldenses. Pamphlets reflecting the feelings and desires of the common people, especially of the peasants, had appeared during the fifteenth century. The best known of these pamphlets propagates the idea of a divine natural law which does not countenance the corrupt institutions of serfdom and bondage but grants all men equal rights to pastures, woods, and waters. (At this time peasants were forbidden to hunt and to fish.) The author of this pamphlet considers communism the order God had intended for the world, but sinful men had corrupted this order. The pamphlet advocates the secularization of Church property and revenues as well as the abolition of monasteries, of donations to the Church, and of ecclesiastical and secular rule. The emperor should be the sole ruler, and only he should be allowed to levy taxes and establish a uniform coinage. But even he is subject to law, and if he fails in the exercise of his duties, the people may impeach him. As the pamphlet says, "The people can exist without the emperor, but the emperor cannot exist without the people."

These early pamphlets anticipate many Anabaptist teachings. Anabaptist doctrine derives its authority not only from the Bible, just as Protestant doctrine does, but also from individual inspiration and conscience, from the presence of God in the individual soul. The preachers of the Anabaptist movement were prophets who expected the early advent of the millennium to fulfill all their dreams and claims. Many of these preachers died for their convictions. The princes and the city authorities, later even the authorities in Protestant cities, drowned and burned the Anabaptist prophets, for they realized that a vast and dangerous revolutionary movement was spreading all over Germany, Switzerland, and the Netherlands, inciting the peasants and the poor people in the cities to rebellion. The Anabaptist movement revived the idea of an evangelical community in which law and rulers would be superfluous, a community in which peace, love, and charity

198

reigned supreme. In accordance with these ideals, the Anabaptists rejected the use of arms and other customs not substantiated in the Gospels, particularly infant baptism and the taking of oaths. The Anabaptists, now known simply as the Baptists, derive their name from this rejection of infant baptism and from the belief that the baptized should actively participate in the sacrament.

The Zwickau Anabaptists did not win Münzer to their movement, but he felt a strong kinship with them, and when the Anabaptists came into conflict with the city authorities, he defended them and was expelled from the city with them. In 1522, after a short stay in Prague, Münzer became a preacher in the Thuringian town of Altstedt where he initiated reforms in the church service, doing away with Latin altogether and reading the Bible from the pulpit. He not only adopted Luther's revolutionary language but actually urged the Saxon princes and people to take up arms against the Roman clergy. "Didn't Jesus Christ say He had not come to bring peace but the sword? . . . And did He not, according to Luke 19:27, command His followers to seize His enemies and slay them before His eyes?"

Münzer also taught a mystical pantheism in which the Holy Ghost is identical with human reason. Faith is nothing but the awakening of reason in man. Through reason man becomes fit to partake of the divine. Accordingly, the kingdom of God is not in the beyond but is to be found and realized here on earth. For Münzer, hell, damnation, and the devil do not exist, but only the evil and greed of men. He saw Christ as a human being, a great prophet and teacher, and the kingdom of God as a classless society in which private property and governmental authority would no longer exist.

These ideas were anathema to Luther. Not only did they go far beyond his religious doctrine, which was strictly based on the Scriptures, but they encouraged social revolution and threatened to discredit the Reformation in the eyes of the princes and of the urban middle class.

Even before Münzer had begun his revolutionary activities in Altstedt, the Anabaptist preachers Storch, Stübner, and Drechsel had gone to Wittenberg where they and their doctrines were well received. Some Wittenberg leaders acquiesced to the ascendancy of the "prophets" or "ranters," as Luther called them; others actually joined them. Carlstadt was particularly taken by the new ideas, and even the cautious Melanchthon wavered, impressed by the arguments against infant baptism and by the Anabaptists' visions. Luther warned his friend against the newcomers and their doctrines: "Those who bear witness of themselves are not to be believed. Spirits must be proved. . . . God never sent anyone who was not either called by men or attested by miracles. . . . Do not receive them if they assert that they come by mere revelation. . . . Pray search their innermost spirit and see whether they have experienced those spiritual straightenings, that divine birth, death, and infernal torture. . . ."

Tumult continued in Wittenberg. Melanchthon was not able to cope with the situation, and he besought the elector to allow Luther to return and quiet the disturbances that were arising in his lands, but the cautious prince refused to do so. On January 11, 1522, the Augustinians solemnly burned all their sacred images. The disorders attracted the attention of Duke George of Albertine Saxony, who not only protested to his cousin, but also complained to the Imperial Executive Council (*Reichsregiment*) at Nürnberg. On February 20, the town council, without consulting the elector, sent an urgent request to Luther, imploring him to return to Wittenberg. Luther appealed to the elector, who again advised him to be patient and to wait until after the next diet. But Luther did not follow this advice, and on March 3 he set out for Wittenberg. From a stop on the way he wrote the elector a letter of apology: "The devil knows I did not hide because of cowardice, for he saw my heart when I entered Worms. Had I then believed that there were as many devils there as tiles on the roofs, I would have leaped into their midst with joy. Now Duke George is still far from being the equal of one devil. . . . Had I been called to Leipzig instead of Wittenberg I should have gone there, even if it had rained Duke Georges nine days, and every duke nine times as furious as this one. . . . I am writing this to your Grace to inform you that I am going to Wittenberg under a far higher protection than that of the elector. I do not intend to ask your Grace's protection. Indeed, I think I shall protect you rather than you me. If I thought your Grace could and would defend me by force, I would not come. The sword ought not and cannot decide a matter of this kind. God alone must decide it without human aid or intervention. He who believes the most can protect the most, and as I see your Grace is yet weak in faith, I can by no means regard you as the man to protect and save me." This letter shows Luther's personal independence as well as his determinism and his view of the Reformation as a purely religious and spiritual matter. Not even in his own interest or in the interest of his cause did he allow a secular power to employ force.

In Wittenberg, Luther lost no time in starting a vigorous campaign against the Anabaptists. In eight sermons he exhorted the people to good sense, moderation, and charity. "I will not compel or force anyone, for faith must be gentle and unforced. Take an example by me. I used no force in my attack on indulgences and on the papists. I only wrote, preached, and used God's Word; and while I drank beer with Melanchthon and Amsdorf and slept, He did more to destroy the papacy than any king or emperor ever did." In saying this, however, Luther forgot the support the elector and the knights had lent him.

Later, when the political situation forced the Protestants to defend their faith, Luther was obliged to permit the use of violence; but he did insist on finding a legal sanction for it. The question of violence was taken up at a meeting of jurists and theologians held at Torgau in 1531. Luther attended this meeting and reported that "the jurists first advanced the theory that force could be repelled by force. This did not satisfy me. They then pointed out that a positive imperial law provided that 'in cases of notorious injustice the government might be resisted by force,' to which I merely replied that I did not know whether this was the law or not but that if the emperor had thus limited himself we might . . . , *as the law permits, resist by force.*" Here we see the modern, middle-class German mentality at its most absurd. Who else but a German would ask whether his oppressor had made it legal to rebel against oppression? German "revolutionaries" have always been inhibited by this compulsion to seek official approval for their revolutionary acts. In 1848, the liberal revolutionaries debated the legality of revolution, and Hitler understood the German mind well enough to see that the people would accept his coup d'état only if it were accomplished "with the permission of the Reichspresident (mit der Erlaubnis des Herrn Reichspräsidenten)."

Luther deviated again from his principle of non-violence when he insisted that the government enforce uniformity in religious practices. "Even unbelievers," he wrote, "should be forced to obey

201

the Ten Commandments, attend church, and conform in all out-ward appearances." Unlike Zwingli, Calvin, and Cromwell, he at least did not insist that dissenters be put to death.

Luther's campaign against the Anabaptists was successful, but their defeat in Wittenberg by no means put an end to their activi-ties. They continued to spread their doctrines elsewhere, and Münzer's influence as a preacher of revolution was instrumental in precipitating the Peasants' War, a major event in German his-tory and in the personal history of Martin Luther.

# 25.

---

## THE PEASANTS' WAR

Münzer had won a great following in Altstedt. Sacred images were removed from the churches; infant baptism was abolished; laws reducing interest and providing for the periodic repudiation of debts were passed; and the right to hold private property was questioned. Münzer also preached inflammatory sermons against the "godless," papists and Lutherans alike. The breach between Münzer and the Lutherans first becomes evident in a letter written in the spring of 1524. Münzer wrote to Melanchthon that the Lutherans did not understand the new religious impulse of the time. Their preoccupation with the letter of the Scriptures stifled this emerging spirit. "Dear brothers," he wrote, "give up your waiting and hesitation; the time of reaping has come. Do not maintain friendship with the godless who keep the Word from full fruition. Do not flatter your princes lest you perish together with them."

Although Luther adopted a number of reforms proposed by Münzer, he still remained basically hostile toward the new movement. Soon Münzer was referring to Luther as "that soft-living lump of flesh in Wittenberg" and taking every opportunity to heap abuse on Luther's head. Luther, for his part, called on the elector and his brother to use force against the Anabaptist revolutionaries. "Truly," he wrote, "here in Wittenberg I have . . . seen that they are intent on overturning the civil government and becoming lords of the world themselves. But Christ says His kingdom is not of this world and teaches His apostles not to be as the rulers of the earth. So . . . I humbly pray and warn your Graces to fulfil your duty as civil governors by preventing mischief and by forestalling rebellion." He urges the elector to "act rigorously against their storming and ranting, so that God's kingdom may be furthered by His word alone . . . and that all encouragement of sedition may cease."

At Luther's insistence the authorities of Altstedt finally drove Münzer from their city. He fled to Mühlhausen, where he joined forces with Heinrich Pfeiffer, an ex-friar and a leader of the town proletariat. Together, they succeeded in expelling the governing patriciate of the city and in gaining control of the city council. Münzer's next step was to join the peasants' movement that his own pamphlets and preachings had helped create.

The grievances of the peasants in the early sixteenth century provided ample enough cause for dissatisfaction that soon took the form of open rebellion. Very few peasants owned the land they cultivated. The vast majority were villeins. They were free themselves, but their land was subject to dues, and they were obliged to perform services for their lords. The "lord" might be a prince, count, knight, bishop, abbot, or even a city. Some villeins paid only a yearly ground rent; others were so overburdened with dues and services that their condition bordered on serfdom. The lowest class of peasants was made up of serfs. Where the amounts of dues and services a lord could demand from the villeins were clearly defined, they were not defined at all for the serfs. The lord could legally demand all a serf's labor and everything he produced, though in many places local customs imposed certain limitations. The villeins formed the backbone of the peasants' revolution. These middle-class peasants, living in a semi-independent community near the estate of the lord, realized that increased dues and services were reducing them to near serfdom and that the village common was fast becoming part of the lord's manor.

Dues were usually collected in produce. Twice a year, in the spring and fall, the peasant had to give his lord a percentage of everything his fields, garden, forest, and animals produced. The lords also made special demands for holidays, feasts, births, baptisms, marriages, and deaths in the manor. Extra dues, taxes, and services were squeezed from the peasant on every pretext; and no allowances were made, even if crops were damaged by frost or drought. The Church, too, took her share of the peasant's harvest. There were three tithes payable yearly: the "great tithe" on

204

corn, rye, oats, wheat, and wine; the "small tithe" on fruit and vegetables; and the "meat tithe" on domestic animals.

Most irksome of all were the *Fronen* or unrewarded services. The peasant had to drop work on his own farm, no matter how urgent, in order to perform these services. The peasants of Stühlingen complained: "One day we must cut wheat; on another we must bind it; on still others we must plow, sow, thresh, cut hay and cart it to the barn, make fences, and help in the chase. We must provide wood, not only for fire but also for building. Often, when we can least spare the time, we must dig roots and pick berries for the lord. Our wives or helpers have to work the flax till it is ready for spinning. We are forced to drain the creeks, which harms us because we need the water. . . ."

Nearly every peasant manifesto complains bitterly of the *Todfall* or heriot. It was the custom for the lord to take from a widow the most valuable article (*Besthaupt*) her husband had left her, the best cow, horse, or even dress. Instead of goods, money was often taken, and the heriot eventually evolved into a regular death tax. "When a man or woman dies," complain the peasants of the monastery of Kempten, "an emissary from the monastery comes and takes an inventory of all the goods. No matter how many children the dead person leaves behind him . . . one half of the estate is always taken." The smaller the estate, the harder it was for the survivors to bear the loss of even a little, since death had already taken away the bread-winner of the family. As we have already seen, the knights tried to alleviate their own financial distress by squeezing more and more out of the peasants. As a class, the peasants were gradually losing whatever independence they still had. It was said that the freeman was becoming a villein, and the villein a serf.

Perhaps the most dangerous threat to peasant independence was the effort of the lords to seize the communal lands or *Allmende*, which consisted of forest, meadow, and heath. Every free member of the community had the right to pasture and wood. From the middle of the fifteenth century on, the lords had encroached on the communal lands by reviving old feudal claims to them, by issuing new regulations on their use, or by outright confiscation. "From earliest times," the peasants of Fürstenberg complain, "we were entitled to the use of the common forest,

205

meadow, and stream. But our lords have taken them away from us by force." If the lord happened to be a territorial prince, he lent these confiscations a semblance of legality by claiming over-lordship. The introduction of Roman law had done much to hasten this process. When a dispute over the use of forest, meadow, or stream came before a Roman jurist, the decision was invariably given in favor of the lord, since Roman law recognized only private property. The idea of communal holdings, so much a part of German peasant life since tribal times, was entirely foreign to Roman law. The peasants were particularly bitter about these transgressions against their rights to common land, and three of the famous *Twelve Articles*, the most important statement of the peasants' grievances, deal with this subject.

The aristocratic sport of hunting placed still another burden on the peasants. They were not allowed to kill game animals that destroyed their crops, and in 1517 the duke of Württemberg decreed that any peasant found carrying a gun or cross-bow off the marked paths in the woods and fields of the game preserves would lose both his eyes. The peasants were often called upon to assist in the hunt, acting as beaters, running after the hounds, and furnishing horses and wagons to the huntsmen. "We have to run after game all day without food and drink. Sometimes we are so tired that we can hardly walk, and for pay we receive only curses and kicks."

Overburdened with taxes, the peasant was often forced to seek loans from capitalists in the cities. The capitalists who held mortgages on the land of nominally free peasants were not satisfied with collecting interest but also demanded dues as though they were lords. Foreclosure of mortgages became so common that, as Luther said, "anyone who had 100 gulden to invest could gobble up a peasant a year with no more danger to his life and property than there is in sitting near a stove and roasting apples."

Luther understood the plight of the peasants very well, and he had no illusions about princes. In a widely circulated pamphlet of 1523 entitled "On Secular Authority and How Far It Should Be Obeyed," he did not hesitate to denounce the princes. "A clever prince is a rare bird, and a pious one is still rarer. Princes are usually either the greatest fools or the greatest scoundrels in the world; hence, little good may be expected of them. . . . We may not, we will not, we cannot tolerate their tyranny and wickedness any longer. . . . If these princes had a city or a castle taken away from them by the emperor, how quickly they would rise in revolt! Yet they consider it perfectly proper to oppress the poor and put down rebellions and then say that it was done at the command of the emperor. Such men used to be called rogues; now we call them god-fearing princes." But despite his awareness of the peasants' condition and the princes' tyranny, Luther would still urge the princes to put down the peasant rebellion with force.

A number of minor peasant uprisings preceded the Peasants' War of 1524-1525. As early as 1476, a peasant piper named Hans Böheim of Niklashausen near Würzburg declared that the Virgin Mary had come to him in a vision and revealed a new order for the world. There would be no rulers, lay or spiritual; taxes would be abolished; and all earthly goods would be held in common. Niklashausen soon became a shrine and Hans a prophet to thousands who came to hear him preach. An army of 34,000 peasants assembled one Sunday at Hans's command. The bishop of Würzburg, lord of the district, had Hans kidnapped, and the peasant ranks were decimated.

In 1493 the Alsatian peasants of the bishop of Strassburg organized a secret movement to abolish all debts, tithes, and dues. They took as their emblem the *Bundschuh*, a laced shoe of the kind usually worn by peasants. This emblem was emblazoned on their banners and from then on it became the symbol of peasant uprisings. In 1502, 1512, and 1514, further *Bundschuh* rebellions occurred, the first in the bishopric of Speyer, the next at Lehen in Baden, and the last in Württemberg. All these uprisings were immediately crushed by local authorities.

The despair that had been growing among the German peasantry ever since the Hussite wars had erupted sporadically in these small, local rebellions, but it was only after Luther and the Anabaptists had supplied the unifying element of religious revolution that the peasantry of the entire empire could rise against their oppressors.

The great Peasants' War of 1524-1525 began in the little village of Stühlingen in the Black Forest. The peasants there rebelled when the Countess Lupfen demanded that her tenants gather snail shells for her in addition to the many other duties they were obliged to perform. The imposition of still another chore, however slight, angered the peasants and evoked a violent response

207

from them. Hans Müller of Bulgenbach assumed leadership of the peasants, gathering a band of 1,200 men and forming a network of peasant organizations.

At about the same time disorder broke out in upper Swabia. An assembly of peasants had presented the abbot of Kempten with a list of grievances which he completely ignored. As a consequence, three contingents of peasants from different parts of the Black Forest and from around Lake Constance met in the city of Memmingen, organized themselves into a Christian brotherhood, and adopted the famous *Twelve Articles*.

Meanwhile, Georg Truchsess von Waldburg, the commander in chief of the Swabian League, assembled 8,000 foot soldiers and 3,000 horsemen. With these troops, he attacked and defeated the peasants at Leipheim. The peasants' leader, Jacob Wehe, was later tried and executed as a rebel. But the peasant movement continued to spread rapidly. Bands of armed men roamed the country, burning and plundering castles and monasteries and demanding recognition of the *Twelve Articles*. Many knights were forced to take service with them and become their leaders. Others did so voluntarily either to gain booty or to strike back at the princes who, a short while ago, had put down the knights' insurrection under Franz von Sickingen. One of these knights was the famous Götz von Berlichingen, a man of unstable personality and shifting loyalties. He had offered his services to the Swabian League, but when the League declined to accept them, he did not hesitate to go over to the peasants and become their commander-in-chief. Together with two other knights, Hipler and Weigand, he hoped to form a working alliance between the peasants and the knights.

Florian Geyer, the leader of the Franconian peasants, was also a knight but one of a different stamp than Götz. He was sincerely devoted to the peasant cause. At the head of his *Schwarzer Haufen*, a well-disciplined regiment of veteran soldiers, he marched on Würzburg to aid the citizens in their insurrection against the bishop of the city. Encouraged by the success of the peasants, the poor people of the cities had begun to rise up and demand a share in government. In Rothenburg ob der Tauber, a blind monk named Hans Schmidt led the people against the city government and reorganized the town on a communistic basis. "There is great division in the towns," the Bavarian chancellor, Eck,

208

wrote. "The poor among the Lutherans take the side of the peasants. The Catholics and the wealthy Lutherans oppose them."

Some members of the governing classes were paralyzed by fear and lack of initiative. Frederick of Saxony was lying mortally ill at his castle in Lochau. Without troops and worn out by disease, he wrote his brother John that if it was God's will that the common man should rule, he would not resist it: "There are 35,000 men in the field against us; we are lost." Others, however, were not so resigned. The troops of the Swabian League under Georg Truchsess, strengthened by additional men and supplies, joined forces with Philip of Hesse and marched against a peasant army of 8,000 at Frankenhausen. There, on March 15, 1525, the revolutionary forces suffered defeat and fled in disorder. More than 5,000 were slain in a few hours. Münzer, who had accompanied the peasant troops as their preacher and leader, was captured and later beheaded.

Complete suppression of the revolt now took only a few days. Truchsess defeated an army of 12,000 men in Württemberg and destroyed many villages. Now that the tide had turned, all the knights defected to the princes. Florian Geyer was the only one who remained loyal to the peasant cause. Once his *Schwarzer Haufen* was destroyed, the recapture of Würzburg was a simple matter, and all organized resistance from the peasants came to an end.

The peasants' rebellion failed because it lacked direction and organization. It was a broad and powerful revolutionary movement, but it had no leader capable of uniting the masses into an effective force. The result was that the trained mercenaries of the Swabian League could easily defeat the poorly armed and undisciplined peasant troops.

The revolt was put down with unparalleled cruelty and bloodshed. Over 100,000 peasants were slain. Fields, houses, and barns were pillaged and destroyed. Determined to take full revenge on the peasants, the lords now made services and dues more onerous than ever before, and the German peasantry sank into a state of despair that lasted for centuries.

All this was done not only with Luther's approval but with his encouragement. In May 1525, he issued a pamphlet "Against the Thieving and Murderous Hordes of Peasants," a truly un-Christian manifesto, which, for violence and brutality, is unmatched

209

even in Luther's writings. He denounced the peasants for calling themselves Christians and said that they were inspired not by Christ but by the devil. In response to the argument that Christianity preaches the equality and freedom of all men, Luther writes: "Baptism does not make persons and property free, but only the soul." He further declares that any prince who refuses to put rebels to death is himself guilty of murder and robbery. God has given the princes "a sword with which to punish evil doers. . . . Therefore, dear lords, . . . stab, slay, and strangle wherever you can. If you are killed in this struggle, you are indeed to be felicitated, as no nobler death could befall anyone. You will die in obedience to God's word and command and in the service of love, trying to rescue the people from the clutches of the devil." Even after the princes had suppressed the peasants with extreme brutality, Luther did not change his views: "My opinion is that it is better that all the peasants be killed than that the princes and magistrates perish, because the rebels took the sword without divine authority. . . . Wherefore no pity, no tolerance should be shown them, but the fury and wrath of God should be visited upon them. . . ."

Luther's behavior during the Peasants' War remains an ineradicable blemish on his life. He understood the background of the rebellion very well. He knew that the princes tyrannized and exploited the peasants, robbing them of their lands, their produce, and their labor. Yet all the crimes and cruelties the princes committed Luther considered authorized by God, while the just revolution of the peasants he denounced as the work of the devil.

A disastrous principle had been established. By separating soul and body and by divorcing salvation from works, Luther had limited the authority of the conscience to spiritual matters alone. In practical and political affairs, the individual conscience was forced to submit unquestioningly to the "God-given" authority of the state, no matter how corrupt that state might be. As Luther himself wrote in his pamphlet "Against the Thieving and Murderous Hordes of Peasants": "God would prefer to suffer the government to exist, no matter how evil, rather than allow the rabble to riot, no matter how justified they are in doing so." This was the new form Luther had imposed on that ancient Germanic desire for both freedom and submission: utter freedom in the realm of the mind and "spirit," utter subjection in the realm of the body and the body politic.

210

# 26.

## LUTHER'S INFLUENCE ON THE GERMAN CHARACTER

THROUGHOUT our survey of Luther's career, I have tried to suggest an explanation for the fact that Luther could accomplish a thoroughgoing religious reform yet respond to the peasant uprisings with a savagery that completely denied the basic tenets of Christianity. Part of that explanation lies in Luther's background. He was never able to free himself entirely from the peasant beliefs he acquired at home, and his violent opposition to the Peasants' War was to some extent an expression of his personal struggle to tame the rebellious peasant in his own character. Luther shared the peasant's belief that demons and devils were at work not only in the natural world but in man as well, prompting him to revolt against the authority of God. The impulse to rebel and the impulse to obey were equally strong in Luther, and in the course of his lifetime, first one, then the other determined his behavior. He defied the spiritual authority of the Church only to uphold the temporal authority of the princes during the Peasants' War.

The struggle between these two impulses was the basic component of Luther's monastic life. Plagued by a sense of ineradicable sin, he submitted himself to extremes of ascetic discipline in the hope of freeing his soul from the demonic forces that seemed to control him. But he could never perform enough good works to satisfy his Judge. It was only when the question of redemption could be divorced from external works and made a purely internal matter that he found a solution to his personal dilemma.

The Bible and the Pauline emphasis on justification by faith provided him with the cornerstone of his doctrine. Since the Bible had given him the answers he had been seeking, he surrendered himself entirely to it, devoting himself to its exegesis and depending upon it as the only valid authority in religious questions. He clung to the literal meaning of the Scriptures, failing to recognize that they are often inconsistent in themselves and that he had chosen to emphasize only those points and interpretations that were particularly meaningful to him personally. The result was a doctrine that erred as much in one direction as orthodox Catholic doctrine had erred in another. The Church's overemphasis on works had led to the abuses of the indulgence trade that Luther had attacked. His own overemphasis on faith and unmediated grace led to the partitioning of the human being that we noted in earlier chapters.

Luther's reform freed men from the rule of the Church, but it brought two new forms of submission with it. On the one hand, his urge to rebel and his desire for freedom led him to advocate spiritual submission to God alone, a submission that amounts to absolute freedom in the personal realm because it is not subject to any kind of human control or supervision. On the other hand, his need for authority and his desire to subdue the demonic forces in himself and in others led him to advocate submission to secular authority in the political realm. In its particular sphere, this secular authority is as binding on the Christian as the authority of the Bible is in the religious sphere. The solution Luther found for his own personal dilemma was also a solution for the basic dilemma of the German character. But the solution engendered new problems that were graver than the one solved. The arguments Luther martialed against the revolutionary peasants give early indication of how useful Lutheran doctrine would prove to be for innumerable tyrants throughout modern German history.

"There is to be no bondage, since Christ has freed us all? What does that mean? It makes Christian freedom a thing of the flesh alone and is therefore contrary to the Scriptures. It is an act of piracy because it robs a master of his bondsman. A bondsman can be a Christian and have Christian freedom just as a prisoner or a sick man can be Christian, even though they are not free. All this talk would make men equal and reduce the spiritual kingdom of Christ to a worldly kingdom. This is impossible, for a worldly kingdom cannot exist without inequality; some must be free, others captive; some must be lords, others subjects."

Luther's indifference to the nature of the worldly government was so extreme that he would even forbid Christians enslaved by the Turks to fight for their freedom: "That would be stealing your body from your master, for he bought it or acquired it in some way, and it is no longer your property but his, like cattle or other goods." In the less extreme circumstances of everyday life, this aspect of Luther's doctrine served to support the existing social and political order, an order supposedly established by God. Every secular calling, every profession or trade, was a true "calling" ordained by God. Consequently, no one was permitted to leave his station in life and move to a higher one unless God, acting through some temporal authority, saw fit to promote him. The stagnancy of German society and the German bureaucracy's hold over the people go back to this equation of divine and secular authority.

Both in his own time and in later eras, Luther's advocacy of unquestioning submission to secular authority exposed him to the charge of opportunism and of servility toward the princes. We have seen, though, that Luther could be harsh and outspoken with the princes, and it is incorrect to ascribe his position on secular authority to subservience. He did not arrive at this position because he was an opportunist but because he was a doctrinaire. He believed his tenets irrefutable because they were demonstrably based on the Scriptures. But he refused to consider that his literalistic readings of the Bible constituted very personal and arbitrary interpretations.

If Luther's mind had not taken the turn it did, he could well have been a great national leader. Instead of focusing on religious reform alone, he could have united and integrated all the social, cultural, and political movements of his age and of his country. Instead of creating just the prototype of the modern German, he could have created a modern German nation. But any speculation on what he could have accomplished is idle, because the fact that he accomplished precisely what he did, the fact that he was a theologian and no more, constitutes what is essentially German in him. If he had been able to become a generalist rather than a specialist, if he had been able to unite rather than divide, then the German character after him would have become different than it is. Yet the evolution of the German character before him would have had to have been very different than it was, for Luther was clearly as much a product of Germany's past as he was a creator of her future. We have seen how the basic conflict

213

in his life is reminiscent of a similar conflict in the life of the Germanic tribes; and we have also seen how Luther's own character was a composite of the peasant, monk, and scholar. In his life as a reformer, all three of these types played a significant role, but in his later life they receded into the background as Luther became, above all else, the prototype of the German burgher. It is perhaps in this his least dramatic role that he has had the most lasting influence on German society. The feasting and drinking, the hearty joviality and *Gemütlichkeit* of Luther's domestic life—all under the aegis of the stern but loving patriarch—these elements of Luther's behavior have persisted to this day as features of middle-class family life in Germany. But more important than this creation of a social type is the fact that through Luther the middle-class morality of the craft-guild cities took on the force of a secularized religion. The humble acceptance of one's station in life and the predominance of collective morality over individual conscience were, of course, features already present in the ethic of the medieval German cities, and they derived from ideas prevalent in medieval Christianity: the blessedness of lowly station and the concept of the community as a *corpus mysticum Christi*, a body in which each member serves the whole. Luther retained these ideas, but by destroying the authority of the Church in the world, he destroyed their specifically religious aspect, secularizing them and transforming them into the essence of middle-class morality in the modern era.

Luther had brought the individual and his God closer together by denying the Church its mediating role between them, but at the same time he drew society and God further apart. In the Lutheran view, God was no longer present in the community as a living force. God had created the social order but then stepped back from it, leaving its administration entirely in the hands of the secular authorities. As a result, German society could never become a true community. It could only evolve into an increasingly elaborate hierarchy in which an unbroken chain of command extended from princes, kings, and emperors down to the lowliest subject. At one stroke, Luther created the ideology that gave rise to the unlimited authority of the modern German ruler and the unlimited obedience of the modern German citizen. When we study the development of the Prussian state, we shall see what the practical consequences of this ideology were.

# Part Three

## THE MODERN AGE

# 27.

## GERMAN LITERATURE
## AND THE GERMAN LANGUAGE IN
## THE PERIOD OF TRANSITION

BECAUSE the Reformation marks the divide between the Middle Ages and modern times, it is only natural that its major figures were transitional figures, men who gathered all the diverse currents of the past together and synthesized them to produce an entirely new world of thought and feeling. Luther was the most significant of these transitional figures, and, as we noted before, Hutten and Sickingen fall into this category, too, the one an admixture of the medieval knight and the Renaissance Humanist, the other of the condottiere and the modern businessman.

Still another personality of this kind is the Nürnberg poet-craftsman Hans Sachs, a contemporary and a great admirer of Luther. As an author, Hans Sachs has very little to offer us today; but in terms of our characterological history of the Germans, he is a major transitional figure. If we trace the development of German poetry from medieval minnesong to Hans Sachs and then beyond him to the Baroque, we shall see reflected in the shifting poetic forms of this period the changes that were taking place throughout German society: secularization, specialization, the increasing importance of the collective as opposed to the individual, the growing influence of the middle class, and the establishment of rigid hierarchies. A brief survey of Hans Sachs's work and of the literary movements during and after his lifetime, then, will serve as our point of departure for a study of Germany in the modern age.

With Hans Sachs (1494-1576), the art, or rather the craft, of the meistersong achieved its high point. The meistersingers considered themselves descendants of the minstrels who introduced the forms of Provençal love songs into Germany and developed medieval minnesong into a high poetic art that would not be equalled again in Germany for centuries to come. The meistersingers were perfectly justified in looking to Walther von der Vogelweide, Wolfram von Eschenbach, and other lyricists of the Middle Ages as the founders of their craft; for with the decline of court society, the medieval minstrels were forced to leave the world of courtly ideals and manners behind, turning to the middle class of the cities and towns for their material and their audience. It is certainly true that the minnesong of the Middle Ages did evolve into the meistersong of the Reformation, but the fact that the one developed from the other does not mean that the one resembles the other. Indeed, the meistersong differs qualitatively from minnesong, and what makes it differ so drastically is the fact that the middle-class, craft-guild mentality of the cities came to dominate it. The craft mentality did more than change the forms and subject matter of poetry. It deprived poetry of its very nature by reducing it from an art to a craft. Poetry was taken out of the hands of poets and put into the hands of craftsmen and scholars. Texts and music had to be written according to established rules similar to those governing any trade, be it carpentry or hog-butchering; and anyone aspiring to become a meistersinger had to undergo guild training just as he would in any other craft, progressing through different levels of proficiency ranging from the lowly *Schüler* (pupil) on up to *Meister*. In poetry as in morality, the collective, not the individual, set and administered the standards. Not only were the forms of meistersong determined by the collective but the themes as well. Unlike minnesong or the courtly epics of the Middle Ages, meistersong did not take individual feelings or popular sagas as its subject matter but became a vehicle for scholarly and didactic treatises. Here, too, meistersong reflects the collectivization and specialization of the middle-class society that was beginning to take shape in Germany during the Reformation. The typical subject of meistersong was not the whole man but only one isolated aspect of human existence.

The origins of the singers' guilds go back to the early fourteenth century when the *Spielleute* or minstrels started to settle in the cities, but actual guilds or *Zünfte* do not appear until the fifteenth century when they began to spring up in the Rhine valley. One of them, established in Mainz about 1450, was particularly rigid in its adherence to the traditional patterns created by the minne-singers. It prohibited any variations on the old tunes and admitted only Scholastic and ecclesiastical topics as subject matter. From the Rhine valley, the singers' guilds spread to the south and east. The most renowned center of meistersong was Nürnberg, and the most renowned of meistersingers was Hans Sachs. Both a shoe-maker and a poet, Hans Sachs must have manufactured poems nearly as rapidly as he did shoes. About 6,000 of his works have come down to us, and it is likely that he wrote many more than that. In this flood of poems, farces, and Shrovetide plays, he dealt with every facet of the cultural and political life of his time. His theatrical writings include allegorical morality plays, social satires, and middle-class adaptations of classical comedies and tragedies, of Christian mystery plays, and of Germanic sagas. There is even a Dantesque rendering of Margrave Albrecht of Brandenburg's descent into hell.

Despite the fact that both Goethe and Richard Wagner pro-claimed Hans Sachs a poetic genius, we are not likely to be moved to the same kind of enthusiasm today. But even if we do not find Hans Sachs's works of great literary importance, we will find in them a rich source of information on his time and on the forma-tion of the middle-class mind in Germany. Hans Sachs stands out above his fellow meistersingers because he surpasses all the rest in vitality, in common sense, and in the wide range of his knowl-edge and interests. His work draws on the past yet points to the future as well. In him we find the whole spectrum of medieval literary tradition represented: minnesong, Scholastic argumenta-tion, Humanistic learning, mystery and passion plays, popular preaching, mock didacticism, and theses on religious reform. At the same time we find him already anticipating characteristic features of German Baroque poetry: its learned, didactic, theolog-ical character; its bombast and verbosity; its amorphousness; its slavish adherence to rules, patterns, and prescriptions; and its cul-tivation in guild-like societies. Through his disciple and close imitator, Jacob Ayrer, Hans Sachs exerted a strong influence on German Baroque drama. Ayrer combined Hans Sachs's motifs and

219

style with techniques and effects derived from the English Comedians who performed at the courts of the German territorial princes from the mid-sixteenth century on.

What Hans Sachs had done for the German drama, Jörg Wickram did for the German novel. Wickram adapted medieval romances to the now middle-class world by replacing the knights of these tales with good, honest peasants or burghers. Wickram is thus among the first writers in German to begin the transformation of the medieval epic into the modern social novel. Another important figure in the development of the German novel was Johann Fischart. His adaptation of Rabelais' *Gargantua* and his translation of the Spanish romance *Amadis de Gaula* established the direction German prose fiction would take during the Baroque period.

German Baroque literature presents us with a wealth of material that is tremendously revealing for a study of the evolving character of the German people. Unfortunately, the scope of this book does not permit us to examine any works of this period in detail. All we can do here is try to relate the main features of the Baroque to our central concerns.

The literature of the seventeenth century could not help showing the influence of the great revolutionary movements the previous century had produced. As we would expect, Reformation, Humanism, and the new natural science all left their mark on the German Baroque. Of these three major influences, however, only the Reformation was German in origin. Accordingly, the tone and direction of seventeenth century intellectual life in Germany were determined primarily by the Reformation and by the growing influence of the urban middle class. The Reformation had a tremendous impact throughout Europe, but in no other country did it overpower all other concerns the way it did in Germany. In France, England, Switzerland, and the Netherlands, Humanism and the new learning were major components of religious reform. Calvin was as much a political reformer as a religious one, and the classicist in Milton was every bit as strong as the Puritan. But in Germany the religious element remained dominant even in areas where we would expect Humanistic learning to assert itself most. German Anacreontic poetry, for example, which consciously drew on classical models, never completely rid itself of Protestant, sermonizing overtones.

220

The Protestant emphasis on the inner life discouraged the free development of outward form. In the seventeenth century, the lack of native forms, indeed, the German aversion to the creation of forms became obviously apparent. Lutheran doctrine declared the concern with external form illegitimate but gave free rein to thought and imagination. The result was that German Baroque literature never developed any indigenous forms. Eager for expression but unwilling to submit itself to the arduous task of creating form, the Baroque literary mind resorted to the indiscriminate importation and emulation of foreign models. The net effect was a plethora of form, an overindulgence in form that led ultimately to formlessness. The German Baroque writers did not assimilate the French and Italian models they adopted. They simply snatched them up like jugs into which their own thoughts and feelings could be poured. Just as the meistersingers were unable to create form themselves and therefore slavishly imitated the models of the past, the Baroque poets, too, insisted on strict conformity with the rules and patterns they derived from their study of foreign poets like Petrarch and Ronsard.

If we consider German Baroque literature in its historical context, we can readily see how its main features are intimately connected with the implications of the Protestant Reformation. Stating the case in a somewhat oversimplified fashion, we could say that the indiscriminate imitation of foreign models that we find in German Baroque literature corresponds, in the social and political realm, to the unquestioning obedience of secular authority that Lutheran doctrine encourages. Conversely, Luther's "freedom of a Christian man," his emphasis on the spirit's complete independence from the body, is reflected in the uncontrolled excesses of imagination and language that also characterize German Baroque literature: the bombast, the verbosity, the endless stringing together of disparate images in poetry, the equally endless episodic digressions and polyhistoric discourses in fiction. In Lutheran doctrine and in Baroque literature, the links between the internal and external life of man were broken. As we saw in our study of Luther, this division of man into separate functions tended to produce subservience of the body and self-righteousness of the soul. In literature, it reduced form to formalism and imagination to self-indulgence.

In all the countries of Europe, Baroque art and literature are characterized by the same formalism and self-indulgence we find in Germany. The ordering principle that the Catholic Church had provided was destroyed, leaving individual and national emotions free to express themselves in orgies of excess. But in Germany, Luther's doctrine actually encouraged this splintering of the human organism into its various functions, and nowhere else does the disjointed, motley character of Baroque life and art appear in such extreme form. The psyche of the German Baroque was a shattered one, ranging hungrily through all the new sensations and diversions that the social and scientific revolutions of the era had produced. This need to encompass all experience, perhaps with the underlying motive of discovering a new order to replace the old, expressed itself in the peculiarly Baroque mania for collecting. Every minor prince and every wealthy man started collecting curiosities of every conceivable kind. (Many European museums would later cull innumerable treasures from the private collections of this period.) The Hapsburg emperor Rudolf II amassed an extraordinary collection of pictures, jewels, books, mosaics, wood carvings, rarities, and natural marvels, all gathered unsystematically as mere curiosities. Rudolf's entire existence was nothing but a multitude of extravagant tastes and dilettante interests—painting, wood carving, astolabes, celestial diagrams, and alchemistic mixtures. He had beautiful horses he hardly ever rode and concubines he never saw or touched. They, too, represented just one more collection.

In active life, the figure corresponding to the collector was the adventurer or soldier of fortune, the man who sought to control chaos by imposing his own order on it rather than by gathering all its disparate elements together. Wallenstein, the central figure of the Thirty Years' War, typifies the Baroque adventurer.

The literary man of this age was an adventurer, too, not by choice, however, but by necessity. Unlike the knightly minnesingers, the craft guild meistersingers, or even the minstrels, he had no definite role in society and belonged to no class or group. He was an isolated individual at the mercy of changing circumstances. This was the point in history when the poet and intellectual became an outsider, a being at odds with society and one obliged to gain a livelihood as a teacher, private tutor, courtier, pamphleteer, or professional eulogizer of any patron who would support him.

222

In *Dichtung und Wahrheit* (II, 10), Goethe gives us a telling description of the German poet's lot in the seventeenth and early eighteenth century: "German poets, being no longer members of a guild that could act as one man, enjoyed no advantages whatever in bourgeois society. They had neither protection nor social position nor esteem unless some other circumstance than their writing favored them, and it was simply a matter of chance whether talent brought its owner honor or disgrace. A poor mortal, fully conscious of his mental powers, had to make his way in life as best he could and squander the gifts he had received from the muses in the struggle to satisfy the needs of the moment . . . and a poet, even if he did not perish like Günther, played a most melancholy role in the world as a mere jester and parasite, so that both in the theater and on the stage of life he was a personage whom anyone could treat just as he wished. . . ." The only position of security a poet could find was as a Protestant minister; and in that epoch of strife and controversy, he had to be a convinced and devout minister if he was to preserve his personal integrity.

Most Baroque writers—men like Grimmelshausen, Gryphius, and Moscherosch—led harried lives, tossed from one country or profession to another, battered in body and mind by the horrors of the Thirty Years' War. They were often servants of princes, of cities, or of rich and influential patrons; and they did not hesitate to change their creeds or loyalties if self-interest so dictated. The life of Martin Opitz was typical of the age. At various times and in various capacities, he served powerful patrons in Germany, Holland, France, Poland, and Hungary. He wrote for Protestants and Catholics alike; and, according to the needs of the moment, he willingly sang the praises of Jesus Christ, Bacchus, or Mars. It would be unfair, however, to condemn Opitz as a completely unscrupulous opportunist. His life and work were also informed by a sincere desire to reconcile the warring creeds and factions of his age, a desire that he shared with other generous and tolerant men in those three centuries of transition and intolerance: Nicolaus Cusanus in the fifteenth, Sebastian Frank in the sixteenth, and Leibniz in the seventeenth century.

Protestant doctrine and the political turmoil that followed the Reformation tended to stunt the growth of a native German literature and to drive the poet and intellectual into the isolation that has characterized his existence throughout much of the modern era. These two factors offer a partial explanation of why the Baroque period is not a major period in the history of German literature. Some recent literary criticism has argued, contrary to my own view, that the Baroque does indeed represent a major phase in German literary history and does not merely prepare the way for Classicism and Romanticism. Granted, the Baroque did produce some writers of real genius, men like Gryphius and Grimmelshausen; and it also produced several minor poets of genuine talent, Weckherlin, Simon Dach, Paul Fleming, Paul Gerhardt, Friedrich Spee, and Christian Günther. But despite these figures, we simply cannot justifiably compare the Baroque with the two truly great literary periods in modern German literature, the one beginning with the *Sturm und Drang* toward the end of the eighteenth century, the other with Realism at the end of the nineteenth. In addition to the factors we have already discussed, still another and perhaps even more crucial one prevented Baroque literature from reaching the high levels of expression these later periods would attain. That factor is the condition of the German language itself.

Baroque literature was necessarily limited because its medium of expression had not yet reached maturity. In his translation of the Bible, Luther had laid the foundations of a common German language; and at the same time he created with that language the only real homeland the German nation would have. Dante, too, created a national language, but Italy had much more than a language on which to base her national experience. She had first claim to the cultural and political heritage of the Roman Empire. Germany, without any common heritage at all, would have to found her national being in the medium of language alone. Forceful and vigorous as Luther's language was, it was still not sensitive or supple enough to meet the needs of an age in which human knowledge and feeling were rapidly leaving behind the known boundaries of experience. In an effort to overcome these inadequacies of the language, German writers and thinkers imported not only foreign forms but foreign terms and idioms as well. Inundated by materials it was not prepared to assimilate, the German language became an unintegrated, unbalanced medium of expression whose structure could not carry the vast burden that had been loaded upon it. The language itself reflected that same collector's mania that characterized so many men of the Baroque period. It, too, gathered up curiosities indiscriminately, then found itself unable to put them to their proper use. As a result, the efforts of several generations, ranging from Opitz' *Buch von der deutschen Poeterey* (1624) to Gottsched's *Sprachkunst* (1748), were needed to purify the German language to the point where Klopstock, Lessing, Wieland, and Herder could transform it into the rich and sensitive instrument it became in the age of Goethe.

# 28.

---

## GERMAN PHILOSOPHY

IN ONE SPHERE of intellectual life, philosophy and the natural sciences, Germany has always kept pace with other European nations. Throughout the Middle Ages and well into the modern period, philosophy and natural science constituted a single field of study, a field in which the German mind could move freely, unhampered by the inadequacies of an as yet unformed literary language. After the universal authority of the Catholic Church had been destroyed by the Reformation, philosophical thought began to follow distinct national lines. To be sure, philosophers in every country of Europe were faced with the same problems; but the French, the Italians, the English, and the Germans all approached and solved these problems in ways that reflected their respective national characters.

Two basic tendencies emerge in Italian thought of the sixteenth century, the great period in Italian philosophy. The dominant strain was a pantheistic one represented by Geronimo Cardano, Bernardino Telesio, Francesco Patrizzi, Tommaso Campanella, and Giordano Bruno, the major figure of this school. Just as religious mysticism had located the living God in the soul of man, the cosmic mysticism of these Italian thinkers located God in nature and posited an artistic harmony in the structure of the universe. Some of the earliest scientific advances of the modern period grew out of this naturalistic pantheism and originated as efforts to demonstrate the presence of God in nature. Because this pantheistic branch of Italian philosophy contains both rational and emotional, both empirical and speculative elements, it could provide a point of departure for later philosophical systems that sought a synthesis of these elements. The other important

226

trend in sixteenth-century Italian thought was a purely scientific one, the empirical method of Leonardo da Vinci and Galileo, who based their conclusions solely on the data of experience and on mathematical calculations.

Rationalism and a desire to control nature by reason are the keynotes of French philosophy, and we find them influencing every aspect of French life. The Cartesian epistemological formula "Cogito ergo sum" recurs with seemingly infinite variation. It informs the politics of Louis XIV ("L'état, c'est moi"), the economics of Colbert, the new psychology of Montaigne, and the standards of French behavior, that perfect mastery of mind, body, and emotions aspired to by the French nobility. The geometrical organization of French rococo gardens is visible evidence of this intellectual impulse to bring nature under rational control and so reshape it for the enjoyment of man.

We need only compare the style of eighteenth-century English gardens to that of French gardens in the same period to see the basic psychological and philosophical difference between the two nations. English life and philosophy are essentially empirical. In the English garden, order is not imposed on nature. Nature is allowed to prevail, and man studies her ways, learning to master her by exploiting her laws rather than by imposing new laws on her. Bacon formulated this empirical principle succinctly, "Naturae imperare parendo," and it is this principle that animates modern English philosophy, psychology, science, politics, and economics.

Unlike France, England, and Italy, Germany had no established national mentality that gave rise to a distinctly German approach to philosophy. Here again, as in so many other fields, Germany's role was one of assimilation and synthesis. In philosophy as well as in literature, Germany drew on the accomplishments of her neighbors; but since philosophy is not as dependent on the medium of expression as literature is, German philosophy was not hampered in its development. Using Latin, it could readily absorb elements of foreign thought and immediately turn them to creative purposes. Consequently, German philosophy was a mature and independent discipline long before German literature was, and its major accomplishment consists in a creative synthesis of all that had preceded it, the uniting of ideas from the past into a new world of thought that had never existed before. From the

227

very beginning of the modern era, German philosophy fulfilled the role that Schiller attributed to the German spirit in a poetic fragment entitled "German Greatness": "The spirit of the world has chosen . . . his German son . . . as the keeper of time's treasures. The German has absorbed and preserved things foreign to him. He has stored up everything of value that other ages and peoples have produced, everything that arose and faded again in the course of time. This precious legacy of the centuries is alive in him. . . . Every nation has its day of glory in history, but the harvest of all time is the glory of the Germans" [editors' translation].

This striving toward creative synthesis is characteristic of all the great German thinkers from the fifteenth century on up to Goethe and Kant. It first appears in the transitional figures who brought medieval German philosophy into the modern era. Nicolaus Cusanus (1401-1464) was one of these figures. He studied in Deventer and Padua, later became bishop of Brixen in the Tyrol, and received an appointment as a cardinal. His thought seeks a reconciliation of Scholasticism and mysticism and, within Scholasticism itself, a reconciliation of nominalism and realism. Like the early nominalistic scientists, Cusanus advocated reliance on the data of experience but only if they were then subjected to rational analysis. Reason, he believed, was the only faculty capable of transforming the materials of perception into actual knowledge. The fact that Cusanus anticipated the essential theories of Copernican astronomy indicates how strong the empirical and rational elements of his thought were. But all the knowledge that perception and reason furnish us provides only a limited understanding of our multifarious and seemingly chaotic finite world. If we are to comprehend the supraphysical, metaphysical coherence of it, we have to call on a higher, mystical faculty which Nicolaus Cusanus called *docta ignorantia*, learned ignorance. This faculty alone enables us to grasp the true, divine nature of the world, which consists in a *coincidentia oppositorum*, a coincidence of opposites.

A similar attempt at harmonizing mystical, magical, and empirical thought was made by two other great transitional figures, the physician Theophrastus Paracelsus (1493-1541) and the astronomer Johannes Kepler (1571-1630). Both these men relied on observation in their efforts to prove that all things and beings in

228

the world were interrelated. Paracelsus took the minutiae of plant and animal life as his point of departure. Kepler began with the movements of the stars. But both of them, each from a different point of origin, arrived at the conclusion that all the forces at work in the universe acted in harmony with each other. Kepler even projected the so-called harmony of the spheres by which the mathematical principles governing musical relationships were reflected in sidereal constellations and orbits.

But of all the men who attempted to unify the diverse elements of philosophical thought perhaps none was more successful than Gottfried Wilhelm Leibniz (1646-1716), the founder of modern German philosophy. Leibniz' amazing erudition and versatility enabled him to draw on practically every branch of knowledge. At the age of fifteen he was thoroughly versed in ancient and modern philosophy, and in the course of his life he became an accomplished mathematician, physicist, chemist, geologist, economist, jurist, historian, theologian, librarian, and diplomat. Immensely productive in every field, he was a prolific writer. His printed works—treatises, memoranda, correspondence with scholars and men of importance all over Europe—fill countless volumes, and a great many manuscripts still await publication. His most famous contribution in a special field was his invention of integral and differential calculus. But what concerns us directly here is his unification of Italian pantheistic thought, French rationalism, and English empiricism.

As I suggested before in our brief survey of the major tendencies in French, English and Italian philosophy, these tendencies are, in each case, the outgrowth of a national mentality which finds expression in even the most abstract of thought. A seemingly dispassionate and disinterested philosophical treatise, whether of French, English, or Italian origin, will still show very clear traces of subconsciously operative preferences and value judgments. Now since Germany lacked a national identity and mentality, German philosophy approached every problem on a universal, abstract, and purely theoretical basis. Since no other components but intellectual ones enter into German philosophy, it remains pure thought, the working out of problems that have come from foreign sources, either ancient or contemporary.

In the German mind, the process of philosophical synthesis acquired a significance beyond itself. German thinkers turned to philosophy in hopes of finding in it a definition of their own national existence, a definition that the other nations of Europe had received gratuitously by way of national evolution and tradition. This is why German ideas tend to become German ideals, for only from thought itself could the Germans hope to build a national identity. This explains the intensity with which Germans devote themselves to philosophical problems, and it also explains their concern with method. Since their very existence depends, in a sense, on what they think, they are particularly careful about the instruments of thought they employ. As a consequence, epistemology, the theory of knowledge, has been the field of greatest interest for modern German philosophers. Epistemological problems have, of course, always been part of philosophical speculation in both the ancient and modern worlds. But in Greek philosophy, just as in modern French, English, or Italian thought, epistemology is an integral part of a philosophical system. When Descartes or Berkeley describes the process of understanding, each tends to describe the dominant mode of thought in his respective country, deductive thought in France, inductive in England. Only in Germany, and starting with Leibniz, does epistemology assume a unique and overpowering role.

In French thought, understanding and knowledge depended primarily on reason; in English thought, on the data of experience. But in both cases, understanding originated from human sources: man reasoned, man observed. Leibniz denies this primacy of human faculties. For him, knowledge does not go back to reason or experience but to "first verities," impersonal logical propositions whose validity is corroborated by both human reason and the laws of nature. The principles of understanding and knowledge exist outside man; they do not arise from his reasoning or his experience. He is obliged to think and act in accordance with logical propositions that are independent of him. Even God's actions are governed by these propositions. But Leibniz carries this separation of man and thought a step further. He separates human consciousness from its content. Thoughts are not coincidental with thinking but exist in potentiality before they are actually thought. The process of thinking does not create thoughts. It simply brings to consciousness "thoughts," or logical propositions, that already exist. It makes conscious what was unconscious, makes actual what was potential.

230

The consequences of Leibniz' epistemology are clear. First, supreme reality—a reality that had formerly been located in God, in thinking man, or in divinely inspired nature—was no longer a reality but a supreme potentiality; that is, reality was identical with potentiality. And, second, the entire substance of existence, which up to this point had been the major concern of philosophy, began to be displaced by a methodology of understanding. This latter tendency was carried to its limits by Kant. In his system, epistemology absorbs and nullifies inquiry into the substance and order of the world. For him, philosophy *is* epistemology. The objective structure of the world is transformed into a subjective mode of understanding.

In terms of the German character, this great synthesizing, unifying impulse in German philosophy has had a curious effect. While German thinkers were drawing together all the threads of European philosophy, they were, at the same time, only deepening the rift in the German character that Luther had created. German philosophy did achieve a major synthesis, and it did create a national existence for the Germans, a national existence, however, that was valid only in the world of thought, not in the world of people and politics. Just as the kingdom of Heaven was, ultimately, the only real kingdom for Luther, so for the German philosophers the nation had its true existence only in the realm of the ideal. The German character is always at odds with itself, at home only in an intangible, unattainable world yet obliged to live in this all too tangible one.

The consequences of this philosophical dilemma for German political life will become clearer in the next two chapters where we consider the formation of Prussia and the character of its ruling dynasty, the Hohenzollerns.

# 29.

---

## THE RISE OF PRUSSIA

EARLIER in this study I suggested that the entire course of modern German history took rise at the Diet of Worms. The Lutheran and Catholic camps that formed there anticipated the division of Germany and of Europe that would follow. The struggle between the forces of the Reformation and the Counter-Reformation reached a climax in the Thirty Years' War, a war that began over religious issues but then developed into a hegemonial contest in which France defeated the House of Hapsburg and won a dominant position on the continent.

For Germany this first great European conflagration of the modern era was devastating. The population of Germany, including Alsace but excluding the Netherlands and Bohemia, shrank from 21 million to something between 13 and 14 million. The destruction of agricultural land and livestock was terrible. The French general Mortaigne declared in Nassau: "I would not have believed a land could have been so despoiled had I not seen it with my own eyes." Although the destructive power of the armies was infinitely less than it is today, the lack of any authority to protect the civilian population from the pillaging armies and the lack of any large-scale relief organizations explain the havoc wrought in this war. Massacre, fire, starvation, and disease accounted for at least as large a percentage of deaths in the civilian population as the armies suffered. Then, too, the loss of homes and property, the displacement of populations, and the constant shifts of civil and religious authority caused a disintegration of the social order that was more grave in its consequences than all the physical damage caused by the war.

But despite all this, the importance of the Thirty Years' War to German history has been vastly overrated. It did represent a major disaster for the Germans, and it did intensify their national inferiority complex, but it is not the cause of Germany's difficulties in the modern era. The explanation for Germany's anomalous position among nations goes back far beyond the Thirty Years' War. The war advanced the social deterioration of Germany but did not initiate it.

The lower classes always bear the brunt of any social disaster, and the Thirty Years' War was no exception in this respect. It stripped the peasants of their homes and livelihood, and, when it was over, left them as much at the mercy of the nobility as they had been before. In the chaos of the war, many drifted to the towns, learned trades, then returned home where they increased their families' incomes by plying their newly acquired skills. As long as the war lasted, the landed aristocracy was unable to prevent this; but when peace came, the landowners acted quickly to restore their hold over the peasants. In Saxony, the nobles compelled the elector, who owed them money, to enact laws forbidding the peasant either to leave his village or to ply any trade at home. In this way, they cancelled out the one improvement the war had brought about in the peasant's lot.

For the middle class, the war meant an increase of intellectual influence but a decline in social and economic power. The independent merchants of the middle class were ruined, and after the war the bourgeoisie began to change from a merchant class to one made up primarily of officials dependent on the princes. Feudal hierarchies were recreated where feudal obligations had long ceased to exist, and caste consciousness flourished even more than in the times when the castes still had real social significance.

The attitude of the German princes and middle class toward the French civilization that dominated Europe after the war was similar to that of their ancestors toward Rome: a mixture of resentment, admiration, and envy. It is interesting to note that the Austrians, whose ruling house was the actual loser in the conflict, were the only Germans to assimilate French influence easily. They were able to do so because the House of Hapsburg, with its Burgundian, Spanish, European, and imperial background, was by nature cosmopolitan and still retained a dignity of its own, even in defeat. Thus, the real threat Austria faced in the modern period was not so much a "foreign" one but the threat posed by the constantly increasing strength of Prussia, her German neighbor to the north.

The contest between Catholic Austria and Protestant Prussia dominated German history from the end of the Thirty Years' War to the middle of the nineteenth century. At this time, Prussia won control of Germany and subsequently broke the power of France in Europe.

How did Prussia come to this dominant position in Germany? Several factors explain her rise to power. First, there is the special character of the land and of its territorial and cultural evolution. What was to become the Prussian kingdom consisted of two territories that originally had no geographical connection with each other. It was not until 1772, when Frederick II (the Great) conquered the land between them, that they became a single territorial body; and this occurred long after the constitution of the Prussian state. These two territories, situated in the extreme north and northeast of Germany, were the Mark Brandenburg and the dominion of Prussia.

The Christianization and agricultural improvement of these two territories were the last, and proved to be the most difficult, colonial undertakings in Germany. It was not until the twelfth century, long after Poland, Scandinavia, and even Russia had been Christianized, that these last pagan enclaves were incorporated into the Holy Roman Empire. For the most part, these territories were made up of sandy lowlands or swampy forests. The population consisted of Slav tribes and Prussians, a people of uncertain origin. The Christianization and cultivation of these areas resembled true colonization in the modern sense of the word. These territories were not conquered by individual rulers but were settled by heterogeneous groups intent on acquiring land, and Prussia has never been quite able to transcend her colonial origins.

The Cistercian monks, the first order to engage in secular works of common usefulness, were the earliest colonizers in Brandenburg. They founded monasteries and farmsteads from which they directed the systematic clearing and cultivation of the land. Under their aegis, knights moved into the territory, and the native population provided serfs for these German or Slavonic lords. It was in this period that *Junkertum*, the rule of the landed nobility, was established. The Mark Brandenburg came into the hands of the Hohenzollern family in 1415 when the Luxemburg emperor

234

Sigismund gave the territory to Frederick of Hohenzollern in return for financial support that had helped Sigismund acquire the imperial crown.

Prussia was similar to Brandenburg geographically, and its inhabitants, the savage and stubborn Prussians, had resisted numerous attempts at conversion. But here the rule of the Teutonic Knights preceded and foreshadowed the administrative achievements of the Hohenzollerns.

The Teutonic Knights were one of the three great orders of knighthood that arose during the Crusades. The other and older orders, Romanic in origin, were the Templars and the Hospitalers or Knights of St. John of Jerusalem, also called the Maltese Knights. As their name indicates, the Hospitalers' original mission was the care of sick or wounded crusaders and pilgrims; but they and the other two orders gradually assumed additional duties: the safe conduct of pilgrims through the endangered regions of Asia Minor and Palestine, the protection of holy places, and the suppression of Mediterranean pirates who threatened sea-faring pilgrims. Combining the qualities of both monks and knights, the orders became permanent advance guards for the Church. Through the membership of powerful European noblemen and the large donations of non-active members, they acquired great wealth and turned to economic activities, the Hospitalers to agriculture, the Templars to commerce. The Templars became the most important bankers of the thirteenth century; but, as mentioned before, their financial power was destroyed when Philip the Fair of France confiscated their fortune by the pseudo-legal methods the French monarchs had already used against local merchants and Jews.

The Teutonic Knights embarked on a different kind of enterprise. In 1226, they had the pope dispatch them on a permanent crusade against the remaining pagan enclaves along the northeastern frontier of the Holy Roman Empire. Their grand master, Hermann von Salza, also succeeded in establishing cordial relations with the Hohenstaufen emperor Frederick II, who granted the order the imperial insignia of the black eagle. Following the call of the Cistercians and the duke of Masovia for aid in Christianizing the Prussians, the Teutonic Knights conquered a large territory which, partially because of its remoteness, became more and more independent from papal as well as from imperial authority. The knights circumvented imperial control by transferring all their holdings to the pope and taking them back as fiefs of the Church. Though nominally subject to the pope, their distance from Rome left them free of papal influence.

In transforming their monastic order into a true collective, the Teutonic Knights developed a military and commercial organization of great power and wealth. Centuries before the rise of Protestantism, they made Christian asceticism secular. Their asceticism focused on the community and not on the individual soul, on the state for its own sake and not for the glory of God. They adhered to the monastic vows of poverty, chastity, and obedience; they continued the practice of confession; and they kept to the monastic schedule of hours and vigils. But where the discipline of the monastic order was intended to isolate the individual for concentration and recollection, the Teutonic Knights turned this discipline into an instrument of the collective. They lived a communal life, eating from common bowls and sleeping in large, lighted halls. All their goods, even objects of daily use, were held in common. They wore uniform clothing, and a similar uniformity prevailed in the construction of their castles. The grand master depended on the chapter for all important decisions. He was responsible to the members of the community, and they could remove him from office. Even the highest offices in the order were subject to strict control by the members.

Long before the consolidation of the territorial states, the Teutonic Knights methodically organized their property, relying on combined military and economic measures that were later incorporated into the Prussian administrative system. They subdued the Prussian tribesmen by force of arms, reduced them to serfdom, wiped out their language and their customs, and conscripted them into a territorial militia. The knights imported German settlers, both noblemen and burghers, and placed them in positions of authority. They founded cities to which they granted municipal and commercial privileges. To prevent any one class from acquiring too much power, they protected the free peasants from the landed proprietors and held the ambitions of the clergy in check. They inaugurated a rigid administration and close supervision of accounting. The management of the order's private property was strictly separated from the management of state property. Uniform law, measure, and currency were introduced throughout the territory, an accomplishment unprecedented in any dominion of that size. The knights competed with the towns they had founded by carrying on extensive trade with the Hanseatic League. In an almost Protestant manner and in sharp contrast to the Romanic orders of knighthood, they were completely honest in their business dealings.

Everything the Teutonic Knights undertook had the sole purpose of increasing the power of the order, power that became an end in itself. The knights did not enjoy this power as individuals, nor, like the Calvinists, did they hold it as a gift from God and for the glory of God. It was not an instrument of national prestige, as it was for the French rulers, or the mark of a patrician elite, as it was for the Venetian aristocracy. It was precisely this abstract, supra-individual concept of power, passed down from the Teutonic Knights, that later guided both the creation and growth of the Prussian state.

In an effort to extend their dominion, the knights had penetrated into Poland and Lithuania. These two countries united in defense, and after a long struggle they defeated the Teutonic Knights at Tannenberg in 1410, just five years before the Hohenzollerns became electors of Brandenburg. With this defeat, the knights began to lose their hold over Prussia.

In 1525, the grand master of the order happened to be a Hohenzollern. In order to save Prussia from Polish pressure, he dissolved the decadent order, became Lutheran himself, and Lutheranized and secularized the territory, which he received as a fief from the Polish king. His relatives in Brandenburg turned this situation to their own advantage and gradually gained control of Prussia through marriage and through bargaining with the Polish king.

The Hohenzollern dynasty is one of several families that came to prominence in Germany after the downfall of the Hohenstaufens and the disintegration of the empire. Their slow, steady acquisition of power stands in sharp contrast to the rapid rise of the Hapsburgs. The Hapsburgs were possessed of a charisma and dignity commensurate with the flamboyant period of transition from the Middle Ages to the modern era. The character of the Hohenzollerns seems better suited for a later age. In viewing their early career, one wonders how such mediocre men were able to improve their position so successfully. The secret of their success was their very unpretentiousness, their shrewdness in seizing opportunities and in bargaining with other powers. English historians of Prussia have called this Hohenzollern trait a "fidelity to attainable ends." The family's career through the centuries has something distinctly bureaucratic about it. The Hohenzollerns progressed from one promotion to another, from burgrave of Nürnberg to vicar and elector of Brandenburg to duke and king of Prussia, until they finally became emperors of Germany for a few decades. Again and again, Hohenzollern fathers urged modesty on their impatient sons. An early elector, Johann Georg, called the Economist, reportedly said to his son: "To become mighty and terrible—that is not the point! Save yourself and Brandenburg from exaggerated ambition!"

Even the earliest Hohenzollern rulers excelled in the skills that their descendents would develop to perfection: economic and military administration. The Hohenzollern talents in these areas were not expressed, however, in the boldness or daring characteristic of a warrior or speculator but in the circumspection of an officer or manager. There is a difference between bellicosity and militarism. Louis XIV was much more bellicose and aggressive than the Prussian monarchs. He really enjoyed the challenge, the adventure, and the glory of war. As he confessed: "J'ai trop aimé la guerre!" The Hohenzollerns did not enjoy war; they enjoyed their army. They enjoyed the disciplined functioning of the military instrument they had developed, the routine, the drill, and the maneuvers. But war itself they found distasteful. Frederick William, the Great Elector of Brandenburg, worried sincerely about the "blood and tears" the army cost his country; and King Frederick William I of Prussia, who perfected the army and made it into the most dreaded military force in Europe, could never bring himself to use it. He wanted war so that he could test his army, but at the same time he shrank from combat and waited all his life for "a right and just occasion." In his political testament he wrote to his son: "I beg you . . . not to be the aggressor in an unjust war. . . . Study history and you will see by the examples of King Louis XIV of France, King Augustus of Poland, and the elector of Bavaria that unjust wars come to no good end. . . ."

When Frederick the Great actually did act as an aggressor and did start unjust wars, he was fully aware that his actions were immoral and that he was betraying the humane, enlightened

238

principles he had professed in his youth and in his pamphlet against Machiavelli. He was a broken man from the day he assumed rulership. He despised himself because he fulfilled the mission imposed on him by the state. "Soyons donc fourbe!" he enjoined himself. "Be a scoundrel!" During the Seven Years' War, he once exclaimed: "Oh God, if there is one, save my soul, if I have one!" And when he had won the war and was receiving congratulations on this, the most glorious day of his life, he replied: "The most glorious day of my life will be the day when I leave it!"

The Prussian monarchs' ambivalent attitude toward war reflects an ambivalence in the German character, a paradoxical commitment to both law and lawlessness. In their single-minded effort to consolidate and then enlarge the Prussian state, they constantly strove to establish a rule of law within the boundaries of Prussia, even if they had to impose law on it by despotic means. At the same time, they readily accepted the anarchy and lawlessness that prevailed in international relations and even considered it their duty to exploit this lawlessness for the aggrandizement of their own state. The consolidation of their scattered territories was no small task, and in the course of this work, the state as institution assumed an overwhelming importance in their minds. It became an abstract entity divorced from the thousands of human beings that constituted it, and the Prussian rulers felt their prime obligation not to their subjects but to this abstract entity, the state. The well-known words "I am the first servant of the state" express perfectly the attitude of not just one outstanding Prussian monarch but of them all.

This unquestioning devotion to the state became a characteristic of the German as well as of the Prussian mind, and there is no doubt that it helped make the total state of the Third Reich possible. The bellicosity of a single monarch or the selfishness of a single dynasty is far less dangerous than this unselfish devotion to the power of the state. In the service of an abstract, idealized state, the most bestial act can be rationalized as a duty performed for the good and the glory of an impersonal, supra-personal being. To be sure, there is an immense difference between Hitler and the Hohenzollerns, between their respective mentalities and standards of behavior. But despite this difference, Hitler could never have come to power if the German people as a whole had not been

239

prepared to accept him. The fact that they were so prepared can be attributed in large part to attitudes instilled in them by the Hohenzollern rulers.

The tenets of the Lutheran faith only reinforced the political ideology the Hohenzollerns fostered in Prussia. Primarily concerned with the secular world, the Hohenzollerns tended to see religion in terms of its value to the state and did not hesitate to change their faith for political purposes. They were quite willing to adopt Calvinism when the acquisition of the Rhenish dominions of Kleve, Jülich, and Berg made this change of religion seem politically useful. But the change to Calvinism was a change in name only. Both Brandenburg and Prussia remained solidly Lutheran, and the Hohenzollerns continued to favor Lutheranism because it provided such obvious support to the kind of regime they had established. In matters of religion, King Frederick William I's actions spoke considerably louder than his words. Though nominally a Calvinist, he appointed only Lutherans as army chaplains. Furthermore, he rejected the fundamental principle of Calvinism—the dogma of predestination—and prohibited discussion of it because he thought debate on the topic had a disquieting influence on the minds of people and therefore worked against the best interests of the state.

In economics as well as in politics, of course, the Hohenzollerns had every good reason to favor the Lutheran doctrine. Where Calvinism encouraged individual competition and the formation of an economic elite, Lutheranism produced diligent burghers and bureaucrats, each with a fixed and limited area of competence. The result was an economy controlled by the state, an economy that did not encourage individuals to compete with each other but encouraged them instead to support the state in its economic competition with other states. The social and political orientation of Lutheranism, in combination with the programs of the Hohenzollerns, was bound to produce a state in which both the human being and religious faith would be made subordinate to economic and political demands of the collective. The thrust of Calvinist doctrine is very different. As we have seen, Luther could separate a prince's religion and personality from his office: "A prince can be a Christian, but he is not bound to rule as a Christian." In Calvinism, however, person and office, religion and politics were not separated. As Calvin wrote in the preface to his

240

*Institutes of the Christian Religion,* "Whoever does not reign to the end of serving God in His glory is not a ruler but a brigand. And whoever expects long prosperity in a reign not governed by the scepter of God and by His sacred word deludes himself." Despite the secularization that has taken place in Calvinistic societies, this theocratic impulse has never been lost. Only in Lutheran Prussia did man become the dutiful servant of the state and of the state alone.

# THE HOHENZOLLERNS

THE PRUSSIAN STATE was the creation of three Hohenzollern rulers: Frederick William, the Great Elector of Brandenburg (1640-1688); King Frederick William I (1713-1740); and King Frederick II the Great (1740-1786). Frederick II was the last major figure of the dynasty, and the task of consolidating the German Reich of 1871 under Prussian leadership would not fall to a Hohenzollern at all but to Otto von Bismarck, one of the few real statesmen Germany ever produced.

The Great Elector prepared the way for Prussia's rise to power. He instituted a standing army, which he was able to maintain, however, only with the help of subsidies from his allies. He defeated the Poles, expanded the dominion of Brandenburg by acquiring Pomerania and Magdeburg, and established an absolute monarchy by limiting the parliamentary power of the Junkers. His son Frederick I received the grant of the Prussian royal crown from the emperor Leopold I. King Frederick William I, building on the work of the Great Elector, completed the domestic consolidation of Prussia and created the Prussian state of the modern era. He developed and perfected the army, making it the nucleus of his entire administration. By strict control of the domestic economy, he was able to support the army without foreign subsidies. Under his rulership, Prussia ceased to be the private property of the Hohenzollern dynasty and assumed an existence of its own. The supremacy the state acquired under Frederick William I is reflected in the fact that the king made all his own property subject to the taxes and regulations of the state. In the reign of Frederick II, Prussia entered the international arena. In the Silesian Wars, Frederick conquered Silesia for Prussia; and by withstanding the combined strength of France, Austria, and Russia in the Seven Years' War, he put an end to Hapsburg domination of central Europe and established Prussia as a major European power.

In considering the accomplishments of Prussia, we must always keep in mind how inauspicious her beginnings were. Her territories were not agriculturally rich, and they had suffered terribly from the devastations of the Thirty Years' War. From the very outset, Prussia was a "have-not"; and the Hohenzollerns, despite the heights they attained, were always regarded as newcomers and upstarts on the international scene. Wherever they turned, they found the Hapsburgs, the French, and the British firmly entrenched in positions of power. They could not afford to compete with these rich and dignified rivals on their own terms. They had to be efficient and economical, turning the resources they had to the best possible use. Consequently, the Hohenzollerns lived and governed like petty bourgeois patriarchs. The few exceptions were Frederick I, who, like other provincial princes of that epoch, tried to emulate Louis XIV; Kaiser William II, who was intoxicated by the idea of his new nineteenth-century empire; and Frederick the Great, whose personal loneliness and intellectual tastes made him a misfit in the dreary atmosphere of his court. But all the other Prussian rulers applied themselves zealously to husbanding and increasing the power of the state. They had to repopulate their lands after the Thirty Years' War and then exact from this new population the funds needed to build up their military strength, strength required not only for enhancing their international position but also for welding together their diverse territories into a coherent unit. Because of the great emphasis placed on the military, the army became the main structural element in the country. Thus, the history of the Prussian state is inextricably entwined with the history of the Prussian army. The Prussian bureaucracy was an outgrowth of the army; and perhaps no other force, apart from Lutheran doctrine, had such a great influence on the Prussian character. Frederick William I was the prototype of both the Prussian officer and the Prussian official, a striking example of that special Prussian combination of military and economic efficiency. "I am the field marshal and the finance minister of Prussia," he said of himself.

Because a mercenary army was prohibitively expensive as well

243

as ineffective as an agent for consolidating the state, the Hohen-zollerns had to build a new kind of army. Steps toward modern military organization had already been taken in the Dutch and Swedish armies. Maurice of Orange and William Louis of Nassau had revived the pattern of the Roman legion to transform the loosely organized troops of the feudal levy into disciplined units. They also dispensed with the services of independent military entrepreneurs who assembled troops for hire. The Dutch princes replaced these "captains" with the commissioned officer and military instructor. The Dutch troops remained mercenaries, however, but mercenaries whose exceptional training and discipline brought correspondingly good pay. The Swedish army of Gustavus Adolphus was the first army raised by draft and the first to combine the element of national spirit with the new methods of training. But even this army was not permanent. In the course of the Thirty Years' War it lost its national character as foreign mercenaries were absorbed into it, and after the war it was disbanded.

Prussia was the first country to create a standing army trained and organized according to modern military principles. Recruiting was conducted by draft and compulsion, and recruiters were completely unscrupulous in their methods. Force was used on Prussian subjects, deception on foreigners. Peasants were simply arrested by their landlords; people "of mean extraction" in the cities were seized and taken to the fortresses. Noblemen received similar treatment, although they, of course, were conscripted to serve as officers. A soldier's commitment was for an indefinite period of time. The regulations of 1726 state in distinctly Lutheran terms: "When one takes the oath to the flag, one renounces oneself and surrenders entirely, even one's life and all, to the monarch in order to fulfill the Lord's will; and through this blind obedience one receives the grace and the confirmation of the title of soldier." Training methods were severe and corporal punishment practically unlimited. The only check on physical punishment was that the captains had to pay for a disabled man. Forms of drill like the goose step were used to break the individual will and subordinate it to the functioning of the collective. Officers were subject to no less rigid discipline. They had to live with their soldiers, unlike French officers who lived at the royal court. They had to wear uniforms all the time. The most minute details of their life were regulated: their religion, their social intercourse, their expenditures. Even royal princes were not spared this kind of discipline. As crown prince, Frederick the Great often underwent severe corporal punishment, and after he once tried to escape with two friends, he was forced to witness the execution of one of them.

The Prussian bureaucracy was an offshoot of the army. It carried military discipline over into civil life and imbued the country with the spirit of discipline. Superannuated officers and noncommissioned officers were transferred to the civil administration, in which corporals and sergeant-majors customarily filled the lower offices. The central organ of the entire administration was, moreover, the General War Commissariat, a military office whose function it was to provide the funds necessary for the maintenance of the army. The new civil administration not only managed the royal estates in the most efficient way possible but also developed a system of economic planning that brought the mercantilistic practices of the epoch under totalitarian control. German political economy ever since has adhered to the guidelines established by this policy.

Spies and unannounced inspectors checked up on the reliability of officials. An official guilty of false reports, delays, or bribery was publicly struck in the face and imprisoned for life, if not hanged. The king's severity toward those who failed him was, however, somewhat offset by his firm protection of those who served him "with unsullied fidelity and untiring diligence. . . . They can be confident that I shall support them against the whole world and permit no intrigues except those intended to improve the civil service. I shall condemn no one before I have personally examined him in the presence of the informer."

The king also went on tours of inspection himself. Undeterred by the worst of roads or weather, he made frequent journeys to all his provinces to review his regiments, meet with his various local officials, examine the accounts of his estates, inspect military stores and magazines, and generally learn as much as he could about local conditions in every part of the country. It was not without reason that George II of England called him "the king of the highroads." One morning, on a walk through Potsdam, he encountered a group of citizens waiting for a postmaster who had overslept. He helped wake the man by smashing windows; then, after thrashing the delinquent with his own hands, he apologized to the public for the laziness of his servant. On these walks, which were called "tours de bâton" because of the frequent canings that occurred whenever and wherever people did not behave as they should, he supervised and observed everything and everybody. An edict of 1723 reads: "The huckstresses and other saleswomen on the streets and in the markets are not to sit with open mouths but are to spin wool and flax, knit, or sew—under punishment of losing their concessions."

Periodic reports on industry and agriculture recorded the number of shops and farms in operation and the size of the work force. Manufacturing was greatly encouraged and consumption placed under government control. Economically useful refugees like the French Huguenots and the Protestants from Salzburg were urged to immigrate to Prussia. Craftsmen, farmers, and experts in special fields were forcibly transported from one province or district to another to meet pressing demands of the economy. The work tempo was accelerated. Mail couriers had to complete their deliveries within a given time. John Toland describes the functioning of eighteenth-century Prussia in the same glowing terms that tourists would use two hundred years later in reporting on the efficiency of countries with Fascist governments: "I may truly say, that, without asking Questions of any Body, a Traveler may distinguish this country by most sensible effects, as soon as he enters it. The Highways are here kept in better order than elsewhere, the Posts are more regular, popular Carriages are more expeditious; and wherever the ways divide themselves, there are strong Pillars erected with as many pointing Arms as there are Roads, bearing, in Letters cut or painted, the Names of the next Stage, and telling the Number of Miles to that Place."

Frederick William I even initiated the systematic breeding of a new, vigorous race of men. Robust human specimens, grenadiers and Dutch peasant girls, were ordered to marry and to provide many children.

Cultural life, too, was under government control. Only those fields of study that were directly useful to the state were encouraged. As a consequence, only professors of economics were highly esteemed, and even they had to take their orders from the king. Frederick William I had nothing but contempt for intellectual activity as such. It was only with great difficulty that he could be prevented from abolishing the Academy of Science that his

246

father had founded. The funds for its maintenance he entered under the heading "Expenditures for the King's fools," and he appointed to the presidency a man whom he actually used as a buffoon. He considered philosophers mere windbags and drove distinguished scholars like Christian Wolff out of the country. Theological controversies were prohibited. "Salvation in heaven is God's province; all the rest is mine." That was the Lutheran motto of the man who created modern Prussia.

Frederick William I was the incarnation of a new social form that Spengler christened "Prussian socialism." But this designation seems erroneous to me, for the focal point of the Prussian state is not the collective itself, not the good of the community itself, but political power as such, independent of the human community. Political power as an end in itself—that was the meaningless meaning of Prussia's unceasing effort to extend her power until she had brought the entire world under her sway.

By tying each individual to a specific function within the whole, the Prussian state carried out the political implications of Lutheran theology. At the same time, it provided the archetype of the modern total state, not only because it assumed control over every sphere of public and private life, but because of its entirely unideological, indeed, anti-ideological character. It did not exist for the glory of God or for the glory of the nation. Prussia alone was not a nation in her own right, nor did she embody the nationality of all Germans. Her sole obsession was accumulating power per se, power that no one enjoyed, not even the rulers who acquired it.

The Prussian state did not grow as France or England did. It was an artifact created by the Prussian monarchs, a kind of social and political homunculus constructed of whatever human materials were available. It later assimilated other social, intellectual, and economic elements in the course of its rise to domination in Germany. It transformed the national impulse of the late eighteenth century into action and, in the Wars of Liberation, led Germany in her struggle against Napoleon. Later in the nineteenth century, it was quick to adopt large-scale capitalism and industrialization and soon became a leading industrial power. Everything that Prussia had been from her earliest beginnings and everything she had absorbed in the course of her history came together in Bismarck's German Reich of 1871. It was during this

Second Reich, long before the Third, that the Prussian historian Heinrich von Treitschke formulated the principle of the total state: "The core of the state is power. The state is not there for the citizens. It is an end in itself. Since the state is power, it obviously can draw into its sphere of influence all human activities insofar as they are apparent in the external lives of men. . . . Under certain conditions, the state will control human life as much as it is able to."

Those certain conditions presented themselves. The state absorbed and assimilated the manifold social, psychic, economic, technical, and intellectual revolutions of the period after the First World War. The result was the totalitarian state of the National Socialists, a state that was both a natural outgrowth of the Prussian experiment and a natural refuge for the German individual who longed to escape from the complexity and loneliness of freedom.

# 31.

## GOETHE AND GERMAN CLASSICISM

THE LAST twenty-five years of the eighteenth century mark a critical juncture in the history of the world, and the events of this period contain the seeds of the crisis we are experiencing in our civilization today. This short span of time represents much more of a break in the continuity of European history than the Thirty Years' War, which, by comparison, seems a relatively minor incident. In the last quarter of the eighteenth century, a great revolutionary change took place, a change whose consequences exceed those of the Reformation in importance. From the perspective of the present, we can see that these twenty-five years signal the beginning of a transformation comparable in significance to the decline and fall of the Roman Empire.

During this short period, the American Revolution, the French Revolution, and the growing importance of industrialization fundamentally altered the political, social, and economic nature of Western society. In Germany, Prussia consolidated her position and became a major power in Europe; German literature achieved the independence and maturity it had worked toward for well over two centuries; and in conjunction with these political and cultural gains, Germany experienced the first awakenings of a genuine national consciousness. In this chapter, we shall focus on the emergence of the new German literature and on Goethe as its major representative. In the next, our emphasis will be on the Wars of Liberation and Prussia's role in the political emancipation of Germany.

Like German philosophy, German literature had to achieve a synthesis of French rationalism and English naturalism; but where those two national principles had only theoretical implications for

249

philosophy, they had practical, stylistic ones for literature. Of the two approaches, it was the English one that had a liberating effect on German letters at the end of the eighteenth century. While all previous influences had imposed various national forms and rules on the immature substance of German writing, English influence, in accordance with the empirical bent of English thought, encouraged the emulation of nature, not an adherence to any prescribed patterns. It was English literature that taught the Germans to trust themselves, to disregard rules and regulations, and to let the irrational and spontaneous prevail.

English deism and pantheism blended the new experiences of empirical science with the emotionalism of the Anabaptists and Pietists, who had picked up the tradition of continental mysticism and carried it still further. God revealed himself in nature and in the laws of nature. The English literature of sensibility evolved in conjunction with this trend in eighteenth-century English thought. Young's *Night Thoughts*, Goldsmith's *Vicar of Wakefield*, and Richardson's novels, together with Macpherson's revival of primitive Gaelic verse forms, all had a tremendous influence on the German literary mind in the second half of the eighteenth century. The other major intellectual impulse of this period was the rationalistic philosophy of enlightenment, originating in France and standing in direct contrast to the worship of nature, genius, and unrestrained emotion. Somewhat tempered and modified by English empiricism, rationalism in Germany culminated in the system of Kant, who imposed on the German mind the most rigid rational discipline imaginable.

As in philosophy, so now in literature, the German mind had to reconcile two opposing tendencies, one giving free rein to emotion and inspiration, the other prescribing rational discipline. This was the situation that confronted the founders of modern German literature. Each one of them had to solve this problem in his own way, striking his own personal balance between emotion and reason, body and spirit, nature and form, genius and discipline. The problem itself became the focal point of literary endeavor and required a conscious attempt at solution from every serious literary artist. This fact accounts for the highly theoretical and philosophical character of German literature. This philosophical tendency occurs in most of the great figures of the late eighteenth and early nineteenth century. We find it in Lessing, in

Herder, in Klopstock, and even in those writers who deliberately stressed emotion rather than reason, the *Sturm und Drang* poets and the Romantics. The most striking example is Schiller, who was as much a philosopher as a poet and, in his poetry, too, much a philosopher and theorist. The unfortunate circumstances of his youth, especially the traumatic experience of the military Karlsschule into which he was forced by Duke Karl Eugen of Württemberg, and the perpetual want, insecurity, and poor health of his adult life motivated him to strive for the realization of consciously determined goals and ideals. This explains why he was drawn so strongly to Kantian rationalism and discipline. It explains, too, his exaggeratedly idealistic attempts to resolve the problem of form by seeking a new, conscious classicism, a conscious state of harmony and balance between nature and intellect, a "sentimental" harmony, as he called it, in contrast to the "naive" harmony of the ancients.

Goethe's disposition and career were fundamentally different from Schiller's. Where Schiller suffered from want, Goethe never experienced material insecurity. Where Schiller suffered from ill health, Goethe was robust and endowed with an elemental vitality. Where Schiller was primarily a theorist, Goethe was primarily a man of the senses, a man of emotion and sensitivity, yet at the same time an artist capable of bringing the stuff of the senses under the control of exquisite form.

But even this favored German felt deeply the chaos of German existence. The very wellsprings of his talent—his excessive vitality, his versatility, his labile temperament—were a danger to him. His early years of study and law practice in Leipzig, Strassburg, Wetzlar, and Frankfurt were dominated by a sense of inner disorder and confusion, of "emotion running riot," as Barker Fairley puts it in his excellent *Study of Goethe*. He felt nature as a whole, nature as an all-pervading, all-embracing element. His inner being merged with the outer world, and he experienced world and self as a transparent unity. At this stage in his life, he lived poetry as an elemental force and as an exalted mode of being. But over an extended period of time, this state of mind became extremely dangerous. The desire to merge with the totality of all existence developed into a suicidal urge. Goethe himself experienced the agonies of his fictional hero Werther, but his own hunger for experience kept him from following Werther's course and taking

251

his own life. He was determined, if he did decide to commit suicide, to do so in a way that would permit him to experience the act to the full. Since shooting himself would have deprived him of this experience, he chose as his instrument of suicide a dagger, which he kept on his night table for months. Thus, the need to experience his own suicide deterred him from rash action and finally kept him from suicide altogether. By 1775, Goethe's inner torment reached its peak; in a letter to Auguste Stolberg, we get an inkling of the tortures his poetic sensibility imposed on him. "Will my heart ever find the true way of joy and suffering, the simple bliss that is granted to man, and no longer be tossed between heaven and hell on the waves of an exalted imagination and sensibility?"

The emotional torment Goethe endured in his early years colored his entire life. The revulsion he came to feel for the underlying chaos of his own nature prompted him, in later life, to condemn his early works, particularly *Werther*. It also explains his refusal to countenance violence in any form, whether in the deeds of the French revolutionaries or in the ideas propounded by the volcanist theorists of evolution. Discipline, cultivation, and resignation became the watchwords of his mature life. But despite his conscious striving toward moderation and form, the explosive emotional potential of his youth remained as a constant and frightening presence. At the age of thirty-seven, having attained the position of minister of state to the grand duke of Weimar, he slipped out of Karlsbad and fled to Italy in order to lose himself in some region of the world where he was unknown. "I have only one existence," he wrote to Charlotte von Stein in 1787, "and I have staked the whole of it on this venture. If I pull through, physically and intellectually, if my nature, my intelligence, my good fortune should overcome this crisis, then I will retrieve for you a thousand times whatever has to be retrieved. If I go down, let me go down, since I was no good any longer anyway."

But Goethe staked more than his own existence on this venture. In a sense, he staked Germany's existence on it as well. If Goethe had killed himself in 1775 or been psychically destroyed in 1787, then German literature and the German consciousness might never have become what he helped make them. German Classicism—not Schiller's theoretical classicism—grew from Goethe's achievements after his journey to Italy. Here again, as with Luther, we see the evolution of the German people pass through the narrow defile of a personal destiny. The age of Goethe abounded in men of remarkable literary talent; but from *Sturm und Drang* to Romanticism, Goethe was always the leading figure. He alone achieved the perfection of German Classicism and, at the same time, the only true realization of German nationality. In conquering the chaos in his own personal life, Goethe also conquered the chaos inherent in German life as a whole. No one before him had accomplished that integration of the splintered German spirit, and no one after him would ever achieve it again. But the fact that Goethe could create a harmonious German nationality in the field of letters does not mean that he was a representative German. Far from it. The integration of Germany he achieved existed only in the intellectual realm. Germany would never experience a similar integration in her social and political life. Perhaps artistic unity was the only kind of unity possible at this stage of Germany's history. Goethe had to assimilate not only the diverse elements of the German character, but also the flood of new knowledge, both scientific and humane, that swept over Europe during his lifetime. This new world of knowledge is not merely incorporated into Goethe's *Faust*; it provides the cosmos in which the drama takes place. The highly symbolic and parabolic story of Wilhelm Meister also unfolds in just such a cosmos. These works assemble and sublimate not just Goethe's personal experience but the entire range of his knowledge and immensely diverse activities.

When Goethe went to Weimar in 1775, the variety of duties and responsibilities entailed in his work contributed a great deal to the recovery of his psychic balance. Mining and afforestation; construction of roads and buildings; the administration of justice, education, theater, and official entertainments all came under his purview. Any one of these assignments alone probably would have been as tiresome to him as his law practice in Frankfurt had been. But since his new office involved such a variety of occupations, it proved thoroughly absorbing for him, maturing his remarkable faculties of observation and leading him beyond purely practical matters into first one branch of natural science, then into another, each branch adding to his understanding of nature as a whole. It was extremely fortunate for Goethe's overall development that he received a post in the small principality of Weimar where all the activities of government were centrally administrated and had not been parceled out to specialized departments.

But despite the satisfaction Goethe derived from his work, he experienced another crisis similar to the earlier one of 1775. Just as the middle-class environment of Frankfurt had palled on him, so the restrictions of court society at Weimar eventually became burdensome to his volatile temperament. What helped him through this crisis of 1786 was the experience of his journey to Italy. He found in that country everything his mind and imagination had vainly sought to achieve at home. In Italy, nature and culture, body and spirit were joined together in an organic whole. Here the unity he had yearned for, emotionally and intellectually, had been attained.

Goethe returned to Germany in full possession of himself but more drastically at odds with his native land than he had ever been before. As we have already seen, his surroundings had been alien to him ever since his *Sturm und Drang* period. *Werther* was the first work of European literature to focus on the conflict between the man of artistic sensibility and conventional society, a conflict that had been evident in the social isolation and insecurity of intellectuals ever since the Baroque period and that would develop into a deep rift between the artist and his world in the nineteenth and twentieth centuries. It is no accident that this conflict became critical in Germany, for Germany had never had a coherent national society that could have furnished an audience for the artist. Thus, when English influence liberated the German literary mind, German writers were unable to find a way into a provincial society and turned instead to self-indulgence and self-glorification.

Goethe, the leader of the *Sturm und Drang* movement, exemplified this conflict more clearly than any other writer, for his genius and vitality far outstripped the society into which he was born. *Werther* and *Tasso* represent two separate stages of Goethe's effort to deal with this problem. In *Werther*, genius still attempts to communicate with society, however vain that attempt proves to be. *Tasso* foreshadows Goethe's final resolution of his conflict with society, resolution through renunciation and spiritual seclusion.

After Goethe's return to Weimar, a period of utter loneliness

254

began. Not even his friends understood what he had gained from his Italian journey. His relations with them seemed worn and faded, and Germany herself, her physical and intellectual climate, aroused in him a bitterness, even a revulsion, that never left him and that manifested itself in innumerable critical remarks about his native country.

The long period of Goethe's maturity and old age is marked by a vast expansion of scope and, at the same time, by an intense economy and abstraction of form. The one necessarily implied the other. The more comprehensive the range of his motifs became, the more rigorous and symbolic the structure and the style of his works had to be. With the parabolic forms he created, he initiated an artistic development that came to maturity a century later in the literature of our own recent past.

If Luther was the first creator of a German nationality and unity, then Goethe was surely the second. The spiritual existence of modern Germany derives from his work. His influence was felt throughout the nineteenth century and beyond, leaving its mark on the style of diverse German authors from Adalbert Stifter to Thomas Mann, Hugo von Hofmannsthal, and Gerhart Hauptmann. His popular appeal, of course, has always been limited. Schiller has had a far greater influence on the general public, an influence that has proved unfortunate because it encouraged a glib idealism that was all too often used to mask rather shabby realities. Schiller's theoretical idealism widened the gap between the spiritual and the physical in German life, just as Kant's rigid idealism opened the way for the materialism and positivism that emerged as by-products of nineteenth-century science and technology. Goethe's work, however, has remained a vital force of far greater importance to Germany and to Europe than Schiller's easy idealism. In his lifetime, he saw the world pass from the gentility of the rococo to the turmoil of the technological age. All this he succeeded in blending together into prophetic, parabolic works that are as much alive today as they were 150 years ago.

But even the achievement of German Classicism and Romanticism—the achievement not only of Goethe but of gifted men like Hölderlin, Kleist, Jean Paul, and many others as well—even this achievement could not bring the Germans together as a nation. German nationality remained a thing of the mind and spirit alone. It was never achieved in the body politic. Napoleonic tyranny incited the German people to struggle for political independence and unity; but once the invader had been defeated, the old ills of particularism reasserted themselves. It remained for Prussia and Bismarck to impose a semblance of national unity on the Germans. But this new German Reich of 1871 would soon prove unable to survive the crises it would have to face.

# 32.

## THE STRUGGLE FOR NATIONAL UNIFICATION

IN CONJUNCTION with the literary awakening of the late eighteenth century, Germany experienced a political awakening as well. Prussia had become a leading European power, and her ruler, Frederick the Great, was admired and dreaded all over the continent. With the emergence of this exceptional and somewhat enigmatic figure, new life stirred in the languishing empire. Germany had in Frederick a great monarch who was both a man of action and a man of intellect, and people far beyond the Prussian borders looked to him as the leader of the Germans. The advances in German literature and philosophy together with Frederick's conquests on the battlefields of Europe released a surge of German patriotism that combined satisfaction and pride in German achievements with increased bitterness over the abject condition of the empire and of German national affairs in general. The major event of the epoch, the French Revolution, only served to heighten these feelings because it acted as a catalyst for a series of revolutions throughout Europe, all of them carried by the same social forces and inspired by the same goals. The effects it had on the entire world were as far-reaching as those of the Russian Revolution would be over one hundred years later. Edmund Burke, the great conservative opponent of the French Revolution, had this to say in 1791: "There have been many internal revolutions in the government of countries, both as to persons and to forms, in which the neighboring states have little or no concern. Whatever the government might be with respect to those persons and those forms, the *stationary* interests of the nation concerned have most commonly influenced the new governments *in the same manner* in which they influenced the old; and the revolution turning on matters of local grievance, or of local accommodations, did not extend beyond its territory. The present revolution in France seems to me to be quite of another character . . . and to bear little resemblance or analogy to any of those which have been brought about in Europe. . . . It is a revolution of doctrine and theoretic dogma. . . . This system makes France the natural head of all factions formed on a similar principle wherever they may prevail. . . . The seeds are sown almost everywhere, chiefly by newspaper circulations, infinitely more efficacious and extensive than ever they were. . . . To what lengths this method of circulating mutinous manifestoes, and of keeping emissaries of sedition in every court under the name of ambassadors to propagate the same principles and to follow the practices will go . . . it is hard to say—but go on it will—more or less rapidly, according to events and to the humour of the time."

The courts of Europe were deeply alarmed and started conspiring against France. The French revolutionary armies, formed by the country's first "levée en masse" (general draft), were soon able to abandon a defensive posture and take the offensive under Napoleon's leadership. The Napoleonic conquests aroused mixed feelings in the German middle class: admiration for Napoleon's genius coupled with hatred for the foreign oppressor. But more important than any immediate reactions to the French Reign of Terror and to French imperialism was the lasting influence of French revolutionary ideas. In Germany, the liberation movement had two aspects. There was a desire to liberate Germany both from the French tyrant and from her own petty tyrants, the German princes and feudal lords. Surprisingly enough Prussia took the lead in this movement for domestic liberation. After Frederick the Great died in 1786, the strength of the Hohenzollern dynasty dwindled, and its weakness made itself felt in a slackening of state discipline. At the same time, the influence of French ideas and of German philosophy and literature pervaded the country and even the government. Berlin became the headquarters of the Romantic movement. Men like Fichte, Schelling, Hegel, Schleiermacher, and Wilhelm von Humboldt were teaching at the newly founded University of Berlin, and there were some sincere patriots and democrats among the statesmen of the country. Among the latter was the Baron von Stein, who inaugurated a comprehensive system of reform: abolition of serfdom, liberation of industry, dissolution of the guilds, reform of taxation and of the entire financial system. For a short time, it seemed as if Prussia were being carried along by the great democratic and humanitarian wave that was sweeping through Germany. This first decade of the nineteenth century, a decade of struggle against Napoleon, was the only point in German history when the great intellectual movements of Germany fused with the military and administrative ability of Prussia and when the ideal of universal freedom animated a struggle for political liberation. The Prussian minister Hardenberg proclaimed: "In this country we shall make a revolution from above."

But, unfortunately, revolutions from above have no lasting effect. The external liberation, the liberation from Napoleon, succeeded with the help of Russia. But the democratization of Germany did not materialize. The attempt at inner liberation was bound to fail because Germany still remained divided into numerous dominions, each ruled by a sovereign who was not prepared to give up his autonomy to form a unified and democratic Germany.

Napoleon had done a great deal to ease the problem of German unification because he had simply abolished several small principalities. But despite this, Germany was still composed of thirty-nine sovereign dominions. Two of them, Austria and Prussia, were major European powers. Bavaria, Saxony, and Württemberg were kingdoms created by Napoleon. Hanover had united with England by royal marriage, Schleswig-Holstein with Denmark. Besides these kingdoms, Germany included three Hanseatic city-republics and numerous principalities, duchies, grand-duchies, and the like. Having rid themselves of Napoleon, the German rulers no longer needed the support of their subjects, and they promptly put a halt to all democratic reforms, joining together under the leadership of the Austrian chancellor Metternich in a solid reactionary front. The spokesmen of national liberation were silenced by one method or another. They were relieved of their positions, deported, or imprisoned. Whoever wanted to make a revolution had to overthrow not just one tyrant but thirty-nine. This fact alone was enough to splinter the revolutionary movement into innumerable local groups and make any coordinated, national action impossible. Then, too, the long training in submissiveness had made the Germans utterly unfit to stage a revolution. We already noted how the revolutionaries at the "Hambacher Fest" debated the legality of revolution. Because of all these factors, the various popular uprisings in Germany during the nineteenth century came to naught. Where the French had been able to reorder their society completely, the Germans fell far short of this goal, achieving only piecemeal reforms that did away with some but by no means all of the abuses of absolutism.

The inveterate antagonism between North and South helped thwart attempts at German unification. Austria and Prussia were able to depend on the regional patriotism of even the most revolutionary segments of their populations. Liberals who fought their local governments at home supported them in the contest for national leadership. The resulting alignments, divisions, and realignments of rulers, territories, creeds and parties are reflected in the seemingly endless constitutional plans developed at the time: universal monarchy or unitary republic; tight centralization or loose federation; a greater German (*grossdeutsche*) confederation, including Austria, under either Austrian or Prussian leadership; a greater German confederation under nominal Austrian but actual Prussian leadership; the so-called Trias, leadership by a board of three powers, Prussia, Austria, and a subordinate organization including all the other German states with Bavaria as their representative; a limited German (*kleindeutsche*) confederation under Prussian leadership within a broader confederation with Austria; a limited German confederation allied with Austria; a limited German confederation excluding Austria and led by Prussia. These are only some of the plans that were under consideration. In the petty infighting of regional rivalry, the democratic impulse was lost; and the dreams of idealistic thinkers and writers degenerated into empty slogans.

The recurrent failure to achieve national unity had a pernicious effect on the German mind. Throughout the modern era, the Germans had suffered oppression at the hands of domestic and foreign rulers; yet during these same centuries they had seen France rise to power and glory, dominating the world politically and culturally in the splendor of her "ancien régime," in the fervor of her revolution, and in the grandiose sweep of her Napoleonic conquests. Then, in the course of the nineteenth century, they

260

watched England build her huge colonial and commercial empire. When they compared themselves with the French and the English, they could not help feeling bitterness at their lack of political power, their lack of economic wealth, and their lack of national and cultural unity. Their national inferiority complex grew, and with it grew the suspicion that they had been duped and cheated through the ages. This suspicion has always made it easy for German rulers to divert domestic discontent toward imaginary foreign "enemies."

Even in the patriots of the Wars of Liberation, in men like Fichte and Jahn, we find a growing resentment not only against foreign peoples, but against the universalistic and humanistic tendency that had guided German letters and philosophy up to that time. German nationalism has always contained this overtone of bitterness and resentment, resentment against the rest of the world and resentment against the universalistic impulse born in the literature and thought of the late eighteenth century. Since intellectuals had been the proponents of universality, German nationalism has always been inclined to lay the blame for Germany's political failure on the intelligentsia. This tendency became all the stronger when the basically anti-intellectual Prussian Junkers took the lead in national affairs. Unfortunately, of course, there is some justice in this censure; for the idealistic, politically inept intellectuals had been unable to translate their thoughts into action and create the national unity that Germany longed to achieve. The unification of Germany, superficial and short-lived as it was, did fall to men of the Junker mentality. It fell to them because German national unity, unlike the national unity of countries like England and France, had no roots in the past. German unity lay in the future; it had to be achieved by an effort of the will, by hard work and collective endeavor. Thus, it is not surprising that Prussia, which had made a state ethic of hard work and had developed the most efficient government in Europe, would assume leadership in the unification of Germany.

Characteristically enough, the first step Prussia made toward German unity was not political but economic, the founding of the German *Zollverein* (customs union) of 1819. Political unity would follow after Bismarck had conclusively demonstrated Prussia's supremacy over Austria in the war of 1866 and after the combined military forces of Germany had swept on to victory over Napoleon III of France in 1870.

In 1871, Bismarck completed the work of unification, drawing all the German dominions except Austria together in the second German Reich. Germany was finally united, and all at once she found herself a world power. She was ill prepared for this new role. She may have been united, but she was far from being a nation; she had no homogeneity, no way of life distinctly her own. She was nothing more than an agglomeration of provincial regimes held together by Prussian discipline. Lacking any other standards, the new Germany tended to equate national identity with material and political power. She tried to offset her intrinsic weakness and instability by constantly acquiring more and more power. After William II dismissed Bismarck in 1890, Germany began to behave like the upstart she was. She became a crass intruder into every sector of an already precarious world order. She upset international trade with her dumping methods, claimed a "place in the sun" as a colonial power, undertook to rival England with her new naval forces, and began to build up her industries as rapidly as possible. In short, this newly established empire threw itself into projects and pursuits that put Prussian military and economic skills to good use. It became increasingly effective and powerful as it adopted methods of mass production, methods well suited to the disciplined collective of Prusso-German society; and it was also quick to follow the Anglo-American lead in developing world-wide capitalistic enterprise. The combination of a disproportionately powerful army, an expanding navy, and a growing industrial potential posed an immense threat to the stability of Europe and the world. It is no wonder that this ambitious German empire disturbed the world's delicate balance of power and no less delicate economy, arousing fear and resentment throughout Europe. But what the Reich undertook in its early years was still done with a kind of naiveté. The empire as a whole would not achieve complete coordination of its forces until the First World War. The union of the old Prussian state and modern industrialism, the complete merger of a militarily organized collective with the work collective of the technological age, was merely foreshadowed before World War I. In the course of that war it became reality.

Before we go ahead to study Germany in the First World War, however, we should first take a brief look at the counter-movement that rose up in Germany and throughout the Western world against the exploitation and repression implicit in industrial collectivization. In the course of the war, the mechanization of society that had begun in the earliest stages of the industrial revolution was carried to its logical and horrible conclusion. But at the same time, the war also brought with it a heightened solidarity among all those who suffered the dehumanizing effects of mass, mechanized warfare and who opposed the unjust distribution of wealth and power that gave rise to such warfare.

Since the beginnings of Christianity, there have been repeated attempts to bring about an equal distribution of property among men; and the teachings of Jesus together with the example of the early Christian community provided a constant stimulus for such efforts. The heretics of the Middle Ages, the French, English, and German peasants, the Anabaptists, and the Levellers of the English Revolution all aimed at a just and equal distribution of goods. But these groups failed to develop into organized social movements for two main reasons. First, their motivation was basically religious; and they expected an act of God, the advent of Judgment Day and of the Millennium, to fulfill their dreams of social equality for all men. Their efforts in this life were therefore more a preparation for the kingdom of God rather than an attempt to achieve it here on earth. It was only after Christianity had lost its authority and only when men realized they would have to act for themselves here and now that they joined together to improve their lot on earth. Second, working conditions in the pre-industrial era isolated the individual worker and provided no base for a workers' collective. The peasants, the journeymen, the weavers of the so-called "domestic" or "putting-out" system were still doing individual work, work that could be performed from start to finish by a single person and without mechanical substitutes for manpower. The mining industry was the first to utilize collective labor, and descriptions of mining in the fifteenth and sixteenth centuries provide us with the first recorded instances we have of working conditions that became typical of modern industry: separation of capital and labor, division of labor itself, migratory labor, job insecurity, the sweat system, the truck system, and, in response to these conditions, armed uprisings on the part of the workers. But since the miners worked in remote sections of the country far from cities and other mining settlements, these uprisings had no impact outside the localities where they took place. Another industry to develop along capitalistic lines and to initiate a division of labor was the textile industry. Being located primarily in cities, the early textile industry made the collectivization of workers theoretically possible; but no such collectivization took place because the tools with which the work was performed did not require collective cooperation. Only in the late eighteenth and early nineteenth centuries when a large work force was needed to service machines did an organized labor movement take shape. And then, ironically enough, it was the discipline of the factory itself that taught the workers the technique and efficacy of organized mass action. Only after "men, women, and children were yoked together with iron and steam, and the animal machine was chained fast to the iron machine, which knows no suffering and no weariness," did the workers learn to act as a unit.

There were three main stages in the growth of the labor movement: the struggle against mechanization, the struggle for legislation protecting the worker, and the struggle against the social order of middle-class society as such, the true class war. The effects of the first stage were felt most strongly in England. In the years 1770 to 1830, the bewildered and desperate masses reacted violently to industrialization, attacking and destroying the machines that threatened their very existence. A law of 1811 made the destruction of machinery punishable by death, but the law had no deterrent effect to speak of.

In the second stage, labor sought to gain basic rights within the established system of middle-class society. This phase is characterized by the English and American labor movement, which, up to recent times, was mainly an economic and trade movement, not a political or social one. The entrepreneurs resisted the labor movement at every stage of its development. Attempts to suppress the English unions through court judgments were made as late as 1913. But despite this resistance from entrepreneurs, economic expansion and the rivalry of the two major political parties helped alleviate the ills of the working class in both England and America. As a consequence, the aims of organized labor in these countries were limited to improving the working man's position within the existing social and economic order.

264

In the third and socialistic stage of the labor movement, the aim is a completely new and radically different social order, a "classless society," in which the individual has not just the equal opportunity supposedly granted him in a capitalistic democracy but an equal share in the fruits of production, a guaranteed living wage for every worker. According to socialist theory, this can only be achieved by collectivizing the means of production.

Modern socialism was a long time in the making. Karl Marx did not invent it out of nothing, and to identify socialism with Marxism alone is to disregard the long, complex history of the socialist movement. For two centuries, men of all nations and classes worked at developing socialist theory, and all its elements were already in existence when Karl Marx synthesized them into his system.

If we look back over the history of socialism, we can see how it arose in reaction to the conditions that economic liberalism had produced. Socialism was at first a purely intellectual movement whose theories had to be inculcated upon a helpless proletariat. Only two of the important socialist leaders, Babeuf and Weitling, were of the proletariat themselves. All the others came from higher social classes: St. Simon was a French count, Robert Owen an industrialist, Thompson an Irish landowner, Hodgskin a naval officer, Hall a physician, Cabet a lawyer, and Proudhon a petty bourgeois. Rodbertus, Fourier, Marx, and Lassalle all came from well-to-do, middle-class families. Only two were Jews: Marx and Lassalle. It is therefore impossible to trace this movement back to either the social or ethnic backgrounds of its originators.

The early socialists did considerable work of a practical nature, and their investigations into existing economic and social evils certainly made them aware of the deep rift between the classes. But as rationalists and true sons of the Enlightenment, they attributed these evils not so much to the system of production as to the corrupting influence civilization had exercised on man's originally uncorrupted state. They hoped to recover those ideal, primeval conditions by educating the ruling classes. They therefore directed their efforts and appeals toward kings, ministers, and industrialists. They planned communistic communities based on the ideas of men like Campanella, Harrington, and Thomas More, whose *Utopia* provided what would become the interna-

265

tionally accepted name for the ideal, still unrealized social order. These perfect communities were to evolve from the "social experiment." Robert Owen had sufficient funds to invest in this experiment, and he actually established a communistic settlement, called New Harmony, in Indiana. This experiment failed, however, because of the social disparity and the human foibles of its members. In the rationalistic, ahistorical view of the early socialists, industrialization was merely an unfortunate episode in the history of mankind. A return to nature, they thought, would cure all the ills industry had created; and the communistic settlements they planned all had a predominantly agrarian character.

Claude Henri de St. Simon (1760-1825) is the central figure in the development of modern socialism and the first thinker to assemble the basic elements of current socialist doctrine: the materialistic interpretation of history; the derivation of all social organization from the law of property; the interpretation of historical processes as a series of class struggles; the awareness that industrialization is irreversible; and the conception of socialism as a world movement conditioned by industrial development. St. Simon observed that the political constitution of France had changed ten times in twenty-five years without affecting the economic conditions that determined the quality of human existence. From this, he concluded that political processes alone are of little significance and that any meaningful political progress must be made in conjunction with economic progress. He even claimed that the metaphysics of the eighteenth century had been determined by the interests of the new economic order.

Industry is the key term in St. Simon's doctrine. Industry, not military power, constitutes the primary strength of a nation; and international rivalry is no longer military but industrial in character. Therefore, economic government was to take the place of political government, and the management of economic projects in the interests of the community was to be the true function of government. The political freedom won in the French Revolution was nothing but an abstraction. It did not lead to social freedom in any concrete sense. The French Revolution had not solved the social problems of the modern era; it had only set those problems. World War I, the inevitable end product of nineteenth-century capitalism and industrialization, would prove just how correct St. Simon's analysis was.

266

# 33.

## WORLD WAR I

THE NINETEENTH CENTURY was a period characterized by an increasing internationalization of human affairs. Industry and technology developed an existence of their own independent of the nations that harbored them. National economics gave way to world economics as capitalistic enterprise reached out to all corners of the earth. Industrial expansion is inherent in the nature of capitalism, and room for expansion seemed unlimited. America had her frontier, and England, too, had frontiers both in her north country, where the big industrial cities of Birmingham, Liverpool, and Manchester grew, and in her colonies, which, in the course of the nineteenth century, developed from mere sources of raw material into industrial markets. All western nations either had colonies or acquired them. In fact, all the nominally independent countries of other continents and all the less developed countries of eastern Europe became objects of colonial enterprise. The major European powers devoted much of their diplomatic energy to the project of dividing up the vast but moribund Ottoman Empire that extended from the Balkans to the Near East and across North Africa to the Atlantic. One advantage of this preoccupation with Turkey was, of course, that it helped maintain peace on the European continent for many years. Like hungry beasts, the European powers circled around the "sick man," as Turkey was called in the nineteenth century, waiting for him to die and preparing to devour him when he did. The dismemberment of the Ottoman Empire was an appalling spectacle characterized by petty bargaining and diplomatic fakery on the part of all the powers involved. But the real importance of this unsavory chapter in European history lies in the fact that it revealed the underlying anarchy of international politics and foreshadowed the great world crisis to come. It occasioned only a few minor wars, such as the Crimean War (1854-1856), the Russo-Turkish conflict of 1877, England's Egyptian and Sudanese campaign, and the first unsuccessful Italian adventure in Abyssinia. But it was the point of departure for developments that led to the First World War. The Moroccan crises of 1905, 1909, and 1911 increased the tension between Germany and the western powers; resentment resulting from the bargaining over Turkey drove Italy into the Triple Alliance with Germany and Austria-Hungary; and constant unrest in the Balkans—the focal point of diplomatic intrigues and of Russo-Austrian antagonism—led to the Austrian annexation of Bosnia in 1908, the Balkan wars of 1912, the assassination of the Austrian archduke Francis Ferdinand, and so to World War I itself.

The First World War resulted primarily from friction between the parvenu nations and the old established powers. Austria, Italy, and Germany resented the fact that they were far behind the other major European powers in colonial acquisitions and in the control of world markets, while France, England, and Russia quite naturally resented the intrusion of these upstart nations, particularly the intrusion of so powerful a rival as Germany, into the world power structure. But the war was an expression of far more than these external conflicts of interest. It became evident in the course of the war that social and cultural crises that had been building in Europe for nearly a century were now making themselves felt with a vengeance. The war not only brought the struggle between labor and industry, proletariat and middle class to a head; it also revealed, with a vengeance, how dangerous the entire thrust of European civilization since the Renaissance had been. The monstrous technology put to use in the war was a direct outgrowth of man's exaggerated effort to master nature by reason and to control his destiny with his rational powers. In short, all the problems of an overly rationalized and therefore dehumanized social order were present before World War I. The war merely brought them to the surface and demonstrated that they were all part of one overwhelming world crisis.

The First World War was a novel phenomenon. It was the first universal war, the first total war, and the first truly revolutionary war, not revolutionary in the sense that it originated from or led to a revolution but in the sense that it represented a fundamental change in the nature of human existence.

Even the greatest wars of former times had all been localized happenings or, at the most, agglomerations of local conflicts. There were always whole countries and peoples that were not affected by them. The war of 1914 was universal in that it drew all the great powers of the globe into its orbit. Every country in the world felt the impact of this war directly or indirectly. Because the growth of a world economy had made all the nations of the world dependent on each other, the war assumed the character of an elemental catastrophe that could no longer be controlled by either individuals or nations.

The First World War was, moreover, the first total war not only because it revealed the interdependence of all the peoples of the world, but because it affected entire societies within individual states. Prior to this war, even the greatest military conflicts had left the major portions of the population relatively unaffected. The Thirty Years' War, of course, did touch the lives of nearly everyone in Germany, but in that war, the people were victims of a process in which they had no active part. In the First World War, every citizen of the countries involved had an active part. War became the end to which all activity was subordinated. The mass-production, assembly-line methods of modern industry took over entire nations and mobilized them into gigantic machines of war. Nowhere was this more obvious than in Germany where the military discipline of the Prussian state had been preparing Germany for this total mobilization for more than a century. For the first time in history, the union of men and machinery that modern industry and capitalism had created was exploited to the full by a despotic government. Total war became the raison d'être of the total state.

Not until this tremendous apparatus of destruction had been set in motion did it become apparent to what extent the human being had become subject to technology. Men and machines chained to each other were the combatants in this war. The battlefield became a deadly factory in which men serviced aircraft, tanks, mines, and heavy artillery. Ernst Jünger, a German writer who served as an officer in the First World War, christened this type of combat *Materialschlacht*, battle of matériel. In this kind of warfare, Jünger stated, men and machines were linked together in collective operations of such vast proportions that no single individual could grasp them as a whole or escape from them. Men as individuals were mere matériel themselves, less important than the machinery they operated and the massed force they constituted. The battle of matériel represented, in the most extreme form, the process German society was undergoing during the war. For the first time, war seized upon an entire people, obliterating their society and culture. Every last man capable of military duty was conscripted; women filled the vacant posts throughout the civil administration; and the whole economy was directed only toward war. Present concepts and methods of planned economy originated in the wartime economics of von Moellendorff and of Walther Rathenau, who later became minister of foreign affairs. Jünger understood these developments very clearly: "War as a military action merges more and more with the broader picture of war as a gigantic industrial process. Along with the armies that meet on the battlefield there are armies engaged in communications, foodstuffs, armaments—the array of industry as a whole. In the final phases of such warfare, there is not a single task, not even that of a woman working at home at her sewing machine, in which, at least indirectly, a military application does not inhere."

The war of 1914 was, finally, the first revolutionary war. By affecting every sphere of human life—social, moral and psychic— as no previous war ever had, it prompted efforts toward a complete reordering of human civilization. For one thing, it was the first war to prove the obsolescence of war. We did not need the beautiful inventions and technical improvements of the Second World War—the napalm, the rockets, and the atomic bombs, not to mention the H-bombs, cobalt bombs, and missiles that have been developed since—to prove that war has become a self-defeating madness. World War I had already taught us that lesson. By showing us that war was no longer an acceptable instrument of politics, it also showed us that power politics were no longer acceptable in themselves. For if we reject war, we must also reject the basic assumption of power politics, namely, that nations may resort to any methods whatever, war included, to acquire or maintain power. Power politics simply cannot function if the threat of war as an instrument of national policy is removed. War and power politics stand or fall together.

But the victorious governments were not prepared to give up

old ways for new. Both within the League of Nations and outside it, the old game of power politics was resumed. The victors had neither the courage nor the determination to change the assumptions on which international life was based, and they treated a vanquished Germany accordingly. The only thing that distinguished their attitude from that of the pre-war period was a new element of weariness. Having developed a bad conscience about war as such through their experience of World War I, they lacked the courage to act resolutely according to the old system of power politics and go to war when the situation demanded, and at the same time they lacked the courage to do away with the system of power politics altogether. The result was that they simply invited aggression.

This lethargy on the part of the victorious nations was one of the revolutionary consequences of the First World War. The consequences in the defeated nations were of a different sort. Defeat had only exacerbated the innate inferiority complex of the Germans. They had watched all their dreams of national glory go down with the Second Reich and had had humiliating terms forced on them by the conquering powers. While the war left the victors war-weary and apathetic, it left the defeated bitter, frustrated, vindictive, and ready to drop any pretense to civilization in still another bid for power. Now, Germany openly practiced the criminality that had always been inherent in power politics. She no longer played the old game according to the old rules, hypocritical as those rules were. She simply disregarded the last remaining vestiges of international order and followed no principle but the principle of might. While England and France still wanted to impose at least the appearance of legality on the international power game, a legality they were obliged to maintain in their domestic politics, Nazi Germany did just the opposite. She imported the lawlessness of international politics into the domestic sphere and began to educate her population to utter ruthlessness. The Nazis were self-proclaimed barbarians whose motto was: Whatever serves the state is right (*Recht ist, was dem Staate nützt*). But despite their all-out preparation for war, the Nazis wanted to avoid it if at all possible, hoping to make their conquests only by the threat of force, not by force itself. But their miscalculations carried them and the entire world into an apocalyptic struggle.

271

These were the revolutionary changes that took place in the governments of both the victorious and the defeated: a wave of ennui on the one hand and of open lawlessness on the other. But there is another revolutionary aspect to the First World War that is more important than its direct effect on governments. For the first time, men in combat began to realize that their ostensible enemies were not their true enemies at all. The German and the Englishman in the trenches were not really at war with each other; their real enemy was the hunger for money and power that ruled their respective countries. The war seemed to be a war between nations, just one more war in a long series of wars fought for political and economic power. But as it progressed, a feeling of brotherhood and community began to bridge the no-man's-land between the trenches. Exposed to the horrors of mechanized warfare, men on both sides felt all distinctions of nationality and class melt away. This war was revolutionary, then, because it was the first war in history to break down rather than reinforce the hold of nationalism on men. Never before had so profound a feeling of human solidarity reached across national boundaries.

On both sides a great resolve took shape: This must never happen again; this must be the war to end all wars; the peoples of the world must take their fate into their own hands and establish their common rights in a constitution to supersede all national constitutions. The young German painter Franz Marc, who was killed in action in 1916, wrote early in 1915: "We in the field of battle feel most deeply that these gruesome months will not mean a mere shifting of political power, but that the blood spilled here will represent an offering made in a profound communion of all peoples for the sake of a common goal. . . . Boundaries shall not be set anew, but broken down. . . . Let us remain soldiers even after the war, . . . for this is not a war against an eternal enemy, as the newspapers and our honorable politicians say, nor of one race against another; it is *a European civil war,* a war against the inner, invisible enemy of the European spirit."

This was the truly revolutionary impulse that emerged from the First World War, an impulse that informed the Russian Revolution and the German revolution of 1918. The humanistic and universalistic spirit of German Classicism asserted itself again. Humanity, fraternity, and the new world order were the great watchwords of German expressionist literature both during and after the war. But nowhere could this revolutionary impulse sustain itself and bring about lasting changes in the social order. The workers, the soldiers, and the progressive intelligentsia of Europe expected the immediate establishment of a new order based on President Wilson's Fourteen Points and on the achievements of the Russian Revolution. Wilson was considered a near saint in those days, and people believed that he would realize his plan for a peace in which there was to be no victor and no vanquished. But he lacked the power to achieve that goal. He foresaw only too clearly, as Norman Angell had done before him, what history was holding in store for Western civilization. At the end of World War I, there was at least a possibility that the coming catastrophe could have been prevented. But history was not ready for Wilson's message. The statesmen of the Allied powers and the people who had spent the war in the "hinterland" had not shared what the soldiers at the front had experienced. And in the overwhelming joy of their victorious homecoming, even the Allied soldiers themselves quickly forgot the rare, spiritual experience of human solidarity they had known in the trenches. The peace Wilson hoped for was doomed from the start.

Perhaps no one did more to thwart Wilson's plans than that grand old man, Clemenceau. Clemenceau could carry on a war, but he was not the man to make peace. An old man guided by long outmoded concepts, he projected the past onto the future and so helped make a diabolical caricature of the past come true. He was keenly aware of the dangers that lie in the German character, keenly aware of its revolutionary, nihilistic tendencies: "There is in the German soul a sort of incomprehension of what life really is, of what makes up its charm, its grandeur. There is a sort of pathological attraction toward death. . . . Those people do not love life, they love death. . . . They alone look on war with sang-froid, and, as a result, they prepare for it; the Frenchman starts thinking about war the day he is mobilized. And as time goes on, war becomes less a matter of courage, of 'panache,' and more and more a matter of preparation."

But Clemenceau's remedy was a shallow, political one. The attitudes of the nineteenth century, the attitudes of the professional politician and the cabinet diplomat determined his course of action; and the peace he achieved for twenty years (he predicted it would last only that long) was an uneasy peace at best, an

equilibrium so precarious that only the watchfulness characteristic of his own generation might have been able to maintain it
a few years longer. It certainly did not permit of the laxity and
self-indulgence the Allies allowed themselves in the post-war
years. Clemenceau saw the course history would take, and he
considered it inevitable. Western society, and French society in
particular, had gone beyond the point where it might have been
salvaged. "Hope?" he said to a friend, "it is impossible! I can no
longer hope, I who no longer believe in what I was passionately
attached to, democracy. I pity you for having to breathe the air
of a stupid bourgeoisie. . . . The French are a people in their
decline. Bolshevism? Not even that! You are too advanced to have
the vigor for a revolution. You will have a deliquescence, and it
will not last long. . . . You will live the gamy peace of decadence.
. . . It will be filthy and delicious . . . as when the ancients opened
their veins in a bath of milk." Clemenceau had the courage to
face facts, and his steady, unerring vision of the truth raised him
above his contemporaries, even above his opponent, Wilson. Yet
precisely the contrast between him and Wilson symbolizes the
great crossroads at which mankind stood in those days. The
choice was between yesterday and tomorrow. The question was
whether the world would follow Clemenceau back into the yesterday of Realpolitik or follow Wilson into the tomorrow of a true
brotherhood among men and nations. We know all too well what
choice was made and what the consequences of that choice were.

In Germany, utter confusion reigned after defeat had put an
abrupt end to the career of the Second Reich and to the dreams
of hegemony the Reich had fostered. The German socialists, themselves products of a hierarchical party organization and bureaucracy, were afraid of their own revolution. They hesitated to use
force against the old ruling class made up of officers, Junkers, and
big capitalists; and whenever violence did break out, as it did in
Bavaria and in the Rhineland, it was immediately suppressed. At
the same time, however, the socialists also began a program of
social and political reform through legislation; but they lacked
the prestige and the material power they needed to break the
opposition of the firmly entrenched bureaucracy. Political reconstruction failed because the Weimar government was betrayed by
its own officials as well as by the Allied powers, and sound economic reconstruction was made impossible because of the huge

274

reparations in machinery, raw materials, and money that Germany had to pay. The shift from a war economy to a peace economy required the import of raw materials and could only be accomplished at the price of further indebtedness. Germany seemed doomed to work indefinitely for foreign countries before she could embark on her own recovery. From the very outset socialist reform had to contend with frustration and despair engendered by defeat and by the hopelessness of post-war economic prospects. It also suffered from the constantly reiterated accusation that the socialists had crippled the war effort by destroying morale on the home front. Demobilized officers and disappointed chauvinistic students formed groups that waged small wars of their own against the workers and enjoyed the support of embittered nationalistic elements in the population.

The industrialists sabotaged the Weimar government at every turn, behaving like the territorial princes whose successors they were. Hugo Stinnes, who created the largest conglomerate in Germany, a huge combine including newspapers, iron and coal mines, shipping, shipbuilding, and several other enterprises, frankly declared: "I am Germany. Whoever is a true German may join me." And since he had jobs to distribute, he was joined by many who then went down with him in his spectacular bankruptcy.

In challenging the Weimar government, the German industrialists had the tacit backing of their counterparts in the Allied countries. French and English industry, fearing that communism would take hold in Germany, viewed the socialistic reform movement with suspicion and did everything it could to strengthen German reactionaries and the German military. The Allied governments discredited the Weimar Republic for the same reason and encouraged the formation of anti-democratic governments, like Mussolini's and Hitler's. The German middle class was all too ready to welcome the rise of totalitarian government. Threatened by inflation and socialist reform, the middle class took refuge in rabid nationalism and refused to recognize Germany's own share of responsibility for her defeat, humiliation, and poverty. Thus, the vast forces massed against democratic reform in postwar Germany made the fall of the Weimar government inevitable and provided a broad base of support for Hitler and the Nazi party.

# 34.

## THE NAZI ASSUMPTION OF POWER

INNUMERABLE theories have been developed to explain the rise of Nazism. The militaristic theory regards National Socialism as a creation of the German army and the German military caste. According to this view, the German military, having lost its ruling position in society after the First World War, tried to regain its power through the Nazi movement. It is true that a direct line of descent leads from the shock troops of the old imperial army to the illegal free-corps that fought against the Soviets, the Poles, and the German revolutionaries during the Weimar period; and the free-corps engendered the Nazi storm troops and elite guards in turn. It is also true that there was collusion between the official army (*Reichswehr*) and these partisan free-corps. But these facts alone cannot account for the success of the Nazis.

Another theory, the capitalistic one, sees National Socialism as a counter-revolution of capitalism. Industrialists and capitalists in Germany and in other countries as well, prompted by their fear of communism and socialism, did help the Nazis come to power. They used National Socialism as a bait, attracting the unemployed with the slogans of socialism while they were in fact destroying any possibilities of economic reform.

A political theory explains National Socialism as the direct result of the Treaty of Versailles. There is considerable truth to this theory because, as we saw in our brief discussion of Clemenceau, the Allies reverted to concepts of power politics in dealing with a defeated Germany; and the harsh terms imposed at Versailles certainly helped create the anarchy and despair that bred National Socialism.

Still another theory attributes the development of Nazism to the

276

national psychology of the German people. The truth of this argument cannot be denied either, for it is clear that certain German characteristics, and especially certain Prussian ones, made the Germans particularly vulnerable to the Nazi movement.

And finally, there is the gangster theory, the assumption that the German people were duped and overpowered by a clique of unscrupulous criminals.

All these theories are correct as far as they go, but no one of them alone is sufficient to explain the complex phenomenon of National Socialism. The roots of Nazism are many and tangled because it represents the final phase of a long historical development. It is not just an isolated episode in European history but the embodiment of a civilization in its last stages of decay and dissolution. In Nazism, we see the logical consequences of a social system based on the assumption that nations, individuals, and economic enterprises are subject to no other law but the law of competition. This assumption first made itself felt in the Renaissance struggles for political power. Later, translated into economic terms, it became the basis for the capitalistic system of free enterprise. It is no mere coincidence that the Fascists and National Socialists were drawn to Darwin's and Spencer's evolutionary theory of the survival of the fittest, a theory, incidentally, on which the free-trade economics of the Manchester School was based. The Nazi movement should not have come as such a great surprise to us. It was novel only because it worshipped power openly. Casting aside all pretenses of Christian or humanitarian principles, even all pretenses of fair play, it laid bare the ruthlessness that had dominated European politics for over five centuries. Nazism exposed not only the criminality inherent in the German state but also in the entire order of Western civilization. National Socialism was nothing new; it was simply the old carried to extremes.

Although Nazism embodied principles that had long been at work in Western society, it certainly cannot be considered an ideological movement like socialism, communism, or even Italian fascism, from which it took rise. Nor was it ever conscious of itself as an ideological movement. It was a link in a universal revolutionary process, but despite its ideological slogans proclaiming a new order in a new Europe, National Socialism never had the slightest awareness of its true function in human history. In and

277

of itself, it was nothing but a criminal conspiracy of national and international proportions. The post-war world was rife with political adventurers, war profiteers, and confidence men like Krenger, Stavisky, Stinnes, and the American bootleggers. National Socialism opened politics, economics, education, and law to this criminal element, then justified this degradation of all civilized activity by invoking Machiavelli, Darwin, and Nietzsche. Nazism did not hesitate to appropriate anything that could serve its purpose, perverting ideas and ideologies only to discard them when they had outlasted their usefulness. But National Socialism had no ideas or ideology of its own. It could not claim even the most primitive of intellectual foundations. This is an essential point to keep in mind if we are to understand Nazism correctly. Nazism had no ideological basis, or, to put it another way, its ideological basis was pure hoax. The Nazi state did not operate on principle but on tactics, and for this reason, it could make such ready use of all the elements present in German society: nationalism, socialism, capitalism, technocracy, Prussian militarism and bureaucracy. The only lasting "principles" in the Nazi bag of tricks were racism, anti-Christianism, and anti-humanitarianism, all of which had permanent value as means of destroying the moral judgment of the population.

The moral anarchy and economic chaos of Germany after the First World War provided an ideal breeding ground for Nazism. Germany was a "dual state," as a historian of that period, Ernst Fraenkel, has called it, a state in which the ruling classes of the old regime—the military, the Junkers, and the big businessmen—managed to retain their power and to turn it against the republican government. They did everything they could to arouse the bitterness and resentment of the population, denouncing "Wilson's deceit" and reiterating the myth of the "stab in the back" that the socialists had supposedly administered to the army during the war. They failed to mention, of course, that General Ludendorff had pressed the government to seek an armistice not because of flagging morale but because Germany's material resources were exhausted. The courts willingly joined in this movement to sabotage the newly constituted democratic government by granting legal protection to every illegal reactionary movement and its most criminal excesses. The men who assassinated republican leaders like Rathenau, Eisner, Erzberger, and Rosa Luxemburg were exonerated because the motives for their crimes were "patriotic." Long before the Nazis came to power the courts had become a tool of Germany's reactionary forces.

In addition to the resistance of the old ruling classes, the Weimar Republic also had to contend with severe inflation and unemployment. The lower middle class was hardest hit by the economic crisis which gradually demoralized the entire nation and destroyed its capacity to reason. The blame for the economic emergency was laid on the republican government, although the chaotic state of the world economy and the intrigues of big industry were actually responsible for it.

Inflation of these proportions was unprecedented in history. One day, a worker's pay would buy food for at least one meal. The next, it would buy only a loaf of bread or a cheap cigar. This was indeed a symbolic event, foreshadowing the destruction of values far more precious than monetary ones. Unemployment resulted from the radical deflation of German currency and from the massive depression that affected the economy of the entire world. It is impossible to overrate the impact of vast unemployment on an impoverished country. The psychic distress that accompanies material need is disastrous for any people, but for the Germans, who had been educated as a nation to see their raison d'être in work, the enforced idleness of unemployment meant total demoralization.

The Weimar government was too ineffectual to meet this crisis. Not only did it have to struggle against both foreign and domestic interests intent on bringing it down, but it was also crippled by its own parliament. Too many parties representing diverse economic interests engaged in endless bargaining, none of which led to any concrete measures that met the needs of the country. This impotent parliament did not inspire confidence in democracy as a form of government, and a cry for a "Führer" went up among the people, a cry for a savior who would cut through all the Gordian knots of post-war German society.

Adolf Hitler's background made him uniquely qualified to fill this position. He was inclined to excessive nationalism by the very fact that he was not brought up in the German Reich and was probably not even of pure German ancestry. He came from a section of Austria where continual friction with the Czechs kept the German element of the population in a permanent state of

279

nationalistic fanaticism. Furthermore, he was a typical petty bourgeois, both in origin and in character. His father, born an illegitimate child, was a shoemaker who managed to rise to the post of customs official. Hitler himself, however, was not only a petty bourgeois but a petty bourgeois manqué as well. The story of his youth is a story of one failure after another. He did not finish high school (gymnasium), and the art academy in Vienna, where he wanted to study painting and architecture, would not accept him because he did not meet the entrance requirements. For three years he lived in a Viennese poorhouse and worked as a peddler until the war rescued him from his miserable condition.

Hitler was predestined to embody the combined resentments of the German patriot, the German petty bourgeois, and the German post-war unemployed. A well-informed, responsible man who understood the complexity of Germany's problems could never have stepped into the role Hitler assumed in history because the people would never have supported him. The German people wanted simple answers to their questions and simple solutions to their problems. Hitler gave them what they wanted. He told his audiences that the Jews, the socialists, the bankers, and the Allies were responsible for Germany's woes. He told whomever he happened to be addressing that their social antagonists bore all the guilt for their poverty and humiliation. He told the people what they wanted to hear, and he told it to them with remarkable effect. The one field he understood thoroughly was propaganda. By studying the methods of American advertising and the Allied propaganda campaigns of the First World War, he developed great skill in manipulating the masses. The only original contributions in his otherwise confused and vulgar book, *Mein Kampf*, are the passages dealing with propaganda. They constitute a worthy supplement to Machiavelli's *Prince*. Hitler's maxim that one must tell only big lies because no one will believe the little ones is entirely in keeping with Machiavelli's principles, and Hitler did not hesitate to act on this maxim. Nor did he hesitate to act on still another maxim which claims that repeated atrocities stifle rather than arouse opposition to them. At first, people do not believe that such things can happen because they are unwilling to believe. Then, when they are forced to believe, they have become so accustomed to monstrous crimes that they accept them as inevitable.

If there was anything of genius in Hitler, it lay in his ability to embrace crime without reservation and to cast off the last vestiges of morality that the ordinary criminal still retains. What is novel in Hitler's career is not that he committed unspeakable crimes against humanity—many others before him had done that —but that he elevated crime to a norm of national and international behavior. The fact that he could overturn the morality of an entire country and that the illegitimate government he formed could receive diplomatic recognition from other nations demonstrates that the world community was perfectly ready to tolerate in its midst the criminal practices of a criminal regime, not only tolerate them but even honor them in binding pacts and agreements. That is the ultimate significance of National Socialism. It marked the point in history when crime became the supreme law in the life of Germany and in the life of the Western world.

# 35.

---

## THE LITERATURE OF NIHILISM

NATIONAL SOCIALISM was completely lacking in anything one could call intellectual foundations. The movement originated in barracks and beer halls, and was led to its triumph by racketeers and latterday mercenaries. The great appeal of the movement lay precisely in the fact that it was anti-intellectual and anti-theoretical. Without any principles of its own, it could pander to any number of contradictory interests and rival groups in the population. The Nazis always exhibited utter contempt for the intellect, heaping abuse on the "gabblers" and "scribblers," the "brain-brutes" and "sidewalk-litterateurs" who had supposedly confused the thinking, paralyzed the will, and shattered the discipline of the nation. Nazi anti-intellectualism was so strong that Hitler even wanted to restore the "blessing of illiteracy" to the people.

But despite the lack of intellectual content in Nazism itself, the movement had been anticipated by very clear developments in the intellectual history of the late nineteenth century. Nearly a hundred years before Nazism demonstrated the bankruptcy of bourgeois society beyond any shadow of a doubt, European literature had begun to expose the corruption of the prevailing social order. Writers of all nationalities recognized the huge gap that existed between society's professed principles and its actual behavior, the gap between its ideals and the wretched reality in which most people were forced to live. They also recognized the distress of the individual who was goaded on by his natural impulses but held in check by the ruling conventions of society. Balzac, Zola, Flaubert, and the German naturalists focused on these particular problems, lashing out repeatedly at the hypocrisy of the middle class and showing how close to the surface

282

the forces of chaos were. In Scandinavia, Ibsen and Strindberg exposed the decay in personal relationships that characterized bourgeois marriage and family life; and in Russia, Dostoyevsky attacked the sanctimony of church and state by contrasting their actions and attitudes with those of true Christianity.

All these authors conveyed an awareness that modern existence made it impossible to live by the principles the middle class professed. They called for a new and honest scrutiny of those principles and of the forces at work in individual and social life. Either Christian and humanitarian principles should be followed rigorously, or the individual should be free to act on his natural impulses. But sharp as these attacks on established morality became, it was only in Germany that the attack developed into an actual denial of Christian and humanitarian values. This denial was unique to Germany because only there had these values failed to become an integral part of each individual and of society itself. Nietzsche led this attack on the traditional ethic of Western culture: "What I am now going to relate is the history of the next two centuries. I shall describe what will happen, what must necessarily happen: the triumph of nihilism. The whole of European culture has long been writhing in an agony of suspense that has increased from decade to decade, as if heading for catastrophe. . . ." But what does nihilism mean? It means "that the highest values are losing their value. . . . The time is coming when we shall have to pay for having been Christians for 2,000 years. We are losing the firm footing that enabled us to live. . . . For a long time we shall be at our wit's end. We are hurling ourselves into a cultural reversal with an energy that could only have been engendered in men by an overevaluation of themselves."

For Nietzsche, the development of mankind since the beginning of Christianity had a meaning just the reverse of the accepted one: he saw that development not as progress but as decline. Using a morality derived from the instincts and requirements of the inferior, the weak had conquered the strong. Christian morality was an intellectual weapon discovered by the lower species of humanity—the "slaves," the "herd," the "masses"—in order to dominate the higher, nobler species. The goal of this morality was the "weakening of the desires; of the feelings of pleasure and pain; of the will to power; a weakening expressed as humility, a weakening expressed as faith, a weakening expressed as repugnance and shame in the presence of all that is natural . . . a weakening expressed as denial of life and as illness. . . ." Christian morality, then, was nothing but an effort of the weak to interfere with nature's tendency to create a higher type.

But this age of Christian morality is on the wane, Nietzsche asserts, and a new, pagan age is dawning, an age that will "restore to man the courage of his natural instincts. . . . Paganism affirms all that is natural. . . . Christianity negates all that is natural." "Belief in the body is more fundamental than belief in the soul." We have overestimated the value of consciousness. "Our valuation of great men and things is . . . natural; we regard passion as a privilege; we find nothing great that does not involve a great crime. . . . From a detached point of view, it is precisely the growing dominance of evil that is desirable, the growth of power, so as to make use of the most powerful forces in nature, the emotions." It is crucial to "re-establish the hierarchy of rank," to know "that there are higher and lower human beings and that a single great man can give meaning to the existence through whole millennia of lesser ones . . . that is, one complete, rich, great human being can give meaning to the existence of innumerable, incomplete, fragmentary human beings." But "what determines a man's rank is the quantum of power he has. . . . Only through war and danger can a rank maintain itself." "I am delighted," Nietzsche writes, "with the military development of Europe, also with its anarchical condition. The period of quietude and Chinese apathy is over; . . . physical values are appreciated once more; . . . handsome men are becoming possible again. The time of bloodless sneaks is past; . . . the savage in every one of us is accepted, even the wild animal. . . . A ruling race can emerge only from terrible and violent beginnings. Where are the barbarians of the twentieth century?" he asks. The destruction of the weak was to be accelerated by weakening them still more, and the rise of the strong accelerated by strengthening them more. The strong enrich life, the weak consume and impoverish it. Indeed, the process of natural selection was to be encouraged by a conscious plan to breed the strongest possible human being. What matters is not mankind, but the superman, not intellect but life; and life is the will-to-power. All this was written in the 1880's.

Nietzsche's work struck all the themes that would later exert such a tremendous influence on the youth of Europe. The Nazis made his prophecies come true down to the last detail. But the form thoughts assume when translated into reality often differs greatly from the thoughts themselves. When Nietzsche dreamed of his "blond beast" or his "superman," he could not foresee that his reaction against the nineteenth century would help bring a nineteenth-century type to power. It is ironic that when the *Herrenmensch* finally became a reality, he was not the ennobled human being Nietzsche had conceived of. He was instead the same stuffy petty bourgeois that Nietzsche had so heartily despised.

The poet Stefan George was the one major literary figure who kept Nietzsche's teachings alive in the post-war period. What particularly drew George to Nietzsche was Nietzsche's cult of the great man. For George, the great man was not a barbaric superman but a complete, harmonious human being in the Greek sense. In contrast to the modern idea of the great man, which emphasizes accomplishment in one specialized field, George's concept envisaged a man whose mind and body are at one. The mind expresses itself in a beautiful body, and the beauty of the body is reflected by the mind. His patterns for emulation were the great European heroes and poets, Alexander the Great, Caesar, the Hohenstaufen Frederick II, Napoleon, Dante, Shakespeare, Goethe, and, above all, Greek youth as it is portrayed in the works of Plato.

George gathered a group of young men around him and trained them in a way that almost amounted to the breeding of a new type. He made such a profound impression on young people that one could recognize a disciple of Stefan George not only by his bearing, his clothing, and his handwriting but also by a striking facial resemblance to the poet. In every aspect of their lives, George's followers felt themselves in opposition to the conventional middle-class world that surrounded them.

The significance of Stefan George for ensuing developments was that he gave Nietzsche's cult of the great man concrete form. Nietzsche was an abstract thinker; Stefan George was not a thinker but a poet and a man of action, a leader after the pattern of the Renaissance princes. His poetry and his Socratic training of youth were only part of an overall design for leadership. He began, however, simply as a poet, following the French symbolists in their "l'art pour l'art" aesthetic and in their defiant hatred

285

of bourgeois society. In a world dominated by the masses, by technology, by naturalism, and by an attitude of "laisser faire et laisser passer," he wanted to "restore the hierarchy of rank" and to set the poet at its apex as the intellectual leader of the state—an anachronistic endeavor if there ever was one. He wanted to create a new elite, and to this end he trained several generations of young people, ruthlessly freeing them from all conventional pseudomorality, from overemphasis of the rational powers, from family life and material interests.

The circle around Stefan George began as a group of poets but soon became a kind of order, an order without specific rules but one characterized by orthodox belief and by the devotion of the disciples to their master. After the First World War, when adherents of this movement occupied chairs in nearly all the great universities and held many important positions in public life, the movement became a secret state within the state, "The Secret Germany" that claimed the future as its own. George's poetry shows the growth of this claim. His early work focuses on the shaping of a personal life; the later poems are sibylline tablets of law for a new society.

By combining opposition to middle-class society with hero worship, the movement that centered around George set a dangerous example for German youth. Hero worship became the link between Nietzsche and Nazism. Trained to worship the hero as such, the youth of the country could no longer distinguish between true greatness and successful criminality. Stefan George himself certainly could. The Nazis wanted to make him an honorary president of the Third Reich, but as early as 1933 he left the country and later died as a voluntary exile in Switzerland. Also, it is worth noting that Count Claus von Stauffenberg, the man who made an unsuccessful attempt on Hitler's life in July 1944, was a disciple of Stefan George.

Nietzsche had introduced revolutionary anti-Christianism and the doctrine of a new elite. Stefan George tried to make this elite real and thus became an intermediary between Nietzsche's theory and the life of the people. Richard Wagner was still another major figure whose work helped set the sage for Nazism, a figure of broader influence but of lesser stature than Nietzsche or George. This brilliant but unstable mind, this "tribune of the people," as Nietzsche called him, is clearly a product of the nineteenth century in every respect. His work draws on every intellectual movement of this era, blending them together into a vulgar, bombastic, and demagogic art. The Romantic and the realistic, the Catholic and the pagan, the intellectual and the sensual are all thrown together indiscriminately. Wagner's tactical use of anything that served his purpose in art makes clear why the Nazis looked to him as their intellectual godfather. His teachings, animated by personal resentments and opportunism, anticipate all the concepts and slogans of the Third Reich. Richard Wagner's pamphlets and Hitler's speeches both spread the same kind of poison.

Wagner too propounded the cult of the "strong and beautiful man," launching violent attacks against Christianity, democracy, and middle-class civilization, which he called "Western" with a special, malicious overtone. He also reintroduced "the people" as a source of power. "Not from our filthy culture of today," he writes, "shall the art work of the future spring. . . . It is not you wise men who are the true inventors, but the people. . . . It is not you, therefore, who should want to teach the people; you should let the people teach you. . . . Our great instructors of the people are in error when they imagine that the people have to know what they want before they have the capacity or the right to want anything at all. . . . The people will take the blind involuntary course of Nature. Like an inexorable elemental force, they will break free from any rule that is contrary to Nature." In this passage Wagner helps provide authority for that mythical, completely undefinable *gesundes Volksempfinden*, that "sound judgment of the people," which the Nazis would later invoke in their campaigns against law, science, and the arts.

For Wagner, of course, "the people" meant the German people in a mythical, tribal, Teutonic sense. In his essay "Die Nibelungen," he interprets the role of the German people in world history in terms of the Nibelungen saga, an interpretation that prophesied, and hoped to justify, the domination of the world by the Germans: "The German people stem from a son of God. His own people call him Siegfried: the other peoples of the earth call him Christ. For the salvation and happiness of his race and of its direct descendants he achieved the most glorious deed, and in accomplishing this deed he suffered death. . . . The heirs to his deed and to the power won by it are the Nibelungen. The world belongs to them to administer in the name of, and for the welfare of all peoples." The hoard or treasure of the Nibelungen is the symbol of all earthly goods and so of world domination.

"The Germans are the most ancient of peoples. Their king, who is of their own blood, is a Nibelung, and as their leader he shall claim world domination. . . . The descendants of the divine hero will always desire the treasure that lends power, . . . but that treasure can never be won in slack quiescence. . . . It can only be won by a heroic deed. This deed, which must always be re-enacted to transmit the heritage anew, contains the moral signifi-cance of blood-vengeance, of the murder of kin. . . ." Siegfried's slaying of the dragon and his death in combat have the same meaning in Wagner's thought as Christ's salvation of the world and death on the cross have in Christianity. But the crucial dif-ference is that Siegfried's deed is not done once and for all; it has to be repeated ad infinitum in order to retain its efficacy.

In Nietzsche and Wagner alike, the Christian interpretation of history, based on the assumption of a single destiny in which all men take part through Christ, is replaced by the pagan idea of cyclic recurrence. Wagner's theory differs greatly from Nietzsche's, however, in its nationalistic bias. For Wagner, the impelling force of history arose from the German people and the German people alone, from their desire for blood vengeance, their desire to reclaim the treasures and the power that had been un-justly taken from them. Both Wagner and Hitler suffered deeply from the national inferiority complex of the Germans, and both of them capitalized on it. In addition to nationalism, Wagner also propounded the related idea of Germanic racial superiority. It was he who first spread racism and anti-Semitism among the German people, promulgating Gobineau's race theory in his *Bay-reuther Blätter*. Nietzsche, we must remember, was never guilty of either racism or anti-Semitism. His theory of the "superman," actually the "overman," the superior human being, was not asso-ciated with any one nation or race. The underlying impulse in Nietzsche's thought was universalistic and cosmopolitan, and the Nazi identification of Nietzsche's "superman" with a "Germanic type" is simply a distortion of Nietzsche's intent. It was not Nietzsche but Richard Wagner who drilled the German people in racism and chauvinism, preparing them for the nihilistic revo-lution of Nazism.

But poets and philosophers do not make revolutions. They can

288

exert an influence on the behavior of a nation only if that nation is prepared to accept their influence. The German people, and especially the young people of Germany, were more than open to the influence of Nietzsche and Wagner. The social, political, and intellectual history of modern Europe through the First World War had been a long, slow movement toward meaninglessness and despair.

The Renaissance and Reformation initiated the decline of Christianity as the sustaining force behind the social order, and a new faith in secular progress arose to take its place. But in the course of the nineteenth century, this new faith too proved to be untenable. European civilization was not moving ahead toward a better, happier future. On the contrary, with each passing year, its corruption and decay became more evident. There was no longer any hope of a life after death, and the possibility of fulfillment in this life had been reduced to practically nothing. Man had been shoved to the edge of the world, as it were, and he stood isolated there, face to face with emptiness and nothingness. Very few people could articulate or explain this malaise, but it affected the entire population of Europe and, in combination with other forces at work in Germany, made the German people particularly susceptible to National Socialism. For the Germans particularly, the First World War had put an end to whatever was left of the optimism and belief in progress that had sprung up during the Enlightenment. Disconsolate and pessimistic, they regarded the values they had held as fraudulent. For them, the idea of progress in history was meaningless.

The prevailing mood in Germany after World War I was bleak indeed, and the great success of Oswald Spengler's book, *The Decline of the West*, can, in part, be attributed to that mood. Spengler's book spread its nihilistic message even among those who had never before been disturbed in their Christian faith or in their faith in progress. Spengler destroyed the notion of continuity in history and, at the same time, the notion that all men have something in common. For him, cultures exist in isolation, each one rising, without rhyme or reason, out of nothingness and sinking back into nothingness. All they share are certain inevitable stages in the life cycle. But though Spengler destroyed the idea of progress for Germans and non-Germans alike, he made good the loss to the Germans by promising them an era dominated by the Germanic, Faustian man. Other cultures, Spengler claimed, had already passed their prime, and though the Faustian culture was at the peak of its maturity, it still had magnificent periods ahead of it, including a period of world domination. It was entering the phase of the great Caesars, powerful, ruthless rulers whom it would inevitably produce, rulers whose power base would be economic, not political. Needless to say, Spengler too regarded democracy and humane behavior as symptoms of weakness and decline. The highest form of man is the beast of prey par excellence, the inventive beast of prey that employs technology instead of tooth and claw.

It is easy to see how these ideas prepared the terrain for National Socialism. But Spengler himself criticized National Socialism severely and called those who greeted it with enthusiasm "lackeys of success." What he rejected in it was its need to win and manipulate the masses which he, like Nietzsche and George, utterly despised. Yet any theory of society and government that ignores the significance of the masses in the modern state obviously fails in its purpose.

It remained for Ernst Jünger to see, with terrible clarity, the role the masses were destined to play in a nihilistic, technological society. Jünger is the only thinker of the post-war period to go a step beyond Nietzsche, and it is he who bears the heaviest responsibility for preparing German youth for the Nazi state, even though he never professed Nazism himself. On the contrary, in passages of his earlier books, particularly in his cryptic parable *On the Marble Cliffs*, he openly voiced his scorn for these "hangmen and their stooges."

But no one understood better than he the mentality of the generation that was the true carrier of National Socialism. He had shared the experiences of this generation, but he differed from them in maintaining critical distance toward his experience. Where he was conscious of what had happened to him and could articulate what he had learned, they were completely incapable of separating themselves from their experience. As an officer in the First World War, he conducted himself with an extraordinary presence of mind that extended beyond military actions and developed into what he called a "second and colder consciousness," an ability to see himself as just one more object in an overall picture and to remove himself beyond the zone of pain and sensation.

290

In the thick of battle he was able to survey the situation he was in, analyze it, and record his observations about it.

As I noted in my remarks on the First World War, he came to understand modern warfare as a technological process, a battle of matériel in which individuals were, if anything, less important than machines. The all-pervading technological process extended to the home front as well, absorbing the entire nation into the enterprise of making war. Jünger carried this analysis a step further. Even in so-called peacetime, modern technological societies are in a condition of permanent "total mobilization"; and in war or peace, this mobilization serves the end of increasing the power of the state.

Total mobilization, Jünger believes, is simply an outgrowth of the basic conditions of an industrial society. No matter where the individual is—in his factory, in a football stadium, or in an amusement park—he is subject to the workings of a mechanized entity in which his own individuality is lost. Marching in one kind of column or another, he is both worker and soldier, a worker-soldier who labors and fights in the service of a collective whose only purpose is the amassment of still greater technological power than it has. For Nietzsche, for Stefan George, and for Spengler, the will to power was a function of the human being, the great individual. For Jünger, it is a function not only of a collective but of a collective lacking any kind of human values.

This new type of collective operates by the law of technology inherent in it. The question of whether this collective is justified in human terms becomes superfluous. The imperialistic, military communism that Jünger proclaims is an inescapable technical phenomenon, and it is idle to speculate on its desirability. The individual can maintain himself in this overwhelming procession of things and machines only by acknowledging himself as a victim, by offering himself as a sacrifice, and by subordinating himself to the machine as completely as possible. The human being can rule only by serving the vast machine of which he is a part. To insist on the personal value and human dignity of the individual, to want life to have a meaning, these are luxuries that no one can afford any more.

Jünger is able to document his analysis of this new collective by pointing to the kind of young people it produced. These young people did not belong to the anti-Christian era, nor could they be called really pagan. It never occurred to them that life should have a meaning; they never inquired after meaning or consciously suffered from the lack of it. If they still sensed that fear of nothingness that had haunted the generation before them, they transformed it into a blind urge to surrender themselves to a collective process that would consume them entirely. Service to the machine took the place of religious service or of service to an ideal. As Jünger points out, these young people combined high organizational capacity with a complete blindness for values. Theirs was a faith without content, a discipline without justification. For them, technology and ethics became one. The functioning of the machine was all that mattered to them, and because they never asked what the machine was accomplishing as it functioned, they became willing accomplices to some of the most heinous crimes in history.

Seen in terms of the German character and its development, the phenomenon Jünger describes appears as an inevitable stage in Germany's history. The German people were ready to surrender themselves to the Nazi state because they had been prepared for the kind of unquestioning obedience it required of them. The psychic needs we observed in the Germanic tribes, the need for both independence and submission, were still operative in the German character when Hitler came to power. But in the course of the intervening centuries, those needs had taken on far more dangerous forms. Luther's division of body and soul had channeled those needs, granting religious independence to the soul and demanding political submission of the body. Under the aegis of Lutheran doctrine, secular authority in Germany assumed absolute power over the people, and the people willingly acquiesced in that assumption of power. Nowhere did the social and political consequences of Luther's thought become more obvious than in Prussia, where the Hohenzollerns created a state devoted solely to its own aggrandizement. In Prussia and from Prussia, the Germans learned the selfless devotion to power that the Nazi state would ask of them.

If Germany's political evolution had been different, if she had undergone the same kind of organic growth that England and France had experienced, if she had acquired some kind of national existence early in her development, then she might not have been doomed to play the role she has played in the history of the West. But the fact that she never did achieve nationhood constitutes her uniqueness among the major powers of modern Europe. She is unique precisely because she continued to lead a divided, splintered existence long after the other countries of Europe had become coherent national units. Her effort to draw the diverse territories of the Holy Roman Empire together was a failure; her centripetal evolution was never completed. Throughout her history, she has been plagued by the particularism that originated in the division of territories and jurisdictions in feudal times and that persisted in the territorial states of the modern period. This division in the political realm extended into other areas as well, making the possibility of political unity even more remote. City stood against country, aristocracy against middle class, power against intellect. Because these forces could never coalesce, the only national existence Germany ever did achieve was the purely intellectual one of German Classicism. Unfortunately, the national impulse that emerged from that intellectual achievement quickly degenerated into the jingoism that characterized nineteenth-century political life in Germany. Once again power and intellect, body and spirit went their separate ways. But this time political power, coupled with the massive physical power of industrialization, gradually destroyed the one Germany of which all Germans could be justly proud. What remained was the military technocracy that Ernst Jünger's "second and colder consciousness" perceived with such terrifying clarity.

# Suggested Reading List

Bainton, Roland Herbert. *Here I Stand: A Life of Martin Luther.* New York: Abingdon, 1950.

Barraclough, Geoffrey. *Medieval Germany, 911-1250.* Oxford: Blackwell Press, 1938.

Barraclough, Geoffrey. *The Origins of Modern Germany.* Oxford: Blackwell, 1947.

Boehmer, Heinrich. *The Road to Reformation.* Philadelphia: Muhlenberg Press, 1946.

Brandi, Karl. *The Emperor Charles V: The Growth and Destiny of a Man and of a World Empire,* tr. C. V. Wedgwood. London: J. Cape, 1939.

Broszat, Martin. *German National Socialism, 1919-1945.* Santa Barbara, Cal.: Clio Press, 1966.

Carr, William. *A History of Germany.* London: Edward Arnold, 1969.

Cheyney, E. P. *The Dawn of a New Era, 1250-1453.* New York: Harper, 1936.

Collingwood, R. G. *The Idea of History.* Oxford: Clarendon Press, 1946.

Dawson, Christopher. *The Making of Europe.* London: Sheed, 1934.

Epstein, K. W. *The Genesis of German Conservatism.* Princeton: Princeton University Press, 1966.

Erikson, E. H. *Young Man Luther: a Study in Psychoanalysis and History.* New York: Norton, 1958.

Eyck, E. *A History of the Weimar Republic.* 2 vols. Cambridge: Harvard University Press, 1962-63.

Friedenthal, R. *Luther: His Life and Times.* New York: Harcourt Brace Jovanovich, 1970.

Harbison, E. H. *Age of Reformation.* Ithaca: Cornell University Press, 1955, 1963.

Hertz, F. *Nationality in History and Politics.* London: K. Paul, Trench, Trubner & Co. Ltd., 1944.

294

Holborn, Hajo. *A History of Modern Germany.* New York: Knopf, 1959.

Huizinga, J. *European Humanism: Erasmus.* Basel: B. Schwabe & Co., 1928.

Huizinga, J. *The Waning of the Middle Ages: Study of the Forms of Life, Thought, and Art in France and the Netherlands in the 14th and 15th Centuries.* New York: St. Martin, 1924.

Kantorowicz, Ernst. *Frederick the Second, 1194-1250.* New York: Ungar, 1957.

Mann, Golo. *The History of Germany since 1789.* London: Chatto & Windus, 1968.

Mayer, Arno. *Politics and Diplomacy of Peacemaking.* New York: Knopf, 1967.

Meinecke, Friedrich. *Cosmopolitanism and the National State.* Princeton: Princeton University Press, 1970.

Painter, Sidney. *Medieval Society.* Ithaca, N.Y.: Cornell University Press, 1951.

Pascal, Roy. *The Social Basis of the German Reformation: Martin Luther and His Times.* London: Watts, 1933.

Pflanze, Otto. *Bismarck and the Development of Germany: 1815-1871.* Princeton: Princeton University Press, 1963.

Pinnow, Hermann. *History of Germany.* London: Dent & Sons, 1936.

Pirenne, Henri. *Economic and Social History of Medieval Europe.* New York: Harcourt, 1937.

Ramm, Agatha. *Germany 1789-1919: A Political History.* London: Methuen, 1967.

Russell, Ch. E. *Charlemagne: First of the Moderns.* New York: Houghton Mifflin, 1930.

Ryder, A. J. *Twentieth Century Germany: from Bismarck to Brandt.* London: Macmillan, 1973.

Southern, R. W. *The Making of the Middle Ages.* 2nd ed. New Haven, Conn.: Yale University Press, 1954.

Steinberg, S. H. *A Short History of Germany.* New York: Macmillan, 1945.

Taylor, A.J.P. *Bismarck: The Man and the Statesman.* Vintage Books (Random House): New York, 1955.

Valentin, Veit. *The German People: Their History and Civilization from the Holy Roman Empire to the Third Reich.* New York: Knopf, 1946.

*Suggested Reading List*

Wedgwood, C. V. *The Thirty Years' War*. London: Cape, 1938 (Garden City, N.Y.: Doubleday, 1961).

White, Lynn, Jr., *Medieval Technology and Social Change*. Oxford: Clarendon Press, 1962, 1963.

# Index

Adelaide 67
Alaric 28
Albigenses 137
Albrecht von Brandenburg 162f., 190, 219
Alcuin 47
Aleander, Hieronymus 184f.
Alexander the Great 285
Amboise, Georges d' 61
Ammianus Marcellinus 30
Amsdorf, Nikolaus 186
Anabaptists 191, 198-202, 207, 250, 263
Angell, Norman 273
Anne, Queen of England 142
Anselm, Saint 135
Anthony, Saint 105
Antinomians 183
Ariovistus 27
Aristotle 153, 158, 181; *Logic* 134; *Ethics* 155
Arnulf 66
Ataulf 28
Attila 29
Augsburg, Peace of 193
Augsburg Confession 190, 193
Augustine, Saint 142, 159, 173
Augustinians 106, 154, 157, 164f., 200
Austria 3, 85f., 194, 233, 259, 262, 279; annexation of Bosnia (1908) 268
Ayer, Jacob 219

Babeuf, François Noël 265
Babylonian Captivity 130-132
Bacon, Francis 227
Balkan wars of 1912 268
Balzac, Honoré de 282
Baroque literature 217-225, 254;

and German character 220; and Lutheran doctrine 221f.
Basel, Council of, and Compacts of Prague 148f.
Benedict of Aniane 105
Benedictines 105
Benno 74
*Beowulf* 32
Berengar of Ivrea 67
Berengar of Tours 134
Berkeley, George 230
Bismarck, Otto von 194, 242, 256, 261
Black Death 150
Bodenstein, Andreas *see* Carlstadt
Bogomiles 137
Böheim, Hans, of Niklashausen 207
Bohemian Brothers 191
Boniface, Saint 91
Boniface VIII (pope) 130
Braun, Johann 154
Brunhildis 40
Bruno, Giordano 226
*Bundschuh* 207
Burke, Edmund 257

Cabet, Étienne 265
Caesar 20-22, 28, 32, 129, 285
Cajetan (cardinal) 165-167
Calixtus III (pope) 161
Calvin, John 142, 202, 220; *Christianae Religionis Institutio* 191, 240f.
Campanella, Tommaso 226, 265
Campeggi, Lorenzo 190
Canon law 25, 95, 180, 183
Capets 60, 62, 65f., 68, 73
Capitalism 262, 264-267, 269, 276; origins of 108-111
Caracalla 23

297

**Library of Congress Cataloging in Publication Data**

---

Kahler, Erich, 1885-1970.
   The Germans.

   Based, in part, on lectures originally presented by
the author at Cornell University, 1951-52, and again at
the University of Manchester, 1955-56.
   "Draws on materials . . . that appeared in Kahler's
earlier work, Der deutsche Charakter in der Geschichte
Europas."
   Bibliography: p.
   1. Germany—Civilization—Collected works.
I. Kahler, Erich, 1885-1970. Der deutsche Charakter in
der Geschichte Europas. II. Title.
DD5.K33          914.3′03          73-21751
ISBN 0-691-05222-0